THE PHANTOM ARMY
OF ALAMEIN

THE PHANTOM ARMY OF ALAMEIN

How Operation Bertram and the Camouflage Unit Hoodwinked Rommel

Rick Stroud

WINDSOR
PARAGON

First published 2012
by Bloomsbury Publishing Plc
This Large Print edition published 2013
by AudioGO Ltd
by arrangement with
Bloomsbury Publishing Plc

Hardcover   ISBN: 978 1 4713 2198 6
Softcover   ISBN: 978 1 4713 2199 3

Maps by John Gilkes

Briti...h Library Cataloguing-in-Publication Data...ble

Printed and bound in Great Britain by
MPG Books Group Limited

To the Commander-in-Chief: Alexandra Pringle

'The use of deception in any action is detestable, yet in the combat of war it is praiseworthy and glorious. And a man who uses deception to overcome his enemy is to be praised, just as much as he who overcomes his enemy by force.'

Machiavelli, *The Art of War*

'It is best to win without fighting.'

Sun Tzu, *Art of War*

'By a marvellous system of camouflage, complete tactical surprise was achieved in the desert.'

Winston Churchill to the House of Commons, 11 November 1942, announcing victory at Alamein

CONTENTS

SICILY

Mediterranean
Sea

Ras el Hil
(False Por

Tripoli

De

Barce

Benghazi

Gulf of Sirte

Beda Fomm

Tripolitania

Cyrenai

El Agheila

L I B Y A

The Desert War in North Africa 1940–43

The extent of the battlefield and the route taken by Geoffrey Barkas on his first recce in pursuit of General O'Connor, who advanced as far as Benghazi before Churchill stopped him. Had O'Connor got to Tripoli, he would have made it much harder for Rommel to use the port to disembark and supply his army. The battles of the next two-and-a-half years swung backwards and forwards between Benghazi and Alamein. The closest Rommel got to Cairo was Alam el Halfa: too close for comfort.

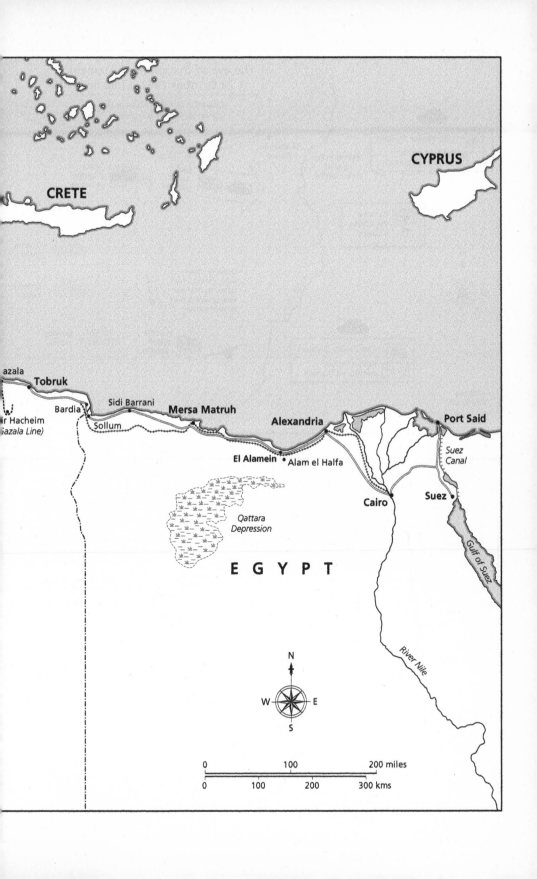

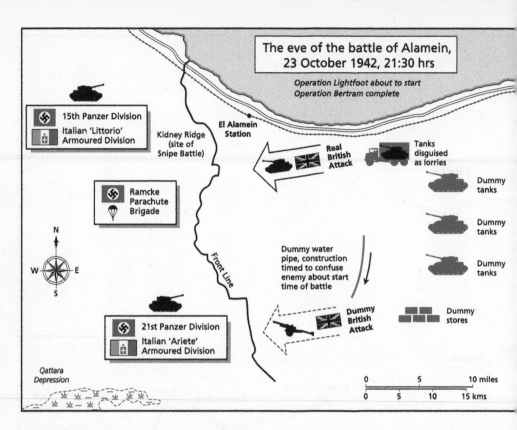

The eve of the battle of Alamein, 23 October 1942, 21:30 hrs

Operation Lightfoot about to start
Operation Bertram complete

15th Panzer Division
Italian 'Littorio' Armoured Division

El Alamein Station

Kidney Ridge (site of Snipe Battle)

Ramcke Parachute Brigade

Front Line

Real British Attack

Tanks disguised as lorries

Dummy tanks

Dummy tanks

Dummy tanks

N
W E
S

Dummy water pipe, construction timed to confuse enemy about start time of battle

Dummy British Attack

Dummy stores

21st Panzer Division
Italian 'Ariete' Armoured Division

Qattara Depression

0   5   10 miles
0   5   10   15 kms

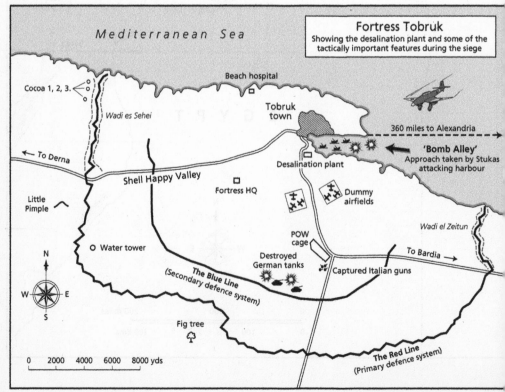

Mediterranean Sea

Fortress Tobruk
Showing the desalination plant and some of the tactically important features during the siege

Cocoa 1, 2, 3.

Beach hospital

Wadi es Sehei

Tobruk town

360 miles to Alexandria

← To Derna

'Bomb Alley'
Approach taken by Stukas attacking harbour

Desalination plant

Shell Happy Valley

Fortress HQ

Dummy airfields

Little Pimple

Wadi el Zeitun

POW cage

To Bardia

N
W E
S

O Water tower

Destroyed German tanks

Captured Italian guns

The Blue Line
(Secondary defence system)

Fig tree

The Red Line
(Primary defence system)

0   2000   4000   6000   8000 yds

Prologue

NOW YOU SEE IT . . .

In Martinique-Avanti in south-west France there is a complex of caves known as Les Trois Frères, named after their discovery by three brothers on the eve of the First World War. Deep within the rock, cut off from all sunlight, lies a chamber known as the Sanctuary. Scored and etched in charcoal on its walls are images of bison, stag, reindeer, ibex, mammoth; around 280 or so animals jostle for space, legs and antlers overlap. The paintings were made nearly twenty thousand years ago. No one is quite sure why our ancestors went to such lengths to make the pictures; they would have had to illuminate the pitch black with fire and work in a space filled with smoke. Stranger still, high above the cave floor and dominating the herd below, is a creature with the head and body of a reindeer and the legs of a man. The figure, dubbed 'the Sorcerer', is thought to be a shaman invoking magic to help with the hunt. On his upper half he wears the hide and skull of a reindeer: his costume—an early form of 'camouflage'—allows him to move stealthily among his prey, to hunt down and kill animals for the food without which he would starve.

The caves were discovered at the beginning of the twentieth century, in an age of total war in which magic and disguise would once more be feted. Men and women would again ascribe to

1

camouflage powerful properties: it didn't just hide people and things, it could make them invisible, invulnerable to attack. Practitioners of camouflage in the modern age were not shamans or sorcerers; they were artists, masters in the arts of visual fakery. The Great War gave birth to the word *camouflage*, from the Parisian slang *camouflet*, literally to blow smoke in one's face, a word which by 1917 had wafted its way to the trenches.

The idea that the Armistice in 1918 would bring an end to total war proved to be wrong. In 1939 the world took up arms again and the authorities rushed to rediscover the lost art of camouflage. By 1940 the British Army had formed the Camouflage Training and Development Centre and once more it was a raggle-taggle group of artists who were called to the camouflage colours. Painters, sculptors, film designers, glass engravers, even a stage magician were pressed into service. At first they worked in Britain, then, at the end of 1940, a tiny group was sent to the Western Desert. The unit was in the vanguard of a team of camoufleurs who were to find themselves working at the heart of the first major land battle fought by the Allies.

In 1942 the war was going very badly for the British. Tobruk fell, Churchill faced a vote of no-confidence in the Commons and, worse, Singapore was overrun by the Japanese. By the end of the summer Rommel stood at the gates of Cairo, apparently invincible. Churchill knew that if he lost North Africa he had lost the war. He demanded a victory and his armies squared up to face Rommel at El Alamein. The Camouflage Unit was called on to work on a gigantic scale and to pull off the biggest conjuring trick in the history of warfare.

2

Their target was Rommel and his *Panzerarmee Afrika*. In six short weeks the Camouflage Unit created a Phantom Army—two armoured divisions of 600 tanks, complete with artillery, stores and supporting vehicles. Straw men manned cardboard tanks and guns. The scheme was called Operation Bertram. The question was: would they be able to pull it off? Could they wrongfoot Rommel and help win the battle of Alamein? The stakes were high. If the Allies lost the battle Rommel would sweep into Cairo, giving the Axis powers control of the Suez Canal and the Mediterranean. Without these vital sea routes the Allies could lose the war in Western Europe.

1

THE ART OF WAR

Tricks and deception have long been embedded in tales of war and military thinking; from the Trojan horse in Virgil's *Aeneid* to Malcolm's army disguised as trees in *Macbeth,* conflict and war have stimulated men's imaginations in sinister and innovative ways. The Greeks defending Syracuse are thought to have created a false beach made of straw laid on a light timber frame. Lured into the trap, the attacking Romans were caught in the wreckage of the artificial beach and faced death by the Greek defenders' swords or drowning in the waters of the incoming tide. In 1513 the defenders of Tournai put up lengths of canvas, painted to look like fortifications, in an attempt to deter the attacking English forces.

Until into the nineteenth century, European armies fought in garish colours, facing each other at a range of hundred yards or so and blasting away with volleys of inaccurate musket fire. Advances in weaponry, optics and transport would change all that. By the time of the first mass mechanised war in 1914, every soldier wanted to be invisible, to either hide or get closer, undetected, to the enemy in war on a scale never before witnessed in history. A century of technological developments had increased the pace and intensity of war. In America, a master gunsmith named Ezekiel Baker produced a muzzle-loading rifled barrel gun that was not only much more accurate than a musket, but had almost twice the range. In 1863, the gunsmith Christopher Spencer developed a magazine-fed, lever-action rifle that could fire twenty rounds a minute and would be used to lethal effect by the North in the American Civil War. By the late nineteenth century, Hiram Maxim had invented a self-powered machine gun that used the energy of the recoil to eject the spent cartridge and load the next, and fired 600 rounds a minute. An improved version of the Maxim was produced by the Vickers company. The Vickers machine gun would provide deadly infantry support for the British Army in both world wars. Its reputation for reliability became the stuff of legend. On one occasion in 1916 ten Vickers guns fired continuously for twelve hours. A million rounds of ammunition were expended and a hundred barrels were used. Not once did the guns jam and at the end they remained in perfect working order.

Rapid-fire weapons would not have been possible without advances in the powder used to propel the bullets. The propellant was originally a black powder, a dirty substance that produced a great deal of smoke and fouled weapons. In 1884 a new smokeless propellant, 'Powder B', was invented. Powerful and clean, it led to the development of the more refined 'cordite', which made it far more difficult to spot where the enemy was firing from. 'The old terror of a visible foe had given way to the paralysing sensation of advancing on an invisible one.' Military thinkers now had to find new ways to locate and spy on the enemy.

An obvious place was from high in the air. The first military aerial reconnaissance flight was in the balloon *L'Entreprenant*, developed by Jean-Marie-Joseph Coutelle, a captain in the Bonapartist Company of Aeronauts. Balloons were used at the Battle of Fleurus to gather information and demoralise the Austrian troops. Coutelle also used his ballooning expertise to help Napoleon plan his never-to-be-carried-out invasion of England. In Norfolk in 1912, during British Army exercises, Royal Flying Corps spotters in aircraft and aboard the airship *Gamma* were able to detect the movements of Earl Haig's 'attacking force'.

Advances in photography allowed aerial intelligence-gathering to make the great leap forward. Between 1903 and 1912, the German engineer Alfred Maul developed the Maul Camera Rocket, which was shown to the Austrian army for use in the Turkish–Bulgarian war. By 1900, George Eastman had introduced the 'Brownie', a simple, cheap camera, and photography entered the mass market. Cameras of all sorts were available and could be used by anyone under almost any conditions. In the First World War many soldiers in the trenches carried the Kodak Vest Pocket Camera. Varying attempts were made to solve the problem of how to get a camera into the air and operate it. Manned and unmanned tethered balloons were tried, as were kites and pigeons, to which were attached miniature cameras with timers. In 1896, Alfred Nobel even built a camera-carrying rocket. In the end it was the aeroplane that proved the most practical camera platform.

With the new technologies of conflict, commanders found that traditional bright costumes of war, originally designed to intimidate or frighten, merely made soldiers better targets. Colours and textures needed to blend in with the natural world. In 1846, a British officer, Harry Lumsden, formed a Corps of Guides that was made up of Sikhs, Pathans and Afghans. Lumsden's corps dressed in comfortable, loose-fitting clothes dyed a muddy colour and known as *khaki*, an Urdu word meaning 'dirt-covered or dusty'. Lumsden's second-in-command, Major William Hodson, said that the uniforms made the men 'invisible in a land of dust'. The outfits confused some of the more conventionally scarlet-jacketed British troops. One officer was only prevented from opening fire on them when one of his gunners shouted, 'Lord, sir, them is *our* mudlarks.'

Other ideas for military camouflage came from observing nature. The nineteenth-century Darwinian zoologist Edward Poulton studied the way animals evolved colours that were used for both protection and aggression. Poulton's meticulous research, examining hundreds of types of insects, was published as *The Colours of Animals*. The natural phenomenon of 'countershading', the colouration that cancels out shadowing caused by natural light, would be harnessed by the modern camoufleurs. In the natural world, the penguin is a good example of countershading. It is two-toned: its top half is dark, so when it is seen from the air, it blends in with the dark waters below it. Its bottom half is light, so when seen from below, it blends in with the sunlit waters above it.

In 1898, during the Spanish–American War, the artist and naturalist Abbott Handerson Thayer, author of *An Exposition of the Laws of Disguise through Colour and Pattern*, suggested to the US government that they paint their ships using countershading. Though they rejected his idea, in 1902 Thayer was granted a patent for 'the Process for treating the outside of ships etc. for making them invisible'. Privately, Thayer called these patterns of contrasting colours, geometric shapes that interrupted and intersected each other, 'Razzle Dazzle'. The idea was to confuse rather than conceal the image and baffle the onlooker. At the start of the First World War, Thayer approached the British government with the idea that they adapt his ideas for the treatment of uniforms: he proposed that rather than flat khaki, the uniforms should be treated to have some sort of disrupted pattern.

By Christmas 1914 the opposing armies were dug in, facing each other along a 500-mile trench that stretched from Switzerland to the North Sea. The front line was more or less static, with nowhere to hide. Technology, so carefully developed over the past hundred years, came into its own. The opposing armies were spied on and photographed by enemy aircraft prowling 3,000 feet in the air. The images were examined in minute detail; defended positions were carefully plotted and then shelled, machine-gunned and attacked without let up. The soldier's search for the cloak of invisibility was on.

Early French camoufleurs apparently devised *cagoules*—'paint-splattered hooded cloaks' that prevented the wearer from being seen from the air. Hidden beneath these hooded uniforms 'was a ghoulish image of the modern soldier, whose finely fitted and brilliant red and blue clothing was replaced by an amorphous costume of drab greens and browns that turned the individual into a frightening form'.

The fashionable French portrait painter Guirand

9

de Scévola, while serving on the Western Front, decided to disguise his 75mm guns by covering them in painted sheets of canvas. De Scévola's work caught the attention of the general staff, who promoted him and put him in charge of the world's first dedicated camouflage unit, the *Section de Camouflage* based at Amiens in 1915.

De Scévola was a fastidious man who wore white gloves as he worked, and recruited artists and designers from among his friends to supervise his projects. At the same time, factories were set up and civilian labour recruited to work preparing materials. De Scévola and his team began to experiment in the field. They mocked up dummy horses and grazing livestock to obscure observation posts. They hit on the idea of using armour-plated false tree stumps with bark camouflage, which could be put up at night in no-man's land: an observer would crawl into the stump at night and spend his day watching the enemy, protected from everything bar a direct hit. By the end of the war, De Scévola had over a thousand men of all ranks under his command and his camouflage factories employed nearly eight thousand civilians.

In England, De Scévola's equivalent was the London Jewish Pre-Raphaelite painter, Solomon J. Solomon. He was a Zionist, President of the Order of Ancient Maccabeans and member of the Jewish Territorialist Organisation; he was also a keen canoeist, studied numerology and believed that his luck was governed by the number six. Solomon frequented London's most fashionable clubs, including the Savage, and was proud to be a full member of the Royal Academy. His portrait painting brought him into contact with politicians and royalty, but he also painted huge biblical and mythological scenes, including a famous depiction of a bound Samson being taunted by Delilah. Like his paintings, Solomon was a larger-than-life character: talented, likeable, but inclined to pomposity.

At the outbreak of war, Solomon joined—as a lowly private—the United Arts Rifles, a volunteer corps for men from the arts too old to join the Regulars or Territorials. They drilled at the Royal Academy, had the playwright Sir Arthur Wing Pinero as their chairman and were known as 'the unshrinkables' because they marched in white jerseys. In January 1915 the war was in its fifth month and casualty figures were already shocking. Solomon wrote a letter to *The Times* arguing the case for a more imaginative use of colour and light and shade to conceal troops. The letter ended with the suggestion that perhaps artists would be useful in the quest to make soldiers less visible. By the end of the year, after a meteoric rise through the ranks, Solomon J. Solomon found himself a lieutenant colonel in the Royal Engineers, in charge of developing camouflage techniques for the British Army and with access to the highest levels of authority—including the prime minister, the First Lord of the Admiralty (Churchill), and the king.

Solomon argued that the arrival of aircraft on the battlefield had made the 'other side of the hill' redundant; there was nowhere to hide any more. His *cri de cœur* was: 'art alone will screen men from the airplane'. Though many staff officers thought that Solomon was insane, he came up with plans to disguise airfields as lakes, gas plants as cabbage patches, and had teams of stage technicians working to disguise observation posts as anything

11

from dead horses to shattered trees. His experience of painting vast tableaux using colour masses led him to a grandiose plan to cover the trenches with miles of painted canvas. He also handpainted tanks in his own particular camouflage designs, covering them with rural scenes and pink sunsets. But when the vehicles were deployed in France, Solomon's designs were thought to attract attention rather than conceal and his work was unceremoniously scrubbed out, painted over in olive drab.

Solomon established a school of camouflage in Kensington Gardens, where one of his designs was for pop-up soldiers made of hardboard. (This idea would be revisited by the British Camouflage Unit in North Africa in 1942.) He also helped set up the Special Works Park at Wimereux which, during the course of the war, deployed one million square yards of canvas, four million yards of scrim (a see-through cloth used for dramatic lighting effects in the theatre), six million yards of wire netting and seven million yards of fish netting.

Solomon's most important contribution was also his most mundane: the camouflage net. Like De Scévola, Solomon toyed with the idea that trenches could be covered with painted sheets. This proved impractical because it was difficult to paint them to match the surroundings and the sheets trapped water. Solomon teased away at the idea and, with the help of F. W. Holmes, head props man at the Drury Lane Theatre, came up with the idea of a mesh 'garnished' with strips of material of any sort: canvas, hessian, cotton, even twigs. So produced, Solomon's nets could be used to cover large objects and stretched between poles to minimise shadows. By the end of the war nearly eight million square yards of canvas netting had been deployed by the opposing armies. Essential to military tactics in the Second World War, camouflage netting would be used with even greater ingenuity by the Camouflage Unit at Alamein.

The Royal Navy also turned to artists for help during the Great War. Naval camouflage presented its own unique problems. Water is a giant reflector, making it very difficult for ships to hide on, and conditions at sea and the ambient light change very quickly. At first Percyval Tudor-Hart, of the Académie de Peinture et de Sculpture, and a small team of artists attempted to use countershading to hide the superstructures of ships, but made little headway. Another team led by the acclaimed marine painter Norman Wilkinson had more success. Wilkinson was a member of the Royal Institute of Painters in Water Colours and later became its president. (His love of naval themes led him to be made Honourable Marine Painter to the Royal Yacht Squadron.) Aged thirty-six at the outbreak of war, he joined the Royal Naval Volunteer Reserve and spent most of his service in submarines in the Mediterranean. Submarines were a new threat. They were difficult to spot and carried a new and lethal weapon: the torpedo, a cheap piece of ordnance that could sink a battleship or destroy hundreds of thousand of pounds worth of merchant shipping and their cargo.

Wilkinson thought that it might be possible to paint a ship in such a way that it would confuse anyone viewing it through a telescope or periscope and allow the vessel to blend in with the existing seascape. He put this idea to the Admiralty and was asked to prove his theory, which he did. Very quickly he commandeered four studios in the Royal Academy, conveniently placed across Piccadilly from his beloved Institute of Painters in Water Colours. There, working with a team of students and artists, he devised a type of ship camouflage that came to be known as 'Dazzle', an echo of Abbott Thayer's Razzle Dazzle.

Wilkinson's designs were first tried out on models in large water tanks at the Royal Academy's studios. The camouflage was examined through instruments designed to simulate the view through a submarine's periscope and successful designs were then sent to the docks, where artists supervised the careful application of the paint schemes onto ships. One member of Wilkinson's team was the Vorticist Edward Wadsworth. Vorticism was the name given by Ezra Pound in 1912 to the style of a group of artists who revelled in the machine age and the modern world. Their work was typified by strong colours and bold, hard lines. Wadsworth was a contributor to the group's magazine *Blast,* and a supporter of the Vorticist Manifesto. Wadsworth's style of jangled, ragged graphics and woodcuts from *Blast* suited the Dazzle style better than Wilkinson's gentle drawings, often displayed in the *Illustrated London News*. So the traditionalist Wilkinson sent an invitation to the avant-garde Wadsworth, who jumped at the chance to supervise the painting of ships. It gave him the opportunity to use his experience of abstract patterning on a larger scale than he could have ever dreamed of in peacetime.

An estimated two thousand ships were painted in Dazzle during the First World War. Though its effectiveness was hard to measure, many believed that the paint schemes succeeded in baffling the enemy. One captain reported that on passing HMS *Ebro* in the Sound of Mull 'it proved that it was almost impossible to say how she was steering'. It was at the very least good for morale, as ships' crews believed it made them less visible. Wilkinson and Wadsworth celebrated the end of the First World War by producing oil paintings depicting the camouflage they had created: Wilkinson in the quiet and sombre *Dazzled Ships at Night* and Wadsworth in the exuberant and edgy *Dazzle Ships in Dry Dock at Liverpool*.

*　　　*　　　*

The final months of the First World War were marked by two land assaults that are classic examples of the use of camouflage and its more sophisticated cousin, deception. The first of these was the German plan to cross the River Aisne along the Chemin des Dames. In March 1918, General Erich Ludendorff attacked the Allies near St Quentin and almost broke through. The frustrated Ludendorff believed that the Allies were on the point of defeat and that if he could attack again, and quickly, he could win the war for Germany. The problem was urgent because American troops were arriving in France and their presence would soon tip the balance in the Allies' favour. His plan was to cross the River Aisne, which was protected by a ridge, the Chemin des Dames, and had seen heavy fighting early in the war. It was now deemed to be impregnable and had become one of the quietest sectors of the Western Front. The French dominated the slopes with machine guns.

Ludendorff's plan was to move his army forward secretly, keeping them hidden until the moment when they could spring up and take the French by surprise.

First he sealed off the area. All civilian movement was stopped and tight security imposed. Every vehicle to be used in the attack had its distinguishing marks painted out. The wheels, moving parts, chains, anything that could make a noise, were muffled with straw, leather or wood shavings; even the horses' hooves were bound in cloth. Everything moved at night and was hidden under the cover of trees during the day. When troops had to move by day they were given orders that in the event of overflying enemy aircraft, they were to about face and march away from the front. The army approached at night and in almost complete silence. When the time came to bridge the Aisne, the din of croaking frogs disguised the noise of the advance. Ghost-like, over four thousand men were moved into position. The attack started with a huge bombardment at 01:00 hours on 27 May, which took the French completely unawares.

By the end of the day Ludendorff had penetrated further into the Allied lines than at any time since 1914. By 3 June, the Germans were thirty-three miles from Paris and had captured 50,000 Allied prisoners and 800 guns. In the end the attack failed, partly through exhaustion and supply problems, but largely because of the arrival of the American Expeditionary Force. Nevertheless, Ludendorff had shown just what effective weapons camouflage and deception could be.

The second great set-piece took place in

Palestine as the Allies advanced up the Jordan Valley, and contained almost all the elements of trickery that were to be used by the Eighth Army twenty-five years later at Alamein. On 17 December 1917, General Allenby took Jerusalem and was faced with the task of getting the Turks and the Germans out of Palestine. His opponents were dug in along the Jordan Valley. Allenby's strategy was to make them think that he was going to attack their left flank when in fact he was planning an attack on their right. The plan was worked out in great detail. First he attracted the enemy's attention to the left flank by simulating a vast amount of troop movement: the Anzac Mounted Division marched down the valley in daylight and were taken back to their starting points at night to repeat the whole thing the following day. They did this at least four times. Meanwhile mules and vehicles were used to drag harrows along other tracks, kicking up huge dust clouds. Dummy camps and horse lines were set up, with straw horses supported by ropes.

A Camel Corps battalion, supported by Arab irregulars, made a raid east of Jordan, destroying a railway station and leaving behind documents and cans of bully beef to signal they had been there. A fake army was created to look as though it would attack the left flank. Agents working for T. E. Lawrence (of Arabia) were sent to buy huge quantities of feed to supply fake horses. At night, bonfires were lit and lights set up to indicate the presence of men. False radio traffic was generated between GHQ and the dummy build-up area. As a further diversion, British local papers carried news of a race meeting apparently to be held at Gaza on 19 September 1919, the day of the attack.

Meanwhile, the real build-up took place in conditions of absolute secrecy. All movement by daylight was forbidden. At night, horses were hidden in orange groves and channels were dug to bring water for them. The newly formed Royal Air Force dominated the skies and kept Turkish and German planes away from the build-up area. Enemy intelligence maps were captured that showed that the Turks had no idea of what was happening on their right flank. By pure chance the Allies had set up a bridging school; the Turks were used to seeing bridges going up on exercise and so no suspicions were raised when bridges were built immediately prior to the attack to get troops across the Jordan.

The attack on the nineteenth was a complete success. In less than six weeks Allenby's forces had advanced 350 miles. On 31 October the Turks surrendered. Allenby's victory was complete. Wavell, who would be one of the Allied commanders pitched against Rommel in the Western Desert, wrote that the campaign 'had, in fact, been practically won before a shot was fired . . . The brilliant conception of the commander, the handicraft of an experienced staff, had combined to prepare one of the most crushing strokes ever delivered in a war'. Wavell's enthusiasm for deception would re-emerge when he became Commander-in-Chief of the army in the Western Desert.

By the end of hostilities, the general staff recognised the importance of camouflage as a weapon, describing it as 'a branch of that important military organisation whose function is to mislead the enemy in accordance with the general plan of operations'. Camouflage and deception had come a long way since de Scévola's early efforts with painted canvas in 1914. The essence of what had been learned was written up in a booklet called 'The Principles and Practice of Camouflage', which concluded: 'The camera is a most accurate witness, and a photograph will always record something. The art of camouflage lies in conveying a misleading impression of what that something means.'

The First World War was meant to be the war to end all wars, a limit to future mass slaughter. To most it was unthinkable that they would ever be called on to fight in another such conflict. The artists went back to their easels and millions of square feet of fragile camouflage netting were destroyed or packed away to rot in stores. Ships at sea lost their Dazzle and battleship grey once more became the order of the day. On 22 March 1919, the art of camouflage saw its 'last expression' when the Chelsea Arts Club held the Great Dazzle Ball at the Royal Albert Hall. Balloons replaced bombs and the *Illustrated London News* correspondent observed: 'One might be forgiven for not expecting wholly to relish the spectacle of Cubist birds, Futurist animals, submarines, Messrs Dilly and Dally, impish pierrettes, Geisha girls, demons, fairies, staff officers, officers of the Grand Fleet jostling one another under multicoloured searchlights that flashed and scintillated. But one did relish it. Enjoyment was the spirit of the hour.'

As the last notes of the band echoed round the Albert Hall and the world relaxed into the embrace of peace, the hard-learned lessons of camouflage were quietly and completely forgotten.

DRAWN B'

AN INTERVAL.

SHOWERS OF BALLOONS.

THE GREAT "DAZZLE" DANCE AT THE ALBERT HALL: TH

The scheme of decoration for the great fancy dress ball given by the Chelsea Arts Club at the Albert Hall, the other day, was based on the principles of " Dazzle," the m
"camouflage" used during the war in the painting of ships to help them in escaping from the attacks of submarines. Many of the costumes were also designed specially

The Great War ended and the world forgot about
camouflage, except for the Chelsea Arts Club, who
gave it back to the artists and held a 'Dazzle Ball' at
the Royal Albert Hall in 1919.

r, S. Begg.

THE GIRAFFE.

OF "BOMB" BALLOONS; AND SOME TYPICAL COSTUMES.

tion on "Dazzle" lines, but there was also a great variety of fancy dresses of the ordinary type.   The total effect was brilliant and fantastic.   During the evening a shower of
ubs" in the shape of coloured balloons descended on the devoted heads of the dancers, and added greatly to the hilarity of the occasion.—[*Drawing Copyrighted in U.S. and Canada.*]

HITLER, SMOKE AND MIRRORS

In 1936 a film based on H. G. Wells's prophetic novel *The Shape of Things to Come* was screened in London. The film is set in 1940—the date Wells predicted as the time Germany would invade Poland, which in turn leads to a protracted world war and the collapse of European civilisation. Early in the film, 'Everytown' (London) is reduced to rubble by fleets of bombers arriving at night. St Paul's can be seen towering over the flames, its dome shattered. The film was designed by Victor Korda and his art director, future British Army camoufleur Fred Pusey. On 26 April 1937, the Luftwaffe bombed Guernica in Spain. The raid took place on market day, reduced the town to rubble and killed over 500 civilians. Newsreel footage of the atrocity was shown all over the world. Wells's prophecy seemed to be coming true. In Britain, committees were formed to look into ways of protecting the civilian population from aerial bombing, and shielding, or at least hiding, factories and industrial complexes. Soon contact was established with veteran camoufleurs and decades-old ideas gently dusted down and examined.

In Germany, Hitler's Third Reich had come to dominance on the back of coercion, manipulation and disguise. Rearmament in contravention of the terms of the Treaty of Versailles had been achieved using a smokescreen of scams and deceptions: 'work creation programmes' to hide weapons manufacture and development; paramilitary organisations with vague aims and frequent name changes; a clandestine airforce, later unveiled as the Luftwaffe; rocket technology; secret military training; underground bunkers, scientific research stations. The Treaty of Versailles contained a 'guilt clause', whereby Germany was required to pay 269 billion golden Marks as reparations for the damage it had done in the First World War. This amounted to about 100,000 tons of gold, nearly half the amount ever mined. The hardship and discontent this caused within Germany made it possible for Hitler to rise to dominance in just over ten years. In 1934, a year after Germany withdrew from the League of Nations' World Disarmament Conference, Hitler told *Time* magazine: 'At the risk of talking nonsense, I tell you that the National Socialist movement will go for a thousand years. Don't forget how people laughed at me fifteen years ago when I declared that one day I would govern Germany. They laugh now just as foolishly when I declare that I shall remain in power.'

Shakespeare describes the affairs of men as having a tide. The problem for the man or woman in the street is that it is impossible to tell where the tide is leading. The currents in Europe in the 1930s were strong, but most people went about their daily business as if nothing was happening. Nazism caught many ordinary young Germans unawares. In 1933, Sebastian Haffner, a student, was training to be a lawyer in Berlin. In his journal he records an event that made him realise just how corrosive the influence of the Nazis had become. On 22 March

23

the quiet of the library where he was working was broken by a disturbance: a door opened and a voice announced that the *Sturmabteilung*, Hitler's private army, were in the building and that 'the Jewish gentlemen would do well to leave'. Another voice shouted out: 'Out with the Jews!' The brown-shirted SA flooded into the reading room and their commander ordered non-Aryans to leave the premises immediately. Haffner did not know what to do; he wanted to get on with his work. He thought to himself, 'Just ignore them, do not let them disturb me.' A brownshirt came up to his desk and demanded: 'Are you Aryan?'

'Before I had a chance to think I had said "Yes",' Haffner writes. 'I had not lied. I had allowed something much worse to happen . . . what a disgrace to buy, with a reply, the right to stay with my documents in peace.' The next day laws boycotting the Jews were passed and by the end of the year, Haffner writes, against his will: 'I was wearing jackboots and a uniform with a swastika armband. We even had a flag, with a swastika of course . . . When we came through villages the people raised their arms to greet the flag, or disappeared quickly in some house entrance . . . they did this because they had learned that if they did not, we, that is I, would beat them up. They greeted the flag or disappeared. For fear of us, for fear of me . . . it was the Third Reich in a nutshell.'

Sebastian Haffner quickly decided that he and Hitler had to part company, and he left the Reich.

For those living outside Germany it was even more difficult to know what was going on, to see the danger beyond the Hitler–Goebbels masquerade of deception propaganda. 'Make the lie big, make it simple, keep saying it, and eventually they will believe it,' Hitler wrote. Few were aware of the monster that was moving on to the world stage, or how insidious his influence had become. In 1936, at the funeral of Leopold von Hoesch, the German ambassador to London, his swastika-draped coffin was escorted along the Mall by detachments of Nazi-uniformed soldiers and bearskinned British Guardsmen in full view of Buckingham Palace. In 1936 the Olympic Games took place in Berlin, filmed by the Führer's tame movie director Leni Riefenstahl. Hitler announced that he hoped the Games 'would connect the countries in the spirit of peace'. For the cinemagoers in their comfy seats in Surrey and Kent, it was hard to see the dark motives behind Riefenstahl's brilliant but fawning images.

Hitler instinctively understood that an important element on the road to victory was to defeat the enemy by sowing doubt and fear in his mind. This was an understanding shared by his favourite general, the 'master of smoke and mirrors', Erwin Rommel. Both men knew that it is not how a thing is that matters; it is what it appears to be that really counts.

*   *   *

One man who saw the Nazi danger clearly was Winston Churchill. In the mid-thirties he came to an arrangement with the Korda brothers, the film-makers who had produced *Things to Come*. The brothers created an unofficial spy network working for the future prime minister. They set up offices of their company, London Films, in several European countries and, thus disguised, they ran Churchill's informal but highly efficient information-gathering service.

At the start of the war many British military figures had little idea of what camouflage was truly capable of and little desire to learn. For most of them camouflage was a time-consuming waste of valuable resources. But Churchill was fascinated by the idea of 'visual warfare'. During the Second World War subterfuge and deception would be his meat and drink—an indispensable element of *léger de main*. He called it 'an original and sinister touch, which leaves the enemy puzzled as well as beaten'. One of Neville Chamberlain's first acts as wartime prime minister was to appoint Churchill First Lord of the Admiralty, a post that Winston had held until the disastrous Dardanelles campaign in 1915. As a moderniser of the fleet, Churchill became enthralled by the possibilities of camouflage, and pushed the development of Q ships, armed decoy vessels disguised to look like merchantmen, coasters and colliers.

The first Q ship, or 'mystery ship', was tasked with trapping a German submarine that operated off Le Havre. With almost schoolboy relish, Churchill wrote to the RN Commander-in-Chief Portsmouth telling him what to do: 'A small or moderate-sized steamer should be taken up and fitted very secretly with two twelve-pounder guns in such a way that they can be concealed with deck or cargo or in some way in which they will not be suspected. She should be sent when ready to run from Havre to England and should have an intelligence officer and two picked gun-layers who should all be disguised. If the submarine stops he should endeavour to sink her by gunfire. The greatest secrecy is necessary to prevent spies becoming acquainted with the arrangements.' Churchill went on to describe what happens next, when the Q ship reveals its true identity: 'By a pantomime trick of trapdoors and shutters they suddenly come into action!'

In October 1939, shortly after Churchill was appointed First Sea Lord, a German submarine penetrated the defences at Scapa Flow and sank the giant dreadnought HMS *Royal Oak*. Over 800 mariners were killed, with the biggest loss of life of boy sailors, youngsters between the ages of fourteen and eighteen, in British naval history. Churchill wept when he visited the wreck, imagining the deaths of 'those poor fellows trapped in those black depths'. He commanded that the harbour defences be protected by deception, by dummy ships disguised as warships. When he was shown the results of his order, he noticed that the dummies had no gulls flying round them: 'You always find gulls above a living ship. Keep refuse in the water day and night, bow and stern, of all these dummies! Feed the gulls and fool the Germans.' Churchill was a natural camoufleur.

Another eminent First World War veteran determined to focus military minds on camouflage was Andrew 'Bulgy' Thorne. In 1936, Brigadier Thorne became Commander of the 1st Guards Brigade. He had attended manoeuvres with the German army and was impressed with the way they took concealment and fieldcraft so seriously, using camouflaged groundsheets and green-painted vehicles to blend in with the northern European scenery. Thorne shared with his friend Captain Liddell Hart a belief that the British Army needed

27

urgent modernisation. Liddell Hart was a radical military thinker: one of the principles of his philosophy was that 'the profoundest truth of war is that the battle is usually decided in the mind of the opposing commanders, not in the bodies of the men'. With the aid of Archibald Wavell, who was with Allenby in Palestine and had witnessed how effective deception tactics could be, Thorne used his brigade to take part in two camouflage exercises conducted in collaboration with the RAF at Farnborough. He used army funds to test how his field headquarters could be disguised using whatever was to hand—pea netting, painted sheets, anything he could beg, borrow or steal. He also built a dummy headquarters out of scrap. His report caused the War Office to start testing camouflage ideas on a large scale, examining the use of disruptive pattern camouflage on vehicles and experimenting with different types of netting.

The same year, 1936, a subcommittee to the Committee of Imperial Defence, dedicated to camouflage, was formed. The Advisory Committee on Camouflage was set up to organise camouflage on a national basis. Its chair was Sir Frank Smith, former Director of Scientific Research at the Admiralty. Also on the committee was zoologist and scientific illustrator Hugh Cott. Cott was a man of action with the mind of a natural philosopher. Born in 1900, he had been too young to fight in the First World War, but later joined the army and at nineteen graduated from Sandhurst. After four years in the Royal Engineers specialising in camouflage techniques and instruction, he went up to Selwyn College Cambridge to read zoology, and then travelled the world. His arrival on the committee would mark the beginning of a long association with the Second World War camoufleurs.

* * *

In September 1938, Hitler demanded to be allowed to take over the Czechoslovakian Sudetenland, the areas on the Czech–German borders occupied by ethnic Germans. His demands precipitated the Munich Crisis. Chamberlain, intent on avoiding war at all costs, travelled to Munich to try and appease Hitler, and failed. Hitler got his way in an agreement signed by England, Germany, France and Czechoslovakia. After the conference Hitler described Chamberlain as 'an impertinent busybody who spoke the outmoded jargon of democracy'.

On the steps of Downing Street, Chamberlain read from the agreement. It contained the sentence: 'We regard the Anglo–German naval agreement as symbolic of the desire that our two nations never go to war with each other again.' Chamberlain concluded: 'My friends, this is the second time there has come back from Germany to Downing Street peace with honour. I believe it is peace for our time.' In private Hitler commented: '[If] that silly old man comes back interfering with his umbrella I will kick him downstairs and jump on his stomach.' In the House of Commons, Churchill declared: 'England has been offered a choice between war and shame. She has chosen shame and will get war.'

The Munich crisis galvanised the work of the Camouflage Advisory Committee. Civil defence became a matter of high national importance and the Treasury at last began to fund projects to disguise aerodromes, factories and runways using camouflage paint schemes developed during the First World War. In an attempt to rationalise matters, the committee recommended that a Camouflage Experimental Unit be established under the control of the Air Ministry. By November 1939 it was placed under the authority of the Ministry of Home Security and given the name the Civil Defence Camouflage Establishment, with headquarters at the Regent Hotel, Royal Leamington Spa. Here air reconnaissance pilots liased with camoufleurs—artists, designers, draughtsmen, photographers and scientists—to work out designs for the most exposed industrial targets, aircraft and ships. Experiments were conducted in a 'vision chamber', making it possible to study the various designs under different lighting conditions, as well as in a 'moonlight vision chamber' for night views. Norman Wilkinson re-emerged and was made Inspector of Airfield Camouflage. Later in the war, when thirty-two million gallons of paint had been expended on airfields, he declared that airfield camouflage was a waste of resources. He was later retired.

During the period of the Phoney War, many camouflage developments proceeded on an ad-hoc basis and were left to the enterprise and ingenuity of individuals. Small, freelance camouflage businesses sprang up, such as Stanley William Hayter's Industrial Camouflage and Research Unit, operating from the architect Ernö Goldfinger's offices at No. 7 Bedford Square, near the British Museum. Hayter was thirty-seven, a printmaker and outstanding technician of the graphic arts. Before the war he had founded a school of engraving and pottery in Paris, the Atelier Dix Sept, which had an international reputation. Among the students were Picasso, Matisse and Chagall. When the Germans overran France, Hayter moved the *Atelier* to New York, leaving behind over a hundred plates and a printing press, all of which were seized by the Nazis. From New York he moved back to London to set up his camouflage company.

Hayter was soon joined by his friends, many of whom he had taught in France. These included the British surrealists, Roland Penrose and Julian Otto Trevelyan. Penrose, a rich Quaker, started as an architect but in 1922 had moved to Paris to study painting. The much younger Trevelyan, a poet, artist and nephew of the historian George Macaulay Trevelyan, gave up a degree in English at Trinity College Dublin to become Hayter's pupil. Soon after the outbreak of war, Trevelyan left Paris for London. Waiting for the ferry on the quay at St Malo, he ran into Penrose and his new girlfriend, Lee Miller—former *Vogue* model, muse to Man Ray, photographer and soon-to-be war correspondent. The three friends arrived in London in time to witness the capital's first air-raid warning. Trevelyan looked at the silver barrage balloons floating overhead like enormous whales and the wardens running around in white overalls blowing whistles and waving football rattles, and wondered if there was anything more surreal than war. Penrose declared that he wanted to be the 'smallest cog in the great machine'.

That first air-raid warning proved to be a false alarm. Nevertheless, Wells's nightmare scenario seemed to be coming true. Londoners waited for the bombs to rain down. Chamberlain's policy of appeasement had failed; Britain was at war and the public believed that it was only a matter of time before Nazi tanks rumbled down the Mall.

The nation saw camouflage as a cure-all. Like the crews of the ships painted in Dazzle camouflage, people believed that camouflage didn't just make things difficult to see, it could make them invisible. All over the country, little corner shops, garages on housing estates, laundries, the roofs of cinemas, were suddenly painted in improvised patterns of brown and green, the magic colours of invisibility. Hayter's Industrial Camouflage and Research Unit came into its own. 'In those early days it was easy to sell any kind of camouflage,' said Trevelyan, conceding that Hayter's team knew precious little more than the man in the street. They had no idea what the buildings they were commissioned to treat looked like from the air or even why they were doing it. 'The fundamental questions were never asked. Against what are you camouflaging? Against the low-flying raider? The night-raider? The photographer? Without an answer to such questions much of our ingenuity was waste.'

Bill Hayter was a very successful salesman and was soon commissioned to camouflage a vast factory complex in the Midlands. He and his staff clambered all over the roofs of the factory buildings, making measurements, taking photographs and gathering information from which models could be made. In the end the surrealist team designed an 'enormous abstract picture to be painted on the roofs and chimneys of an industrial town'. The client paid up, but the scheme was never realised. Trevelyan later wrote: 'We were not alone in neglecting these aspects of the problem, and it took the various camouflage departments of the services a long time to realise their importance.' Ernö Goldfinger was more direct: he described Hayter's company as the biggest con he had ever been involved in.

As the initial terror of air attack passed, enthusiasm for camouflage flagged and Hayter ran out of clients. He kept everyone busy dreaming up schemes for camouflaging guns and tanks and lorries; experiments were made, mock-ups were designed, none of which came to anything. Eventually the work of the unofficial camouflage organisations was banned and the work coordinated from Royal Leamington Spa under the Civil Defence Camouflage Establishment.

The Phoney War dragged on. In October 1939 over 150,000 men of the British Expeditionary Force were settling in to positions across the Channel, dug in along the French–Belgian border. France was standing strong; no one imagined that in just a few months the country would fall. Meanwhile, members of the artistic community came forward to offer their expertise to the War Office. Forty-four-year-old Freddie Beddington had served as a sniper in the First World War: he had very good eyesight and was regarded as an excellent shot. He spent much of the war concealed in no-man's land, blending in with the mud and the trees, and lying quite still for many hours, waiting for a victim to cross his sights. He developed his own theory of concealment. Nature, he thought, likes soft, round shapes; man, on the other hand, makes shapes with straight lines and smooth curves. One's eyes are naturally drawn to the geometrical, which is why, he said, we can walk past a deer in the forest without seeing it; the deer's very form, as well as its colouring, make it hard to see.

After the Great War Freddie studied at the Slade School of Art before going into the City. Outgoing and gregarious—his natural habitat was clubland, Piccadilly and St James's Street—he was well known as a 'godfather' to young artists. Soon after the outbreak of hostilities, Freddie Beddington offered his services to the War Office. He was taken on as a civilian advisor and in early 1940 was astonished to be appointed 'Camouflage Advisor to the British Expeditionary Force's Engineer-in-Chief in France' with the starting rank of major. The BEF had no camouflage organisation or even any officers trained in that art; he would be starting from scratch. Very quickly Freddie found himself promoted to colonel and charged with the additional task of forming 'The Royal Engineers' Camouflage Development and Training Centre' at Farnham Castle on Surrey's western border. Freddie Beddington's job was to track down suitable candidates from the artistic community and recruit them to the world of camouflage.

Freddie's older brother, Jack, was already harnessing the talents of an array of artists. Before the war, as publicity director for Shell-Mex and BP Limited, and working out of the sumptuous new Art Deco headquarters at 80 The Strand, he hired creative people—sculptors, painters, writers and film-makers—to promote the work of the company around the world. Jack Beddington was a clever man and his protégés included the artists Paul Nash and Graham Sutherland. He commissioned a series of guide books, the *Shell Guide to England*, which the poet John Betjeman produced in collaboration with the artist John Piper. By 1940 Jack would be appointed director of the Ministry of Information Films Unit, orchestrating hundreds of wartime propaganda films. The formidable Beddington brothers—affable, suave and very well connected—used their contacts to scour the creative world for recruits for 'Freddie's Camouflage Development and Training Centre'.

One of the artists to be approached by Freddie Beddington was John Hutton, an artist and glass engraver from New Zealand who had moved to England in order to work for Shell-Mex. Jack Beddington had recommended him to several important architects, including Brian O'Rourke, interior architect for the Orient Line ships. In 1939 Hutton was recruited by Freddie and commissioned as a second lieutenant into the Royal Engineers. Before his military duties proper began, Hutton marked time in London, painting anything from large murals on the sandbagged hoardings that had been put up to protect buildings against bombing, to the exterior of the Orient Line headquarters, to small greengrocers' shops. His work and that of other artists was displayed in the 'Art Replaces Sandbags' exhibition at the Building Centre in New Bond Street in January 1940.

Trying to find a useful role in these uncertain times was forty-two-year-old Geoffrey de Gruchy Barkas, MC, a veteran of the First World War. In peacetime Barkas had earned a good living directing films. He loved being behind the camera and enjoyed the travel and excitement that went with it. But in the last few years the work had dried up. For a while he joined Jack Beddington's outfit at Shell-Mex as director, stage manager and administrator for a travelling exhibition called *See How Your Car Works*, but a few weeks into the war Barkas received news that the exhibition would be scrapped; private car ownership would almost cease to exist and the tour would be meaningless. Barkas found himself, once more, without a job. He wrote to the Ministry of Information offering his services, thinking he might be asked to make propaganda or training films. To his dismay he received no answer.

Instead he and his wife Natalie received a letter telling them to report to the Permit Branch of the Postal and Telegraph Censorship Department in Liverpool, where they were to start work as censorship examiners. Geoffrey Barkas entered a world of endless tedium and bureaucracy. In the outside world the Germans and Russians brutalised Poland, while in the Liverpool docks, the war became more and more apparent. Great liners were converted into troop ships; neutral tankers and cargo boats flying strange flags chugged in and out of the harbour; coastal vessels sprouted anti-aircraft guns and occasionally destroyers or torpedo boats appeared decked out in grey-blue and white zigzag patterns, an echo of the last great conflict. Overhead saggy barrage balloons lolloped about the sky.

In the Censorship Department spy fever and paranoia ruled, and caused chaos. The mania for secrecy became almost surreal. The angle at which a stamp had been stuck on a roll of newspapers was seen as sinister evidence of fifth columnists at work. One examiner was ordered to open a parcel of 200 whistles and test every one of them to see if they contained anything untoward. Oddly spaced lines

36

and dots on a package immediately aroused suspicions of coded messages and espionage.

On 9 April 1940, Germany invaded Norway. The Phoney War was over. Barkas had stuck it out in the censorship office for several months, but could stand it no more. In desperation he telephoned his old patron Jack Beddington, now director at the Ministry of Information. This time there was no lifeline. Just before the call ended, Beddington mentioned that his brother, Freddie, was starting up some sort of camouflage organisation and might be looking for recruits. 'Possibly be worth a try? Perhaps give him a call?'

Barkas made the call, secured an interview, took two days leave, and caught the slow, troop-filled train to London. The capital had been transformed into one huge military camp. Air defences overhead, uniforms everywhere, government buildings protected by walls of sandbags and adorned with huge, officious, black and white signs. He walked down the Strand from Trafalgar Square, heading for an address in the Aldwych. There he expected to see Freddie Beddington; instead he was introduced to Captain Richard M. Buckley, a man with neat military bearing, red hair, a trimmed moustache and something of the appearance of Colonel Blimp. Buckley was a fellow First World War veteran and holder of the Military Cross but, as Barkas would discover, Buckley was a progressive, not at all Blimp-like, and a dedicated camouflage expert.

Barkas explained his background and experience. He sketched in the last two decades of his life since he had begun directing films in 1925 aged twenty-nine. He was especially proud of a short documentary, *Wings Over Everest*, which he had

37

directed with Ivor Montagu. The film had won an Academy Award for Best Short Novelty Feature. He had also co-directed a film about decoy vessels, named *Q-Ships*. He talked about working with the novelist, MP and reformer A. P. Herbert, who had written the film *Tell England,* a war story that Barkas had co-directed, and about directing the exterior scenes for *King Solomon's Mines* starring Paul Robeson.

Buckley did not seem impressed. He put down his pen and sat in silence, staring at something behind Barkas's head. Then he asked if he had any technical qualifications. Was he a designer? A painter perhaps, an architect or sculptor? Barkas answered no: the tools of his trade were his eyes and his typewriter. As the interview came to an end Buckley asked him what he had done in the last war. Barkas explained that he had enlisted aged eighteen in 1914 and had served as a subaltern, first in France and then in Gallipoli. He had gone 'over the top' several times. Buckley began to talk about the importance of camouflage; how he believed the art had been lost in the twenty years of peace and it was only old-timers like him who knew anything about it. Confused, Barkas left the interview.

While film-maker Geoffrey Barkas waited to hear if he had been accepted by Buckley, and John Hutton squeezed the last drops from his life as a painter in London, another *artiste* searched for a role. Jasper Maskelyne, music-hall illusionist and magician, was the third generation of a family of entertainers. His grandfather, John Neville Maskelyne, had written the bestselling *Sharps and Flats: A Complete Revelation About Cheating at Games of Chance* and ran an entertainment empire

38

from the Egyptian Hall in Piccadilly—dubbed 'England's Home of Mystery'. At the outbreak of war, Jasper had an international reputation as a conjurer and entertainer; he was handsome, charming, with a sparkling smile and movie-star looks. However his last tour had flopped and funds were dwindling. He applied for a commission, wangled an interview and presented himself at the War Office wearing his 'finest Harry Hall suit'. (In return for free tailoring, Harry Hall Esq, Bootmaker and Tailor, had plastered the underground with posters of Maskelyne sporting the company's new look.) Maskelyne was turned down: he did not have the required educational qualifications. Somehow Jasper managed to get an interview with Buckley, who reasoned that if Maskelyne could make the lady vanish, he might be able to do something similar with a tank, and so offered him a place on Freddie's new camouflage course.

By Christmas the painter, sculptor and engraver Steven Sykes had come into the Beddington brothers' sights. Sykes was twenty-five and a graduate of the Royal College of Art. On the day war was declared, he and his fiancée Jean Judd had been on a cycling tour of England. When they reached Burton Bradstock in Dorset they were informed that their hostel had been requisitioned by the British Army; the trip was over and they travelled back to London by train. Sykes spent the last days of 1939 as an air-raid warden in Chelsea, scanning the skies for bombs that never fell. He tried to join the Royal Marines, but they would not have him. He visited one of his old Royal College of Art tutors who happened to be on the look-out for recruits for Freddie Beddington. Soon Sykes was in front of Buckley, who offered him a commission in the Royal engineers, told him to buy a uniform and put him on standby for Freddie's camouflage outfit.

In early February 1940, Steven Sykes and Jean Judd were married in a brief ceremony at the Catholic church on the Fulham Road. A photograph taken afterwards, outside La Speranza restaurant in Knightsbridge, shows Sykes, trilby in hand, gazing lovingly at Jean; she is holding a cyclamen as a posy and smiling at the camera in the pale winter light.

Weeks later Steven Sykes was in France, assigned to No. 693 Artisan Works Company, a civilian construction firm that had been converted, lock, stock and barrel, into a military unit—a posting to which Sykes, a talented artist with no construction experience, could hardly have been less suited. The commanding officer of 693 Company put Sykes's artistic skills to good use by asking him to decorate the mess for parties, or getting him to draw caricatures of visiting guests. For several weeks, Sykes found himself manning a telephone in Calais linked to an office in Arras and reading the names of unfamiliar bits of equipment down the crackly, antiquated telephone line to the sapper officer at the other end.

Salvation came on 26 April in the form of the all-seeing, charismatic Lieutenant Colonel Freddie Beddington, dapper and resplendent in an immaculate uniform. He had come to find Sykes and tell him that he would soon be posted back to England, where his artistic talents could be better used. All Sykes had to do now was wait for his orders. They were very slow in coming. It was the lull before the storm.

On 10 May the Germans invaded Belgium and then crossed the French border. The rapid German advance would lead to the collapse of the French army and the surrender of the French nation in an advance referred to as *Blitzkrieg*, lightning warfare. Hitler's initial plan, 'Führer Directive No. 6', had assumed a modest conquest to the west across the French border and then a pause, possibly for several years, while the military built up their resources. But suddenly, against his general staff's advice, Hitler ordered that everything should be accomplished in a few weeks. His luck was that he had two generals, Heinz Guderian and Erwin Rommel, who were headstrong and prepared to disobey orders. On 13 May the Germans crossed the Meuse River into France at Sedan with the heaviest air bombardment the world had ever seen.

The advance was so swift it completely unnerved Hitler and his high command. By 14 May, General Ewald von Kleist ordered Guderian to stop, dig in his tanks and halt the advance. The next day the French Ninth Army surrendered. Rommel took immediate advantage, disobeyed orders and broke loose, advancing thirty miles, refusing to let his troops rest and losing communications with his superior, General Hermann Hoth. The following week the Germans had the BEF trapped and were poised to take Dunkirk. Between them, the two tank commanders had rescued Hitler and, on the way, 'invented' the idea of *Blitzkrieg*. They had beaten the French, an apparently superior enemy with better armour. Just as Liddell Hart had theorised, the Germans prevailed because they had dominated the minds of the enemy commanders. The notion of *Blitzkrieg* had been sown in Allied minds and would prove a weapon of profound psychological power.

By 24 May, German Panzers surrounded Calais. The few thousand British and French soldiers at the port, the last line of the defence between the Germans and the BEF, were told to resist at all costs to allow Operation Dynamo, the main evacuation at Dunkirk, to take place. Churchill wrote of Calais's plight: 'One has to eat and drink in war, but I could not help feeling physically sick as we afterwards sat silently at the table.' There was terrible fighting in the streets. More and more wounded arrived, evacuated by trains from the battles taking place not very far to the east. As German dive-bombers attacked overhead, Steven Sykes saw his first dead body. A French officer had been caught in the open area along the docks and a bomb had landed almost on top of him. The explosion spattered his body along the wall of a hangar. 'It was the first corpse I had seen and perhaps the strangest throughout the entire war, because he was not so much a corpse as a splash of red, but still human.'

That night a train-load of badly wounded men pulled into the sidings by the shattered quayside and Sykes was ordered to load the men onto the cargo ship the *Ben Lawers* and remain on board. In the early hours, to his immense relief, Sykes felt the vessel start to edge out of the harbour; shells from a German battery dug in at Sangatte exploded in the water around them. The ship was filled with the sounds and smells of the dead and the wounded. On reaching Dover they were turned away: the port was already too crowded with shipping to take them and they were forced to spend the night moored off Southampton.

In the morning Sykes stumbled down the gangplank onto the quay. Ahead of him men began to unload corpses covered with Union Jacks. He was filthy and unshaven, wearing his service dress uniform, trench coat and steel helmet. He carried his revolver, an abandoned Lee Enfield .303 rifle, which he had picked up on the quay at Calais, and around his neck were bandoliers of ammunition. The tranquillity of England came as great shock. He wrote in his diary: 'Country looks heavenly, beautiful and heavenly.'

Meanwhile, Freddie Beddington's preliminaries were over. Buckley had identified the first draft of thirty trainees, weeded out from 300 applicants. Geoffrey Barkas was one of them. Now he was about to catch a train bound for Kent. His orders were to proceed to Napier Barracks, No. 1 Training Battalion Royal Engineers, Shorncliffe, where he would join the other students of No. 2 Camouflage Course. He wondered if there had been a No. 1 Camouflage Course, and if so, how it had gone.

The thirty fledgling camoufleurs heading for Napier Barracks were the vanguard of an unlikely group of individuals who, through innovation and dedication, would bring the skills and imagination of the artist to the battlefield and help lead the Allied armies to victory.

3

A MATTER OF LIFE AND DEATH

Many of the soldiers waiting on the platform for the Shorncliffe train that sunny May morning wore the RE cap badge and shoulder flashes. Officers, non-commissioned officers and other ranks congregated into separate groups. Barkas headed for the officers standing about at the far end of the platform where the first-class carriages would draw in. He moved towards them, picking his way past the kit bags of the NCOs and other ranks, briskly returning their salutes. Ahead of him he saw a group of young subalterns in brand new uniforms and wondered how many of them were bound for the camouflage course.

Barkas soon realised he was the oldest man of the group and stood out because his uniform had medal ribbons, from the Western Front and Gallipoli, stitched over the left-hand pocket of his tunic. The train arrived, and Barkas and the others lugged their suitcases into the carriages. Eventually everybody sat down, cigarettes were lit and uneasy conversations started. There was a strong smell of new leather and the squeak of shiny, unbroken-in shoes. He stared around him; these men were mostly artists, Barkas thought, men who probably only a few weeks before had dressed in casual bohemian style, now wore stiff, tailored uniforms, tight, uncomfortable shoes, polished Sam Browne

44

belts, gloves and peaked caps. On their shoulders were their new badges of rank—mostly the pips of a second lieutenant fixed by brass tags through the cloth of their epaulettes.

The train chugged through the English countryside, first following the course of the Thames and then, reaching the wide waters of the Medway at Chatham, it headed south-east for Folkestone. When they arrived, Buckley was waiting for them. Sheepishly they approached their new commanding officer, and 'hived around him, offering him almost every variety of salute, except possibly the one laid down in the rule book'. A row of taxis waited outside the station, requisitioned by Buckley. Soon the group was on its way to Napier Barracks, where they were to be briefly indoctrinated in the basics of military discipline. Geoffrey Barkas was about to relive a part of his youth.

The intake for No. 2 Camouflage Course unpacked and settled into the shared rooms, their home for the next few weeks. They dined together in the mess and Barkas had a chance to assess his fellow students. He was surrounded by a huge variety of artists: painters, illustrators in woodcut, stained-glass window specialists, sculptors, architects, poster artists, designers, art directors. There was even a celebrated restorer of Old Masters. He felt like a cuckoo in this nest of creatives.

Some people he already knew. Hutton, tall, dark and slim, 'reminded him of Dante'. P. E. Phillips—known to everyone as 'Pep'—was a painter with a 'long flowing moustache and the cut of a cavalry officer'. Michael Bell was another painter. He recognised too the tall, dark-haired figure of Edward Bainbridge Copnall, a young, talented sculptor with big, powerful hands. Copnall had recently completed the bas-relief carvings on the Warner Cinema, Leicester Square. On the far side of the room he spotted a fellow film man, twenty-seven-year-old art director Peter Proud, a brilliant artist in pen and wash who already had a string of film credits to his name. Julian Trevelyan, Jasper Maskelyne and Roland Penrose had also been accepted onto the course and would form part of the second draft, No. 3 Camouflage Course.

Barkas's thoughts were interrupted by the arrival of senior officers from headquarters at Farnham Castle: Buckley, Freddie Beddington and the school's chief camouflage instructor, zoologist Captain Hugh Cott. Beddington explained that Cott had just finished a major work called *Adaptive Colouration in Nature.* In it he argued that military camouflage should be organised along the same lines as nature and stressed the importance of countershading. The next day each student was presented with a cyclostyled copy of Cott's article from the *Royal Engineers Journal* entitled 'Camouflage in Nature', which they were expected to digest quickly. Cott left his fledgling camoufleurs with something to think on: all animals except man and apes, he told them, were colour blind, so the saying 'a red rag to a bull' was nonsense—the matador would be better off with a shining white cape. It would be some time before the trainees realised that he had made an important point about the difference between colour, tone and movement.

The three senior officers left the room, leaving Barkas wondering how he was going to find a role for himself in which his total lack of technical ability would go undetected. He did not know why

Buckley had chosen him. He hoped that it was for his background, his maturity, and the fact that he had already served in the army and knew how the military machine worked.

The next day a sergeant major with shiny boots, barrel chest, and parade-ground voice began to drill the new officers. He shouted his orders with such snap that Barkas's service cap 'vibrated for at least a second after his body had frozen into immobility'. Little seemed to have changed in twenty-five years.

At the end of basic training the small band of recruits was marched into Shorncliffe town and allowed, at their own expense, to buy rounds of .450 ammunition, which they carried to a gravel pit and fired from borrowed revolvers. The artists had come expecting to be shorn of their identities and hair, and be made to sleep in vast dormitories, losing all possibility of a private life. In fact they were treated very well. Buckley and Freddie Beddington would look in from time to time to see how things were going. John Hutton wrote home to his wife: 'I had the misfortune to pass a colonel and had to salute. Did the best I could.'

In France the situation had deteriorated. The BEF, with its back to the sea, had been cut to pieces. One day the parade-ground drill was interrupted by the arrival of a convoy of lorries from which jumped small parties of sappers commanded by impossibly young subalterns. They began to load boxes of explosives, reels of cable and more boxes of detonators. The ordnance was bound for Dover harbour, which they were going to destroy if the Germans invaded. Convoys of lorries came and went all through the day and far into the night as the harbour, the rail and road bridges were made ready for demolition.

Basic training ended and No. 2 Camouflage Course began in earnest. The students were taken to the Royal Artillery Camp at Larkhill, Wiltshire, where they were to live under canvas. On arrival the group found a new recruit had joined them: Steven Sykes. He carried all his possessions in a brown-paper parcel tied up with string. When Buckley asked him why he did not have a uniform or a proper suitcase, Sykes explained that he had lost everything in the frantic evacuation from Calais.

On the first night, Buckley gathered his officers in the anteroom of 'B' mess. As they lounged in comfortable old chairs, smoked and drank what Barkas considered a particularly good Madeira, Buckley told them how they would be spending their time. He talked to them with the fervour of a zealot, explaining that it had taken a lot of arguing to persuade the War Office to provide expensive resources like cameras, developing and printing facilities and access to reconnaissance aircraft; the course was a great opportunity and they were not to waste it. Once trained they were to go out as disciples and spread the camouflage gospel: this was that every soldier had a personal responsibility to understand the principles and importance of hiding what they were doing; every track made by every driver, every badly concealed heap of spoil, was an invitation to German bombers and artillery and, by definition, a danger to other soldiers.

Making soldiers realise that their own initiatives contributed in a major way would be one of the main tasks of the camouflage officers working in

48

North Africa. 'We were, in fact, to go out in the world as evangelists, but we were to preach our faith only where it could save souls,' wrote Julian Trevelyan.

For Barkas and his fellow students, fresh from art studios, film sets and drawing offices, it was hard to believe that soon they would be putting their lessons into practice in an environment where people would be killing and maiming each other. The glorious weather and the school-like atmosphere conspired to heighten the sense of unreality. Days later the trainee camoufleurs listened as Churchill warned the nation that the French would soon probably lay down their arms. The broadcast was met by a deep and worried silence. If France fell, Britain would be next. The silence was broken and the atmosphere lightened by an officer who quipped: 'Well, that's one thing we'll never do. Got no bloody arms to lay down.'

The real nature of the war was brought home to Barkas one hot summer day in early June. They had been given a few hours off. Barkas and another student sat on the grass outside, revelling in the view, 'a glorious sweep of English countryside drenched in sunshine and flecked with the shadows of little lazy clouds'. The land rolled away, grassland met wheat, and beyond the wheat newly ploughed earth, and on the horizon a grassy slope leading to a great belt of beech woods. There were no sounds, no aircraft; all he could hear were the birds and the grasshoppers. 'There below us, clear and placid, flowed the stream. The war was somewhere else, a million miles away. We peeled off and slipped into the pool.'

On the way home, the two men came across a

long, slow, straggling procession of soldiers, stumbling and slipping on the grassy slope that led back to the barracks. The men were ragged, dirty, unshaven, caked in mud, oil and dust. Some had no boots, others were hatless. 'They stumbled on like zombies, dead but walking'—the remnants of the BEF, just evacuated from France, silent stragglers on the last stages of their painful journey home from Dunkirk. Only Steven Sykes had any clue what the men had gone through.

The No. 2 Course was intense. In the classrooms at Larkhill and Farnham they learned, about light and shadow, textures, and the difference between colour and tone. They wrote detailed notes about camouflage netting, which, properly garnished with strands of fabric, hessian, or other materials like steel wool, was the camoufleur's secret weapon. There were various patterns and colours of garnish, devised according to the terrain in which it would be used: dark greens and olives might work well in northern Europe, but would be useless in snow or the scrubby yellow and grey landscape of the desert. The members of the Camouflage Unit spent many hours working out how best to garnish nets for all topographical conditions and circulated their conclusions by way of pamphlets drawn by the unit's graphic designers.

They learned about infra-red photography, wavelengths and the properties of chlorophyll. They studied aerial photographs of Stonehenge and saw how evidence of man's activity can remain visible as scars on the land for thousands of years, impossible to remove. A modern army makes a huge mess, with its marching troops, columns of vehicles, encampments and dugouts. The marks it leaves tell a very clear story to the aerial reconnaissance camera, a story that can have lethal consequences. They were shown relics of camouflage from the First World War: the dummy trees that had been used to hide observers and plaster heads that could be popped above the parapet to draw enemy fire, helping to pinpoint the sniper's nests concealed in the debris of no-man's land. They were taken to the film studios at Denham, where they were shown scenic film techniques such as plaster moulding and set construction.

In spite of the intensity of the training, the students could not suppress their creative instincts. Sykes recalls that John Hutton found it impossible not to sketch during the classroom lectures, managing to take in the complicated detail of the lessons while drawing his classmates.

Buckley ensured that the course balanced the theoretical and the practical. His trainees roamed Larkhill playing hide-and-seek in camouflaged sniper suits, or dug trenches disguised with camouflage nets. Miraculously, Buckley and Beddington managed to wheedle from the RAF at Boscombe Down and Farnborough light aircraft—Lysanders or whatever could be cadged—so that course members could fly over their attempts at disguise and see how successful their efforts had been. Julian Trevelyan grew to know 'Buckles' very well and to love his various moods. 'It was continuous April weather to be near him,' he recalled. His laugh was 'Homeric'.

Buckley would often lecture while looking into space, giving off-hand answers to important questions, but could also flare into a temper. He had thought out the problem of camouflage from

© The National Archives

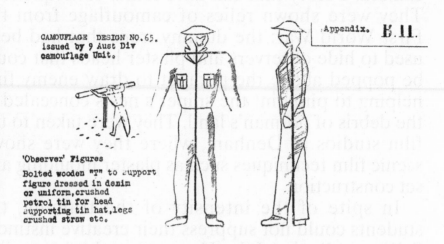

CAMOUFLAGE DESIGN NO.65.
issued by 9 Aust Div
camouflage Unit.

'Observer' Figures

Bolted wooden "T" to support
figure dressed in denim
or uniform, crushed
petrol tin for head
supporting tin hat, legs
crushed straw etc.

Dummy head in loophole here; real sniper behind concealed
loophole.

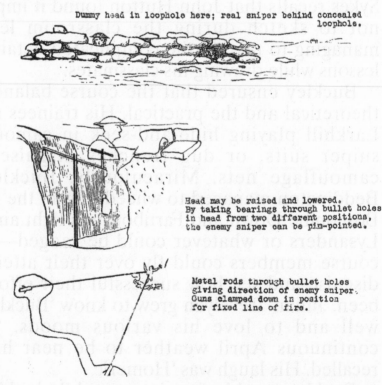

Head may be raised and lowered.
By taking bearings through bullet holes
in head from two different positions,
the enemy sniper can be pin-pointed.

Metal rods through bullet holes
giving direction of enemy sniper.
Guns clamped down in position
for fixed line of fire.

Design for dummy to locate enemy sniper positions.

first principles and would not stand for sloppy thinking. Artists like Bainbridge Copnall, John Hutton and Steven Sykes could be prima donnas and, at times, handling them took its toll on Buckley. But while he could get angry, he never let his rank ride roughshod over the men in his care. On one occasion an order from an untrained senior officer to camouflage something using coal-tar varnish led to a row between Buckley and Major Pavitt, a future tutor at the Camouflage Development and Training Centre. Afterwards Buckley wrote to him in longhand on blue writing paper:

Dear Pavitt,

I am sorry if I have hurt your feelings—as evidently I have. I most certainly did not mean to. When you were here I was tired to the point of being unconscious. However that is no excuse for being rude. I don't know what the stuff about coal-tar varnish versus chippings is all about. I have no particular views and was probably putting the case of the cheaper stuff because nothing, not even the most expensive, will hold on concrete until is has had the laitance [a by-product of over-wet concrete] knocked out of it. However that is a suggestion and no more . . . I probably expressed myself roughly or badly & perhaps rudely. And if I put it badly or unfairly or clumsily or rudely, as evidently I did, I apologise. I am very well aware of the efforts you have made and are making in this cause.

So I am sorry, very sorry that I hurt your feelings and I apologise.

Yours,
Richard Buckley

When No. 2 Camouflage Course came to an end, none of the graduates had any idea what would happen next. In the summer of 1940 the RAF was fighting and winning the Battle of Britain and the War Office was trying to put back together an army that had escaped from France by the skin of its teeth. Thirty newly trained camouflage officers, with no other military qualifications, were not much of a priority. For now they were scattered around the country in a variety of posts. Steven Sykes was sent to an anti-aircraft division in Newcastle, where he rented a flat and was joined by his wife and mother-in-law. John Hutton continued to kick his heels while Geoffrey Barkas and Michael Bell received postings to Northern Ireland.

Barkas felt that much of the course had remained beyond his grasp. When it came to wielding a pencil or brush, he was the undisputed holder of the wooden spoon. However, Buckley had infected him with a new vision of what camouflage could become and what it could do to save the lives of the fighting men. On 4 July, Barkas received his orders and began to get an idea of the role he was to play in camouflage. On that day he awoke and breakfasted as a second lieutenant; by mid-morning he had been promoted to first lieutenant and by teatime he was on his way to his new job with the rank of captain and 'in the style of General Staff Officer, Third Grade'. Michael Bell accompanied him as his staff lieutenant.

*   *   *

In Northern Ireland, Barkas and Bell felt daunted by their task. Their orders were to teach the army how to hide its vulnerable parts and intentions from the enemy. What had seemed simple and logical in the classroom now seemed a huge and almost impossible job, beyond the capabilities of just two men. This was a problem that would come up over and over again in the next few years. Effective camouflage is highly labour- and material-intensive; hard-pressed local commanders were usually unwilling to allocate the resources that the camoufleurs demanded. Barkas learned several lessons: one was that if he and Bell were to succeed in selling their ideas, they must become crowd-pleasers. They must be as much entertainers as instructors. Barkas decided to write a pamphlet; he wanted it to be memorable and unlike any other training literature. The product was a doggerel poem, 'The Sad Story of George Nathaniel Glover'.

Driver George Nathaniel Glover
Despised the use of natural cover
And never, never could be made
To park his lorry in the shade.
In fact his favourite parking places
Were vast and treeless open spaces . . .

Driver Glover thinks that all he has to do is cover his lorry in an ungarnished net and his lorry will instantly become invisible. The words were scarcely out of his mouth,

When German planes arrived in herds
And landed several tons of Muck
Right on top of George's truck.

Emerging later, safe and sound,
His comrades searched for miles around

55

But not one trace did they discover
Of Driver George Nathaniel Glover.
And I am also very sorry
To say, they never found his lorry.

The moral is, as all can see
Ungarnished nets are NBG.*
(* No Bloody Good)

Barkas's verse aimed to hit home: get camouflage wrong and it can lead to death. The top brass were won over and soon Barkas and Michael Bell had access to equipment and manpower to enable them to mount large-scale camouflage demonstrations. Barkas learned another very useful lesson that would serve him well in North Africa: camouflage would only be taken seriously if it had backing at the highest level of command. In one exercise they took sixty vehicles, complete with accompanying troops, and hid them under camouflage in a field. Then a spotter plane flew over with the pilot briefed to drop flour bombs wherever he thought he could see the hidden equipment or men. Everybody understood what would have happened if the bombs had been high explosive rather than flour. The message was clear: hide it or die.

In Newcastle, Steven Sykes found his duties with the ack-ack batteries taxing and diverse. The ack-ack company had its headquarters in a large park defended by a series of pillboxes. He decided to camouflage the headquarters as a glasshouse and outbuildings, which earned him high praise from his divisional commander. Sykes, too, was learning the importance of having friends in high places.

Sykes was also beginning to find that strange and dangerous little adventures seemed to happen to him more frequently than to other people. He would often have to cadge flights with the RAF so he could assess his work from the air. Sykes had to inspect some heavy gun emplacements outside Newcastle and begged a ride in a Fairey Battle, an unusual little aircraft with a long canopy, nicknamed 'the greenhouse'. Sykes clambered aboard and was placed face down over an open hatch from which, Sykes supposed, bombs could be dropped or observations made. They flew at 10,000 feet in freezing cold. Suddenly a loud klaxon started. Sykes looked up to see the pilot making a thumbs-down sign. Suddenly, the plane went into a steep, terrifying dive. The plane pulled out of the dive and landed. Sykes got out, shaking with fear and only just able to control himself. The pilot explained that a flight of Free Czech Air Force Hawker Hurricanes had been on their tail. The pilot thought that the Czechs had mistaken the Fairey for a German Junkers and were going to shoot him down. The dive was his solution to the problem.

Barkas, meanwhile, was not the only one writing pamphlets. Camouflage seemed to attract eccentrics. One Norman Demuth, late of the London Rifle Brigade, produced 'Practical Camouflage'. The booklet was published by John Crowther Ltd, whose wartime list included 'How to Get Eggs', 'ABC Invasion Law', and 'Wills in Wartime'. Demuth's most popular work was 'Harrying the Hun', which had been reprinted five times and contained such gems as how to deal with a captured enemy airman: 'Stand well to the side as you march him in and keep him covered. If he tries to run off shoot him . . . one live Home Guard is worth more than two Huns, alive or dead.'

Even though the Blitz had started, trained camoufleurs, including Hutton, Trevelyan and others waiting to join No. 3 Camouflage Course, had to dally a few months before they were pressed into service. For them both, painting became a thing of great urgency. Julian Trevelyan found himself feverishly working to fill every minute of his soon-to-be-lost personal freedom. Suddenly subjects abounded: boys on roller skates, the fish and chip shop on the corner, and the mad barrage balloons that now filled the London sky.

On 7 September, Trevelyan heard the familiar noise of the sirens, something which, after many false alarms, Londoners had come to ignore. None of them knew that this time *Reichsmarschall* Goering was watching from the cliffs at Cap Gris Nez near Calais as the biggest air armada ever launched flew towards London, codenamed 'Target *Seeschlange*' (Sea Snake) and 'Target Loge', after a character in Wagner's Ring Cycle. They arrived in daylight and inflicted terrible damage on the docks before turning back to Germany just after six in the evening. Two-and-a-half hours later the second raid started and went on until dawn. London had never experienced anything like it. During the night the German planes dropped over 1,500 tons of incendiaries and high explosives. Nearly five hundred people died and 1,500 were seriously injured. The East End was on fire, the Surrey Docks were destroyed and flames stretched from horizon to horizon. For Trevelyan, surrealism acquired a new slant. He saw for the first time the bizarre effects that high explosives could produce. Uneasy fear became his constant companion and he found that, suddenly, it was possible to make new and deep friendships.

On 14 October 1940, Buckley once more stood on the platform at Shorncliffe waiting to greet the new intake. On the journey Trevelyan had been reunited with his old friend Roland Penrose, whom he described as 'not like the rest of us'. After leaving Bill Hayter's freelance camouflage company, Penrose had become a civilian lecturer in camouflage at the Home Guard School based in Osterley Park. The school had been set up by Tom Wintringham, who used his experiences as a member of the International Brigade in the Spanish Civil War to teach demolition, street-fighting and guerrilla warfare.

At Osterley, Penrose invented a practical way of showing how the smallest movement could be visible from the air. He tied a button to a length of thread and hid it in a patch of grass and around it assembled his Home Guard students. The button was invisible until Penrose tugged on the thread, pulling it rapidly across the grass, making it immediately visible from above. The collar stud could have been a military convoy and the eyes of the students could have been staring through the bomb sights of a dive bomber, he explained.

During the No. 2 Course, Buckley and Beddington had urged the trainees to make camouflage as interesting and entertaining as possible, and encouraged their students to invent rude stories and risqué jokes to capture the imaginations of the soldiers they would be teaching. Penrose now went a stage further. He persuaded his lover Lee Miller to strip naked and be painted in camouflage colours. He then draped a net over her, placing strategic tufts of grass over bits of her anatomy. The resulting photograph would be woven into his camouflage lectures and used in the highly popular pamphlet 'Home Guard Manual of Camouflage'.

Penrose stressed the importance of personal camouflage: 'The Home Guardsman may have many dangerous tasks to accomplish, but there is little doubt that, from his own point of view, the most dangerous thing he may carry about with him is his own naked face.' He knew that the stakes in the coming battles would be very high, and made no bones about it in the closing line of his pamphlet: 'Camouflage is no mystery and no joke; it is a matter of life and death—of victory and defeat.'

HOME GUARD MANUAL OF
CAMOUFLAGE

by ROLAND PENROSE
Lecturer to the War Office School for
Instructors to the Home Guard

Penrose's manual went into several editions
and sold thousands of copies.

GHQ CAIRO AND OPERATION COMPASS

On 10 June 1940, *Generalmajor* Rommel reached the French coast at Les Petites Dalles near Dieppe and on the same day Mussolini declared war on England and France. *The New York Times* described *Il Duce*'s actions as having 'the courage of a jackal at the heels of a bolder beast of prey'. Franklin D. Roosevelt said that 'the hand that held the dagger has stuck it in the back of its neighbour'.

In the spring of 1940, Mussolini had watched the Third Reich take less than three months to annex most of Western Europe and defeat the four-million-strong French army. He wanted to start his own war of conquest. Italian territories already encompassed what is today's Libya in the west, and in the east, Italian East Africa stretched as far as the Horn of Africa. Separating the two parts of the empire, and blocking the path to the Suez Canal and the Arabian oilfields, were the British in Egypt. Mussolini aimed to grab Suez and create a New Roman Empire. His battlefield would be the thousand-mile strip of land that lay parallel to the sea along the north African coast. The fighting area was forty miles wide, bounded in the south by the impassable Qattara Depression and in the north by the sea. It was considered to be ideal tank country and Mussolini had plenty of tanks: 600 in all. He could also muster nearly 300,000 troops, 1,600 artillery pieces and an airforce of 230 aircraft. Once he crossed the Egyptian border, all that would stand between him and his new empire was General Wavell with an underequipped army of 36,000 men, 275 tanks, 126 artillery pieces and 142 aircraft. Numerically, Mussolini held the whip hand. He thought his campaign was going to be a pushover.

On 7 September, after some shilly-shallying, Mussolini's Commander-in-Chief, Marshal Rodolfo Graziani, was ordered to attack Egypt from Italy's bases in Cyrenaica. Italian newspapers screamed 'Nothing can save Britain Now', and the world imagined Italian tanks racing across the shimmering sand, heading for Cairo.

To fight the much larger Italian force, Wavell appointed Major General Richard O'Connor. A modest man with a reputation for bold and unorthodox thinking, O'Connor had the ability to handle mobile forces and make the most of what little resources he possessed. Unlike his famous successor, Montgomery, O'Connor's style was reserved and low key. General Galloway, who knew both commanders, said: 'The difference between O'Connor and Montgomery was that O'Connor detested publicity and Monty lived on it.' Diffident or not, O'Connor had the complete trust of his troops and was possibly the best general fielded by the Allies in the Desert War, and a man who was the equal of Rommel in his ability to ruthlessly exploit an advantage.

Graziani's original orders were to begin the invasion on 8 August. At the end of that day his army had not moved. Graziani did not believe an invasion was possible. His army was dogged by incompetence; it lacked fuel, and suffered from poor vehicle maintenance. It took Mussolini nearly a month of bullying, but on 13 September, Graziani at last began the campaign proper. First he shelled British frontier posts, not realising that they were empty. Then, advancing at twelve miles a day, he crossed the Egyptian border. The Italians immediately came under pressure from British skirmishing forces and were stopped at Sidi Barrani, eighty miles short of the Allies at Mersa Matruh. The Suez Canal was still a very long way away. Mussolini was furious.

Throughout October and November, Graziani prepared for the next phase of his slow progress. He built a water pipeline and a metalled road to supply him from the border and erected a monument to celebrate the glories of the advance so far. He intended to sweep into Egypt past Alexandria along a pillar-lined route stretching all the way to Cairo. He called the enterprise 'The Road of Victory'.

On the other side of the hill the Allies were looking to launch an offensive of their own. In this Dick O'Connor was aided by his friend, the intelligent, perceptive but unpopular Irishman, Brigadier 'Chink' Dorman-Smith, whom many people found arrogant and overbearing. He was a close friend of Ernest Hemingway (who based the character Wilson-Harris in *The Sun Also Rises* on him). Wavell asked Dorman-Smith to look into the feasibility of an Allied counterattack and Chink detected a gap in the Italian lines south of Sidi Barrani. His report led to the first major Allied offensive of the campaign: Operation Compass.

By December, O'Connor was poised to launch Compass, a campaign that continued throughout the winter until February. He wanted his tiny Western Desert Force to attack the Italians in an initial five-day assault. O'Connor's army was short of everything: he did not have enough three-ton trucks to ferry his soldiers and their supplies, and with no tank transporters and towing equipment his armour moved under its own steam, wearing out irreplaceable engines and tracks. The supply problem would be solved by leaving concealed dumps of ammunition, food and water all over the area between the British and the Italian lines.

Wavell communicated prior to Compass: 'I do not entertain extravagant hopes for this operation but I do wish to make certain that if a big opportunity occurs we are prepared morally, mentally and administratively to use it to the fullest.' O'Connor would make such an opportunity and would follow through as hard as he was allowed. He wrote of his superiors, 'I felt they did not plan for a success . . . only for mediocre results.'

*   *   *

That autumn, Geoffrey Barkas had been warned by Freddie Beddington to be on standby to go to North Africa. His work in Northern Ireland had made its mark. Buckley had been instructed to send a small contingent of camoufleurs to North Africa. he chose Barkas to command the unit and ordered him to set off with an advance party of three officers. They were to be followed a few weeks later by a larger contingent, which would include Steven Sykes and Jasper Maskelyne. What they were to do when they got there was not made quite so clear: Buckley told Barkas that he must use his initiative,

65

seize opportunities where he could and make things up as he went along, just as he had done in Ireland.

By now Buckley had established himself in what were to be his permanent headquarters at Farnham Castle in Surrey. Barkas received his embarkation papers one November afternoon and opened them while lounging in the late autumn sunshine on the castle lawns. He was to sail from Liverpool on the *Andes* on 15 November.

The day of departure dawned fresh and windy as Barkas and his wife Natalie approached Liverpool docks. Far ahead they could see the buff and black funnel of the RMS *Andes* and, beyond, the grey outlines of the escort vessels. They stood together for a few final minutes together at the guarded barrier beyond which Natalie could not pass, and waited for the moment of separation. They had shared fifteen years of happy marriage. It would be two years before they saw each other again.

On board, as darkness fell, there was still no sign of the rest of Barkas's small command. When they at last arrived, their train from London having been badly delayed by the Coventry Blitz, Barkas was relieved to recognise a couple familiar faces. He knew John Hutton and the moustachioed 'Pep' Phillips from No. 2 Camouflage Course. The third man was Captain Blair Hughes-Stanton, a small, keen chap with unruly hair and dark eyes; he laughed a lot, and when he did, his eyes seemed to disappear. Barkas thought he seemed to inhale his laughter. Blair was a highly skilled wood engraver, but his first career choice had been the Navy, which he had joined as a boy sailor. He was a close friend of Henry Moore, a founder of the English Wood Engravers Society, and in 1938 won the International Prize for

Engraving at the Venice Biennale. He had also made ten tail-piece engravings for T. E. Lawrence's *Seven Pillars of Wisdom: A Triumph*. (Hughes-Stanton remembered the legendary hero as 'an arrogant little chap'.) Blair had applied to be an official war artist but the authorities found his portfolio 'too pornographic'. Barkas remembers that Hughes-Stanton had unusual hands, 'very capable-looking and apparently double-jointed in all fingers'. He and Barkas hit it off at once.

That evening the four men met in the bar of the *Andes* and drank to the future success of their mission, whatever it might turn out to be. Barkas went to his cabin that night very pleased with the team Buckley and Beddington had assigned to him.

The Mediterranean was too dangerous for merchant shipping, so the *Andes* travelled to Port Said the long way round, south down the west coast of Africa before turning north for the Suez Canal, a journey of 12,000 miles that would take an agonising six weeks. Along the way they picked up more ships until they were a convoy of ten fast passenger ships, with an escort of six destroyers, 'questing like sheepdogs'.

Aboard the densely crowded ships the passengers were quickly organised for defence. Barkas volunteered to man an anti-aircraft gun and was given a twenty-minute lesson in its use, after which he still did not have a clue how to operate it. Life on board the luxury liner was comfortable but tedious. Barkas and his party killed time playing deck tennis and giving impromptu camouflage lectures to the troops on board. He also volunteered to undertake the duty of censoring the soldiers' letters, something that he saw as necessary but that should be handled with sensitivity. News of the success of the first stages of Operation Compass filtered through the static on the wireless, making the slow voyage all the more frustrating. The convoy sailed south; the weather turned mild, blue sky replaced the wind and rain. Eventually the escort disappeared, leaving the convoy with only speed to protect it from the U-boats that prowled the Atlantic.

Back in England, Steven Sykes was booked to sail on the steamship RMS *Samaria*. He managed to spend the final days with his wife, who was expecting their first child. The pair made a last-minute shopping trip for a sun topee, but with no success. In the dressing-up cupboard at his mother's home at Formby, he discovered his father's First World War uniform. There, amongst Mickey Mouse costumes, gnome outfits and old furs, capes and obsolete fashion items, he found his father's topee and khaki shorts. He wrote in his diary: 'It will do.'

Joining Sykes on the *Samaria* were eleven fellow camouflage colleagues, including sculptor Bainbridge Copnall, magician Jasper Maskelyne, film designers Peter Proud and Fred Pusey, painters Robert Medley and John Codner, commercial artist Edwin C. Galligan and Garrett C. Clough, who would find international fame after the war as an anthropologist.

After dinner on the first night Sykes quietly made his way on deck where he looked into the skies for the Plough: he and Jean had made a pact before he left that they would both look at the stars of that familiar constellation every night at ten o'clock, a sort of comfort that they could share for the period they were separated.

*   *   *

Christmas found Geoffrey Barkas on the *Andes* manning his ack-ack gun. The sea was as 'smooth as mother of pearl. Flying fish winged their smooth and agitated course', he wrote. He scanned the sky for aircraft and the sea for periscopes while the soldiers sang 'Once in Royal David's City' and 'Hark the Herald Angels Sing'. The reek of engine oil mixed with the smells of Christmas cooking. At New Year 1941, the *Andes* sailed slowly up the Suez Canal towards Port Said, where the advance guard of camoufleurs disembarked for the final leg of their journey to Cairo. The four men stood leaning on the rail of the boat deck. Along the banks of the canal they could see the extent of the Allied army, huge workshops, depots and store dumps, hutted and tented camps, anti-aircraft batteries and defence works; thousands and thousands of troops and vehicles throwing up huge clouds of dust and sand. The depots stretched for miles. Was this what they were supposed to camouflage? 'The first cold drops of realism began to fall,' wrote Barkas.

During the voyage the camouflage officers had discussed in detail the problems that lay ahead of them and had come to conclusions uncluttered by reality. The huge encampment spread before them on the beige carpet of the desert was a small fraction of what they would have to deal with. Soon more troops would pour in from all over the Empire. They had no idea where to begin.

As Barkas stepped off the gangplank onto the

dockside at Port Said, he reflected that twenty-five years ago to the day he had stood in exactly the same place, a young second lieutenant with twenty men under his command, covered in lice and newly evacuated from Gallipoli.

* * *

On 30 October, the Italians invaded Greece. The Greeks retaliated by invading Italian Albania and set in train a series of events that would eventually put O'Connor on the back foot. The first phase of Compass—an attack on the fort at Nibeiwa, held by 2,500 Libyan soldiers and supported by seventy Italian tanks—had been a great success. O'Connor's forces had approached in two stages. On 7 December, tanks and lorries rumbled forward, carrying the soldiers in the three-tonners huddled against the bitter cold of the desert night. Overhead flew the bombers of the RAF on their way to hit the Italian airfields. Out to sea, the monitor HMS *Terror* and the gunboats HMS *Aphis* and HMS *Ladybird* bombarded the towns of Maktila and Sidi Barrani. By morning the bombers had destroyed or crippled twenty-seven aircraft. Daylight came, the convoys of lorries stopped and the troops waited. O'Connor sat calm in his concrete command post at Maaten Bagush, wondering if his advancing columns would be discovered. Night fell and the columns moved on towards the unsuspecting Italians.

At 05:00 hours on 9 December a barrage began and forty-eight British Matilda tanks stormed into the western side of the fort. The assault was shocking and swift. Twenty-three Italian tanks, positioned to guard the entrance to the camp, were destroyed before their crews could reach them. In less than ten minutes the crews themselves were dead, along with their commander General Maletti, who died in his pyjamas, gunned down firing a machine gun from the entrance of his dugout. Soon the remaining Italian armour had been captured, leaving the defenceless Libyan infantry to surrender. The fort had fallen in less than five hours and the battle for Sidi Barrani had begun.

Throughout the fighting, O'Connor toured the battlefield in a staff car accompanied by an office truck crammed with administrative equipment: typewriters, carbon paper, official rubber stamps, ink, pens and all the other unmilitary paraphernalia needed by a modern mobile army. The quiet, scholarly general's message was simple: 'Offensive action wherever possible'; 'Attack with the utmost violence'. By 11 December the battle for Sidi Barrani was over. Thirty thousand Italian prisoners marched in long, chaotic lines through the squalor of the battlefield. Four generals were among the captured; between them the Italian army had lost seventy-three tanks, over two hundred guns and thousands of tons of supplies, including rifles, ammunition, petrol, food and water. Ambulances bounced about carrying wounded and dying men; paper blew everywhere. Exhausted British troops watched their sometime enemies disappear into the distance, vast crowds of dazed, filthy men, no longer an army, trudging through the smoke past burning vehicles and scorched armour, and into captivity. He may have won the battle for Sidi Barrani, but General O'Connor was far from finished.

His sights were now set on Benghazi, and he would get there via the ports at Bardia and Tobruk.

But first General Wavell had some bad news for him. The 4th Indian Division was needed, immediately, for an attack on Eritrea. Overnight, O'Connor lost half his force.

By New Year, O'Connor's men, soon to be renamed XIII Corps, were ready to attack the tiny port of Bardia. O'Connor had tasked the Australian general Iven Mackay (known to his men as 'Mr Chips') with commanding the assault. As was usual in Compass, the Allies faced a larger, better-equipped force: 45,000 Italians under the command of General 'Electric Whiskers' Bergonzoli. *Il Duce* himself ordered that Bardia must be defended to the last. Bergonzoli replied: 'In Bardia we are and here we stay.'

The town was surrounded by minefields, an anti-tank ditch and huge quantities of barbed wire. Before the tanks could go in, the engineers had to clear a path. The men of 7th Armoured were ordered to remove the exhaust baffles from their tanks. Without the baffles the powerful tank engines could be heard miles away. At dusk the tanks roared into life, the stupendous noise echoed across the desert and they set off spending the hours of darkness driving up and down the roads outside the town. The noise battered at the ears of the terrified enemy, who thought that a gigantic force was assembled against them.

Convoys of Allied three-ton trucks lurched forward, carrying shivering Australian troops through the freezing cold to the start line. Each man carried 150 rounds of ammunition, hand grenades, magazines for the Bren guns, and enough food for three days. The heavy support teams cradled their two-inch mortars, bracing themselves against the sides of the lorries, trying to stop the weapons sliding around as the lorries jolted forward, as tin boxes of heavy mortar rounds slid and tore the skin off their shins. The sappers crawled forward, heading for the weak points they had found in the fearsome tank ditch. Behind them they dragged 'Bangalore Torpedoes', a weapon used for clearing mines and barbed wire, made of five-foot-long sections of pipe packed with explosives, which could be screwed together under fire, pushed forward under the wire and detonated. The engineers carried captured Italian wire-cutters stuffed into their belts.

At 5.30 a.m. the artillery opened up and simultaneously the Bangalores were detonated. Before the sand and gravel thrown up by the explosions had stopped falling, the sappers dived into the ditch, pulling its sides down with pickaxes, making a bridge for the tanks to clatter over. It took an hour to clear two lanes, and then the tanks surged towards the centre of the town, engines screaming, firing round after round of high explosive into the Italian dugouts. Behind them came the infantry, bayonets fixed. By eight o'clock the battle began to die down: 8,000 Italians had had enough. Fighting continued to the north and south but by the end of the next morning it was over. The town had fallen, its harbour and water supply intact. Signals poured into Wavell's headquarters: the enemy had lost 40,000 men—captured, killed or wounded—along with 400 guns, 120 tanks and, most useful of all, nearly 800 trucks. While the Australian troops lunched on Italian food and toasted themselves with Italian wine, O'Connor was already on his way west to Tobruk.

Churchill, on the other hand, was having second thoughts about the direction of the war. For some time it had been his ambition to establish a 'Balkan Front' made up of Turkey, Greece and Yugoslavia, which would put the Romanian oil fields, vital to the German war effort, within reach of Allied bombers. He later wrote: 'It was our aim to animate and combine Yugoslavia, Greece and Turkey. Our duty, so far as possible, was to aid the Greeks.' It was an idea that was developing into an obsession. Two days after Bardia fell, he wrote to Wavell: 'Although perhaps by luck and daring we may collect comparatively easily most delectable prizes on the Libyan shore, the massive importance of . . . keeping the Greek front in being must weigh hourly with us.'

* * *

Barkas and his small group arrived in Cairo, where he had orders to report to GHQ Cairo at No. 10 Tomolbat Street, a Belle Époque-style apartment block requisitioned by the army at the beginning of the war and known to all as 'Grey Pillars'. To get to the smart Garden City district in which GHQ was located, Barkas drove along streets where local cars, tiny Fiats and Austin 7s, jostled with British staff cars, army lorries, donkey carts piled high with fruit and vegetables, flocks of sheep and even tanks. Buses and donkeys sported blue beads to ward off the evil eye.

After witnessing the privations of wartime Liverpool, Barkas found the sheer plenty of parts of Cairo shocking. Department stores like the 'Salon Vert' offered glass, crockery, fabrics, clothes and cosmetics, things that had become impossible to find in Britain. The smell of fresh coffee wafted from the dozens of small bakeries. One, 'Groppis', offered pastries cooked in clarified butter. Eggs, sugar, oranges and dates were freely available, as were giant cauliflowers and cabbages grown in the warmth of the fertile Nile Delta. There were clubs like the Muhammad Ali and the RAC, which were as exclusive and luxurious as any in the world. The wealthy were interested in intrigue, racing and fine clothes, while beyond the grand main streets the poor lived in disintegrating mud buildings with no sanitation, working for a pittance, and in the narrow alleys their children played in muck and filth.

Grey Pillars stood at the heart of Wavell's vast command. From it he controlled an empire that straddled two continents and contained nine countries. GHQ was his nerve centre, manned by staff officers who worked long hours doing their best to see that wherever the fighting men were sent they would arrive in the right place, at the right time, with the right equipment, stores, food, fuel and ammunition; a complex and highly demanding task. The men working in GHQ spent nearly two years planning the build-up of the supplies, reinforcements and base developments that would enable Montgomery to defeat Rommel at Alamein. In addition they had to service the requirements of General Wavell's campaigns not just in the Western Desert but also in Greece, Eritrea, Syria and Iraq.

But such a huge headquarters attracted what one officer who worked there has described as a 'fringe element of conmen' who gave Grey Pillars a bad name and magnified the divide between the front-line troops and the staff personnel, a divide found in every army. Soldiers, on short leave from the rigours of the desert, and unaware of the real work that was going on behind the façade of their HQ, saw British officers who had stopped work at midday to play tennis, swim at the Gezira Sporting Club or drink champagne, hock or local whisky on the terrace of the Shepheard's Hotel, before staggering through the Moorish Hall, a cool refuge from the heat, its sweeping stairway flanked by ebony caryatids, to the restaurant, where they luncheoned on traditional British food, chicken pie, roast beef or ham and chips. Some skipped lunch and succumbed to the pleasures of the Long Bar, presided over by Joe, who was Swiss and reportedly a spy. The fighting men nicknamed General Headquarters personnel 'The Gabardine Swine', a reference to the material of their uniforms. The name could be unfair, as some of the officers on that terrace at Shepheard's were themselves on leave from the desert, a place to which in a few days they must return. One staff officer remembers that 'during the hot weather we had a break from 1300 to 1600 and returned to work probably to 1900 or later. This was essential as we had no air conditioning. I don't recall that we ever had time to indulge in the delights of the Gezira Club and champagne!'

Outside, other ranks flooded the streets, frantic to make the most of their short leave from the desert. Most of the soldiers were under thirty, young men who had never been further from home than Blackpool or Margate, who now bargained for souvenirs in the markets, had their pockets picked and got drunk in sleazy bars where bands played behind wire mesh to protect them from flying bottles. Military policemen stood guard round the red-light district, vainly trying to keep the soldiers away from the girls. Noël Coward's impression of the city was that 'somewhere in the vague outside world there might be a war of some sort going on. All the fripperies of pre-war luxury are still in existence here, rich people, idle people, cocktail parties, dinner parties, jewels and evening dress', while photographer Cecil Beaton wrote that a combination of the military and the heat played 'upon a man's moral fibre as relentlessly as upon his physique'. Lawrence Durrell described it as: 'this copper pan of a blazing town with its pullulating, stinking inhabitants . . . its cripples, deformities, ophthalmia, goitre, amputations, lice and fleas'. However one took it, for those arriving from Britain, Cairo was overwhelming.

* * *

Barkas's taxi dropped him at the guard post to Grey Pillars. Once through the barbed wire and military police guarding the entrance, he joined the hordes of khaki-clad figures milling about in what seemed to be chaos. Clerks scurried about carrying armfuls of files, or pushed even larger piles on trolleys. Doors opened to reveal sweating staff officers sitting at desks in kitchens, bathrooms and converted bedrooms, trying to make themselves heard over the clatter of typewriters and the irritable trilling of telephones. At the foot of each staircase were signplates, bristling with pointers, sporting only baffling initials; acronyms sprouted everywhere: MEBU, NABU, SABU, MEFU. The building changed on an almost daily basis as

77

departments were split into sections, the sections into subsections and sub-departmental offices. It was 'like a beleaguered department store, manfully trying to cope with major alterations,' wrote the journalist Alexander Clifford. At one level GHQ was a huge bureaucracy, with its share of complacent men disconnected from the war they were trying to fight and men who, like the conmen, tarnished the reputations of their hard-working brother staff officers to such an extent that Durrell found: 'There was something definitely and deeply wrong about the attitude of the British Army.'

Barkas, on the other hand, said of the personnel at Grey Pillars: 'I have yet to encounter any set of men who could have wrestled more effectively with overwhelming difficulties, or produced more sense and less "flannel" in the ever-shifting conditions which beset them.'

But, on that first day, Barkas toured the corridors trying to find anyone who knew anything about him. The officer who had sent for him had long vanished, posted back to England, taking with him the reasons for the Camouflage Unit's mission. Eventually some of the files relating to the unit were found: Barkas's remit was both vague and far-reaching, it seemed that he was to undertake to camouflage the entire army of the Nile. Barkas was put under the direction of Lieutenant Colonel G. B. S. Hindley RA, a regular officer and director of staff duties ('DSD'). Barkas found him patient, helpfully critical and always encouraging. He later described him as 'the kind of boss I would have chosen had I been given my pick'.

Hindley solved the immediate problem of an office by finding Barkas a half share in a trestle table in the despatch riders' room. It wasn't much, but it was a start. Undaunted, Barkas began to work out the practicalities of his task. Since becoming a camouflage officer he had developed a theory: he thought that everywhere, even in a place as flat and featureless as the desert, there would be patterns, natural or manmade, which could be used to hide, or at least blur, the army's intentions from the enemy. He now had to find those patterns and work out a way to use them. Hindley agreed and quickly secured an RAF reconnaissance aircraft to survey the area.

*   *   *

On 11 January, after the fall of Bardia, Hitler issued 'Führer Directive No. 22', a decision to send German troops to Libya. The move would begin on 15 February. O'Connor, though he did not know it, was fighting against the clock. It took only three days for him to get his force from Bardia to Tobruk. He knew that he was up against considerable Italian opposition: 32,000 men, 65 light and medium tanks and 220 guns. At 05:45 hours on 21 January he began his assault on the port. An artillery barrage was followed by an armoured assault, the tanks fanning out through the town. The fighting went on all day. By nightfall the Italian artillery had been silenced and the port's commander, General Petassi, had been captured.

The following afternoon Tobruk fell, and with it the port's water supply, a desalination plant that could deliver thousands of gallons of water a day and which had been taken intact. Without the desalination plant military life could not be sustained. The

Camouflage Unit would be instrumental in protecting this vital lifeline. The Italians had lost 25,000 troops. More importantly, O'Connor had a new base to supply his ambition to roll up the Italian army in West Africa once and for all.

* * *

On 22 January, Barkas and Hughes-Stanton peered out of an unarmed Lysander reconnaissance aircraft and surveyed the battlescape; it was immense. 'This desert warfare has to be seen to be believed,' wrote Winston Churchill. 'Large armies, with their innumerable transport and tiny habitations, are dispersed and scattered as if from a pepper pot over the vast indeterminate slopes and plains of the desert, broken here and there only by a sandy crease or tuck in the ground or outcrop of rock. The ground in most places, especially on all commanding eminences, is rock with only an inch or two of sand on the top, and no cover can be obtained for guns or troops except by blasting.'

Far to the west, on the coast, they could see clouds of black smoke hanging over Tobruk, the town that would soon play an important part in their lives. The two men discovered that the desert was not nearly as featureless as it appeared from the ground. Stretching across the war-scarred landscape they noticed distinctive patterns to which they began to ascribe names: the Wadi pattern, the Polka Dot, Figured Velvet. The positions of these regions were noted down for closer scrutiny on foot.

Two days later the intrepid camoufleurs climbed into a Chevrolet staff car to start their land recce.

Behind them, in support, was a fifteen-hundredweight Ford truck. Both vehicles were crammed to bursting with all they would need for three weeks of reconnaissance and camouflage experiments. One of the most important things they wanted to test was whether camouflage could be used aggressively in the front line. Would they be able to hide troop formations so that the enemy would be unaware that an attack was planned? This idea would grow over the coming months and would bear fruit at the siege of Tobruk.

Into the two vehicles sacks of potatoes and onions were dumped on top of rolls of camouflage nets, miles of cord, garnish, wire, picks and shovels, Primus stoves, bivouac tents and blankets. Canvas map cases bulged with large-scale maps covering desert wastelands from the Mersa Matruh to Benghazi, yellow, featureless documents that might as well have been charts of the sea. Petrol was stored in standard-issue, almost useless, leaky four-gallon cans; water was carried in two fifteen-gallon 'fantasies'. Rolls of canvas cleated with wood—essential to help them out of soft sand if they got bogged down—were hauled on top of everything else.

Hughes-Stanton and Barkas had been assigned a couple of Royal Army Service Corps drivers for the trip, a Cockney and a Mancunian. The Londoner was Lance Corporal Dowse, who was reputed to know a lot about how to navigate and survive in the desert. Tall, slim and as 'sharp as a needle', he had 'an engaging hint of impudence in his sharp face'. His driving partner, Tom Parker, was shy and taciturn; Hughes-Stanton described him as having a 'lumpy resemblance to Fred Astaire'. The two

81

drivers were perfect foils for each other. If anything went wrong, even if it was something he had done or not done, or ordered to be done only minutes before, Dowse would blame Parker very loudly. This was all carried with good humour and Parker would nod and reply, ''Appen you're right.'

The two-vehicle convoy swept out of Grey Pillars and headed off in the direction of Tobruk, hoping to catch up with General O'Connor's galloping army. Barkas wanted to put their theories into practice at the 'sharp end'. Passing the Pyramids and the vast camps of the British Army of the Nile, they turned west off the main Alexandria road and headed up the coast past a big sign that announced: 'You Are Now Entering the Western Desert'. Here they joined the endless line of military vehicles, stretching to the horizon and groaning with the tens of thousands of tons of materiel for the fighting men at the front. They drove through a featureless, fawn-coloured valley. To their left was yellow sand and rock; to their right, white sea dunes. The valley gave on to straggling plantations of fig trees; white-robed Arabs walked behind oxen, harrowing the stony ground.

The road stretched on interminably. Mile after mile of endless uniform drabness speckled here and there with dusty, sage-green scrub; colour became a distant, almost forgotten, memory. On a series of switchback ridges leading to Mersa Matruh, the heavily laden vehicles ground, in low gear, up the last hill and as they topped the crest were confronted with the water of the Mediterranean, glittering blue, emerald, turquoise and purple; after the miles of desert the colour was overwhelming, as though they had been 'slapped in the face by a rainbow'. Through the glitter they could see the pure white buildings of Mersa Matruh.

For the rest of that day the world contracted to the view through the windscreens, the roaring of the engines and the zip of the heavy tyres on the road. Whenever they clambered out of the vehicles for a break, small Arab boys appeared from nowhere ready to bargain; eggs were the currency. For five eggs you could fill your enamel cup with sugar; the rates for tins of bully beef, butter and everything else were the same from Bardia to Benghazi. Barkas wondered who the far-off Egg King was who controlled the trade and fixed the rates.

As they reached no-man's land near Sidi Barrani, the scene of General O'Connor's recent victory, they saw graffiti-covered walls, vestiges of the beaten Italian army: 'Believe, Obey, Fight', 'The Duce is Always Right'. Then they came across the road that General Graziani had so carefully started to build, his 'Road to Victory'. It had never been finished—only the foundations had been laid, enormous blocks of concrete that jolted the vehicles so badly they were forced to take to the flatter, sandy bush where the going was smoother.

At a small settlement called Buq Buq they came across the first signs of battle, where the Italians had fought a rearguard action and the Allies had captured many prisoners and large amounts of equipment. There were shot-up tanks, some overturned, burnt and caked in oil; abandoned equipment lay strewn everywhere. They drove against an endless stream of trucks packed with Italian prisoners, which slowed their progress. These were the men captured at Tobruk and now on their way to POW camps in Scotland or Canada. Barkas was surprised at how cheerful they all looked.

Nearing Tobruk, they entered the battle zone proper. On the outskirts of the town the wind got up, blowing in a sandstorm. The world went yellow and visibility dropped to almost zero; empty ration tins and cans, caught by the gale, clanged and banged through the murk. They spent that night sheltering in the lavatory of a hospital block.

By morning the storm had cleared to reveal the astonishing sight of Tobruk harbour choked with ruined ships: some burnt-out floating hulks; some sunk, their superstructures still visible. A waterlogged seaplane rolled in the swell, its wings under water. The jetty was a wreck, dynamited cranes and hoists lying where they had crashed down. British ships of war and picket boats nosed about, trying to get the harbour working as quickly as possible.

They continued on through the ruined outskirts of the town. Pictures of Mussolini stared out from smashed walls; on the side of the barracks a soldier had drawn a caricature of a debauched, drunk-looking Churchill smoking a cigar and scrawled underneath: 'I am the friend of the little people'. Eventually at a point called Kilo 5, where they were warned that the road was under direct observation and might be shelled, they had found the war. Overhead a Lysander buzzed in circles, directing the fire of the British batteries. Barkas had forgotten how noisy war was, and how frightening. He and Hughes-Stanton could not stop flinching every time a shell exploded, as if each one had been aimed directly at them.

The battle quickly moved on. Desperate not to

be left behind, Lance Corporal Dowse put his foot down and sped through the blinding dust. They overtook a lorry and hit an oncoming vehicle. Their car slewed sideways, bounced and came to rest on its side. After a long silence Barkas heard someone say 'Are you all right?' He replied: 'I'll tell you in minute.' They had narrowly avoided a terrible disaster. The car was a write-off, Barkas's chin was cut to the bone, and Hughes-Stanton's nose poured blood—he thought he had broken it. Driver Dowse had a huge lump swelling up behind his ear where he'd hit his head on the doorframe. The next hours were spent stumbling about, salvaging what they could from the wreck.

The Royal Engineers brought up a big bulldozer and, with a lot of shouting and waving, pushed the wrecked Chevrolet off the road. For a moment the air was full of the noise of breaking glass and crumpling metal as the heavy vehicle rolled over on its back, crushing the dented roof flat. The troops in a passing lorry cheered and the bulldozer backed off, and rumbled on up the road in search of new prey.

In the morning Barkas had his chin dressed. While queuing to be seen, he sat next to an Arab woman waiting for an ambulance. Her arm had been blown off at the shoulder when the donkey she was leading trod on a mine.

After this they saw a lot more suffering civilians. At one halt Barkas noticed that the ground was littered with Italian hand grenades, brightly coloured objects that looked like toys. A little later he saw a middle-aged man sitting on the ground wrapped in a blood-stained blanket. Where the man's hands should have been were two stumps wrapped in balls of wadding; he held the stumps up,

85

turning his head from one side to the other, his eyes now bloody, sightless sockets. The man had picked up one of the grenades and taken the pin out. The last Barkas saw of him, he was being led away on a mule by his friends.

*　　*　　*

Hundreds of Allied tanks, trucks, armoured cars, carriers and staff cars were now in full cry, following the retreating Italian army. The retreat turned into a rout and the race for Benghazi was on. Soon the desert was covered in hundreds of broken-down vehicles. Any vehicle that could move was pressed into action: captured Italian SpAs, Fiats, motor-tricycles, lorries towing other lorries, anything to keep the advancing front line supplied. For Barkas it was 'as though all the junk from all the motor cemeteries of the world had come to life for one glorious spree'.

The camoufleurs kept up as best they could in their overloaded truck. At one stage they were shouted at by a fierce brigadier whom they nicknamed the 'Ball of Fire'. His name was Horace Robertson, an Australian who had fought at Gallipoli. Robertson was hellbent on winning the 'Benghazi Handicap'. They saw him standing on a heap of stones by his command vehicle, chain-smoking impatiently. The brigadier beckoned Barkas over and said in a quiet, kindly tone, 'I've seen you before haven't I? Who are you again?'

'Camouflage officer from GHQ sir, doing a recce of camouflage conditions,' Barkas replied.

The brigadier smiled and seemed pleased. 'Yes, I do remember,' he replied thoughtfully. And then he exploded, hurling his cigarette to the ground: 'AND GET YOUR TRUCK OFF MY BLOODY ROAD IMMEDIATELY!'

Barkas obeyed.

*   *   *

Richard O'Connor had fought the length of the desert. His vehicles were on their last legs and his supply lines were stretched to breaking point. But he was determined to get to Benghazi before Churchill took the rest of his army away from him and sent it to Greece. He used every last gallon of petrol he could lay his hands on and any means to keep the vehicles going, including cannibalising non-runners. His troops were in uncharted territory that the Italians had thought to be impassable. The historian Correlli Barnett called O'Connor's advance 'one of the epic marches of history'. Between the Allies and Benghazi on the right flank stood infantry, guns and tanks under General Babini; on the left, a division holding Derna, a wadi with sheer sides reaching to 700 feet. O'Connor resolved to smash through on the right, but Babini gave O'Connor the slip, withdrawing under cover of darkness. To his enormous frustration, O'Connor had to wait while fresh supplies of fuel, petrol and ammunition were brought up. The Italians were slipping from his grasp.

The question of supply was the enigma of war in the Western Desert. The better you did and the further you advanced, the longer your supply lines became and the more difficult it became to manoeuvre. This problem bedevilled O'Connor, as it would Rommel and Montgomery—although

Monty partly solved the problem by being supremely cautious in his pursuit of the enemy. O'Connor was in a frenzy to get on: Dorman-Smith described him as being like 'a terrier ratting'.

Thirteenth Corps had only fifty usable cruiser tanks. The logistics were stark. Before joining the battle O'Connor had to advance 150 miles across unknown territory to face a much bigger Italian force. His tanks would arrive and start fighting with a full tank of petrol and whatever ammunition and food they could carry. He could count on enough resupply to last him two days and that would be it; he would have no more supplies of any sort. O'Connor applied for and received Wavell's permission to resume his advance.

O'Connor followed the advance in his staff car. On the roadside more and more British tanks stood broken down and abandoned. At one point his worries overcame him and, uncharacteristically, he asked Dorman-Smith, 'My God, do you think it's going to be all right?'

The Italians continued to withdraw with nothing to stop them. Then a small mobile flying column of 2,000 men under the command of Lieutenant Colonel John Combe managed to hook behind the retreating enemy and cut them off at a place that those who fought there would never forget: Beda Fomm. 'Combe Force', made up of the 11th Hussars, the King's Dragoon Guards, the 2nd Battalion the Rifle Brigade, an RAF armoured car squadron and the Royal Horse Artillery, had a few anti-tank guns, the weapons on their armoured cars, Bren guns, mortars and rifles. They faced 20,000 Italians, sporting 60 medium tanks and over 200 artillery pieces.

The battle raged for three days. By the end, the fighting was hand to hand. For a time it looked as though the Italian tanks would break through: they had advanced right on top of Combe Force. Twenty-five-pounder field guns were ordered to open up on Combe Force's own position; shells dropped on friend and foe alike. One rifleman remembers that when the shells started to land, everyone—British, Commonwealth, Italian—dived for whatever cover they could find. It was a desperate measure but it worked, the enemy tanks ground to a halt, turrets blown off, tracks ripped apart.

At the very end a regimental sergeant major who had run out of ammunition captured an enemy tank by hitting its commander over the head with a rifle butt. The Allies had come out on top and the shattered survivors from both sides watched as General Bergonzoli surrendered to Captain Pearson of the Rifle Brigade. There were no cheers; the only noises were the burning vehicles, exploding ammunition and the moans of the dying. Wind caught the heavy black smoke, mixed it with sand, and blew it against men's faces, burning their eyes. General O'Connor signalled to his commander Wavell, 'Fox killed in the open'.

Barkas and Hughes-Stanton were less than twenty miles away, on an airfield littered with the wreckage of Italian aircraft. They drove towards the burning hangars, where soldiers were lighting campfires, brewing up. No more shells were falling; all the urgency of the last few days had gone. Barkas jumped out of the lorry and asked what was happening. 'Don't you know? The war's over. We've taken Benghazi.' It was 7 February 1941.

Later that day an enormous Italian staff car

drove past, leading a truck, both filled with braid-covered high-ranking Italian officers. The leading despatch rider gave a huge thumbs-up as he shot by. The camoufleurs glimpsed General Bergonzoli, his generals, including Babini, his ADCs, and headquarters staff being driven into captivity.

O'Connor now wanted to dash to Tripoli, where Italian troops and equipment had disembarked on their way to fight the Allies. Churchill stopped him. He sent Wavell a telegram congratulating him on the capture of Benghazi, which ended with the fateful words: 'Your major effort must now be to aid Greece and/or Turkey. This rules out any serious effort against Tripoli . . . We should try to get into a position to offer the Greeks the transfer of to Greece of the fighting portion of the Army which has hitherto defended Egypt.'

Churchill was talking about XIII Corps, O'Connor's army. The Germans had marched into Greece and Churchill had become consumed by his obsession with helping the Greeks who, in a declaration made in 1939, Britain had undertaken to help with 'all the support in her power'. O'Connor protested, but to no avail. This was a major strategic blunder on Churchill's part. If he had given O'Connor his head, XIII Corps might have reached and even captured Tripoli, thereby denying the Germans a port to land their troops. Even if they had not got there by 14 February, the day the Germans began to disembark, XIII Corps would have caused immense disruption. O'Connor might have fought Rommel in the Battle of Tripoli; he was easily Rommel's equal and it is likely he would have won.

Unaware that their leaders were arguing, Barkas

and Hughes-Stanton turned and retraced their steps to Cairo. They had learned a lot on the trip. They had worked with soldiers of all ranks and arms—gunners, infantry and sappers. In their attempts to put their Farnham theories into practice, they had found the soldiers willing to help with experiments to find ways to hide guns, men and equipment on the unpromising surface of the desert. Barkas was certain that he could use camouflage to hide the build-up to a battle, but they had a lot to learn and he knew it would be some time before the planners would include camouflage in their tactical thinking.

It was a solemn drive back through the chaos of war: their noses full of the smell of burning oil and gasoline, and the stench of rotting corpses. The two men felt flat and futile. Barkas could not get the blinded, handless man and the woman whose arms had been blown off out of his mind. Dying animals snarled at the truck's tyres as it sped by on the narrow road.

The route to Cairo took them from Benghazi to Barce, Derna, Tobruk, Amriya, Halfway House, Giza, to Cairo—over 2,000 dusty, suspension-wrecking miles of road. On the road to Barce they came across a British Army tank; alongside it were two soldiers who looked as though they were sleeping. The tank had hit a mine, the sleeping men were dead. Painted on the barrel of the tank, in gay scrolls and flourishes, were the words 'Spirit of Fun'.

5

TOBRUK: THE CAMOUFLAGE UNIT'S LUCKY BREAK

Hitler received news of the Italian military failures with rage. He accused his allies of defeatism. Planning for Directive No. 22, the order to send German troops to North Africa, began immediately and was codenamed Operation *Sonnenblume* (Sunflower). On 6 February, the day that Bergonzoli surrendered Benghazi, Hitler summoned Rommel and gave him command of the new army, the *Deutsches Afrika Korps*.

Days later, on 12 February, Hitler summoned Rommel back to Berlin. The most powerful man in Europe was speechless. In his hands he waved translations of the major articles in English and American newspapers describing O'Connor's victories. 'See what they say?' raged the Führer: '"Masterly Coordination Between Armoured Land Forces, the Airforce and the Navy".' The British had triumphed despite being outnumbered three to one.

Rommel set off for Libya at once. He had been ordered to disembark his troops and proceed with caution, but he was determined to seize every opportunity to engage and beat the enemy. *Blitzkrieg* had been pioneered in France and would be put to use in the desert. Later he wrote: 'In view . . . of the sluggishness of the Italian command, I decided to ignore my orders and take command at the front with my own hands as soon as possible— at the very latest after the arrival of the first German units.'

By the fourteenth, Rommel was in Tripoli, standing on the quayside watching the disembarkation of the first elements of his force. He ordered the work to continue round the clock. Arc lights blazed through the night as men, tanks and heavy equipment poured off the transport ships. Rommel instructed that dummy tanks be built of wood and canvas and mounted on Volkswagen cars to fool aerial reconnaissance into thinking his force was larger than it was. Every opportunity would be seized to outfox the enemy. Rommel held a parade in Tripoli and made his new division drive through the town, passing the same point several times again to make it look as though he had a bigger force than he actually did. Many of his own men did not spot the trick. One officer did, though, and wrote: 'After a quarter of an hour I noticed a fault in the chains of a heavy Mark IV Panzer, which somehow looked familiar to me . . . Only then did the penny drop, as the Tommies say, and I could not help grinning.'

For the Camouflage Unit, as for the rest of the Allied armies in the desert, the arrival of Rommel changed everything. The war was back on and there was plenty for the camoufleurs to be getting on with. Barkas was back in action and impatient for his next contingent to arrive. The *Samaria* was still making its slow way round Africa; its twelve camoufleur passengers were all extremely bored. Jasper Maskelyne was doing his best to keep everyone on the ship entertained with his magic tricks. He was helped in this by another camouflage officer, Lieutenant R. J. Morrison, who had worked for Maskelyne as a stage manager. Morrison treated the famous illusionist as a sort of minor god and was always at his side.

Conditions on the *Samaria* were not agreeable for any of the troops. The sentries' and men's quarters were 'one mass of hammocks . . . They were all eating, living and sleeping in the same cramped place.' Sykes fell ill with malaria and for some days was confined to his sweaty cabin. Robert Medley and Peter Proud set up a portable gramophone to entertain him. He spent his days listening to Tino Rossi singing 'L'Ombre s'enfuit' and reading T. E. Lawrence's *Seven Pillars of Wisdom*.

The sixty-five-day journey passed without any contact with the enemy. Maskelyne had proved indefatigable in his efforts to make the trip go smoothly. When the ship docked at Cairo, the 'Officer Commanding Troops' handed Maskelyne a star-struck letter, thanking him for the work he had done trying to keep everyone amused.

> *My Dear Maskelyne,*
> *Our long voyage is fast drawing to a close and I feel I must convey the grateful thanks of everyone aboard this ship for the wonderful entertainment you have provided on many occasions throughout this journey. I would like to personally thank you for your tremendous loyalty and for the great many sacrifices you have made for the troops on board, whose discipline and wellbeing has been your unstinting concern . . .*

94

*I would also like to congratulate you on your
very fine personal style and for the healthy
comradeship you have constantly displayed
throughout the voyage, not forgetting the real
'pep' you have instilled in everyone on the ship.
With many thanks and every good wish,
Yours sincerely,
H. M. Davis. Lt Col RA.*

Somehow Maskelyne had taken it upon himself to assume command of his fellow camoufleurs. On 10 March 1941, Barkas received a scrap of paper containing an urgent, handwritten, message: 'Please tell Major Barkas that I am stranded here with all eleven officers and that we have no money at all.' It was signed 'Jasper Maskelyne'.

'How disappointing,' thought Barkas. 'You'd have thought, being a magician, he'd just say "Hey Presto" and five-pound notes would fall out of the sky.'

*   *   *

When the group arrived in Cairo, Barkas threw them in at the deep end, sending them straight out into 'the Blue'—what the soldiers called the desert. He knew they were spread very thin, and before they set off he instructed them to make what they could with whatever was to hand. Initiative and improvisation were to be their watchwords.

Barkas had a special role for Maskelyne, one that he thought would make good use of the magician's unique skills: he wanted him to set up a Camouflage Experimental Unit and come up with ideas that could be transferred to the desert. The

95

Experimental Unit would be based in two large huts at Wingate Barracks just outside Cairo, where the army had established its huge engineering workshops. Barkas handed the magician a narrow piece of buff card. On it was what looked like a child's drawing of a tank, with a sort of canopy over it. Above the drawing was written: 'Is it a wild idea that a tank could be camouflaged to look like a lorry?' Below the picture the same person had written: 'It might be useful during approach march etc.' The 'might' had been crossed out and replaced with an emphatic 'would'. The drawing came from the Commander-in-Chief Middle East, General Wavell himself.

Maskelyne looked at the drawing and asked Barkas if he could take Morrison with him to help set up the Experimental Unit. Barkas agreed.

Later, Maskelyne wrote home: 'Of course I have not told you that I have been put in charge of the Camouflage Experimental Unit. I handle all ideas and inventions for the Midell [sic] East; or at least I have done since I arrived out here—I am now a captain! It has been great fun as I started with myself and one man in a small room. Now I have thirty-five men, several buildings and garages. My staff consists of carpenters, plasterers, fitters, photographers, draughtsmen and office staff. On top of this I have one CQMS and three sergeants.' The master showman was greatly exaggerating the number of men under his command.

*　　*　　*

Churchill's fixation with helping the Greeks had now turned into a full-scale operation. Codenamed

Lustre, which would see the despatch of thousands of British and Commonwealth troops from North Africa to Greece. Operation Lustre started on 6 March. At three-day intervals convoys left Alexandria, bound for Piraeus, the Greek harbour outside Athens. The convoys siphoned off some of the best men and materiel from the Western Desert Force. O'Connor's highly trained and triumphant force melted away. With them went two of Barkas's best camouflage officers, his friend Blair Hughes-Stanton and Garrett Clough. Barkas wrote in his diary: 'Day after day, clanking and rumbling eastward along the battered coastal road and through the dust and slime of the inland tracks went the freshest of the fighting units, the soundest of the trucks, tanks and guns, the cream of the desert army.'

When Barkas tried to find out where Lustre Force was going, he met strong resistance from the middle-ranking officers at Grey Pillars. The information was top secret and could not be passed on. When he asked if he could at least be given some clue as to the colour and nature of the terrain—was it perhaps yellow, brown or green, was it lumpy or flat?—he was told that that too was classified information. In desperation he asked how big the force was, so that at least he could work out how much camouflage material to assemble for it; but no, he could not be told that either. He asked when, roughly, the force was due to depart so that he could get an idea of how long he had to prepare: no, that was classified. Finally he made a direct approach to his most senior officer, the Director of Ordnance Services, and, at last, was let in on the secret. Somehow he would make sure that the camouflage element of Lustre set off with the right equipment.

The mania for secrecy was spreading everywhere and was later summed up in the song 'Hush Hush', from the musical *Salad Days*.

> *But all my job appeared to consist of,*
> *Much to my chagrin and dismay,*
> *Was a painfully comprehensive list*
> *Of things I mustn't do or say.*
> *Don't ever ask what job you're on*
> *It's hush hush.*
> *Don't ever ask where the Empire's gone*
> *It's hush hush . . .*
>
> *If you invent a code that's new*
> *Nobody must be able to*
> *Decipher the code*
> *Not even you.*
> *It's hush hush . . .*
>
> *Don't ever ask who won the war,*
> *It's hush hush.*
> *Don't ever ask what the war was for*
> *it's hush hush.*

At Wingate Barracks, Maskelyne had taken Wavell's suggestion and mocked up a wood-and-canvas-framed lorry big enough to fit over a tank. Barkas watched the first trial. Twelve local Egyptian labourers carried the heavy wooden prototype cover towards a Crusader tank while Maskelyne explained that he had codenamed the device 'Sunshield'. The name stuck.

The canopy was in two hinged parts. When in

98

place it made the tank look like a huge, toy, cardboard lorry. He asked Maskelyne how the Sunshields were to be transported. 'By lorry,' came the reply, 'two to each vehicle.' The Royal Engineer sergeant supervising the work gave a sign for the tank driver to start up. The engine bellowed into life and the huge machine clattered into the desert, slipping and skidding as it went. Very quickly the canvas shield began to wobble and come apart, much to the delight of the Egyptian workers, who cheered and clapped as each new bit fell off. The tank came to a halt like a bedraggled monster, wood and canvas hanging in tatters from its hull. The driver climbed out, hauling himself with difficulty from the wreckage.

Nevertheless, Barkas thought that the idea was a good one, even though the prototype was crude, unpainted and had problems. He was sure it would be very effective when seen from the air. Maskelyne told Barkas that he would have a Mark 2 prototype ready as soon as possible. Barkas nodded and said he was worried about its weight.

Maskelyne's Mark 2 Sunshield was a big improvement. He and his stage manager, Morrison, came up with a much lighter tube and canvas construction, which could be put in place by two men. He estimated that a three-ton lorry could carry at least nine Sunshields. The Mark 2 was strong enough to survive the hammering it took when mounted on a tank and the rough manhandling it received at the hands of men who put it in place. Pilots flew test-runs over the prototype and confirmed that from 500 feet in the air the tank looked like a lorry.

The Sunshields would be one of the most used

camouflage devices in the next two years of the Desert War. At Alamein and in the Allies' deception finale, Operation Bertram, it would be the most important single element. They were cheap and easy to make. A Camouflage Unit report outlines the basic materials needed to manufacture 300 Sunshields:

110,000 feet of ¾ inch black steel tubing; 25,000 feet of ⅜ inch flat mild steel; 30,000 x ³⁄₁₆ inch flat mild steel; 15,000 yards of canvas jute; 15,000 feet of ½ inch cord; 500lbs of sewing twine.

The figures give an idea of the scale that Barkas and the Camouflage Unit were starting to work with, and why they would always be on the look-out for storage space, material, workshops and labour.

*   *   *

In Tripoli, Rommel continued his round-the-clock build-up of the *Afrika Korps*. Meanwhile, the codebreakers at Bletchley Park were reading Rommel's Enigma signals and trying to piece together a picture of his plans. Rommel had a reputation for moving with great speed. The year before, in France, his 7th Panzer Division had earned the nickname *Die Gespenster* (the Ghost Division) because it moved so fast and reappeared behind enemy lines with such shocking force and surprise that no one, not even the German high command, knew quite where it was. It had set a record for the longest advance achieved by tanks in one day, nearly two hundred miles.

Wavell was privy to the Ultra–Enigma decrypts and received a signal from Bletchley warning him that Rommel was on the verge of launching a major assault. Wavell ignored the warning. On 30 March he assured his staff that Rommel could not possibly be ready to go on the offensive for at least a month, possibly more.

The next morning, at 09:44, the first armoured cars and tanks of the *Afrika Korps* began an attack eastwards. They were supported by Stuka dive-bombers and the much-feared 88mm, high-velocity anti-aircraft guns, used in an anti-tank role, a technique Rommel had pioneered in France. At the same time the last detachments of the troops sent to Greece were stumbling down the gangplanks in the harbour at Piraeus. By 2 April, 58,000 men and all of their equipment were in Greece and moving into position. With them were not only the two young camoufleurs, Hughes-Stanton and Clough, but also a huge stock of camouflage supplies: hundreds of large nets, thousands of feet of garnish, miles of cord, plus wood, nails and tools, none of which would ever be seen again and which, in the coming months, the Camouflage Unit would sorely need.

*   *   *

One of Barkas's most urgent problems in North Africa was the concealment of airfields. Aircraft are big objects, and they create big problems; airfields are huge; runway patterns are difficult to hide from the air and the hangars where aircraft are stored and serviced cast large, black shadows. It was John Hutton, working with architect Maurice Green, who came up with the solution. They decided to disguise the airfields as civilian housing complexes. They achieved this by painting giant murals on the roofs of the hangers, the surrounding fields and the runways, in a version of Hugh Cott's countershading. They called the scheme the 'Shadow Houses'. It was a very complicated task.

Hutton worked out the designs, drawing on all his knowledge of colour and perspective. Maurice Green supervised the execution. First the engineers marked out the designs on the ground, then hordes of mystified local workers, using road-sweeping brooms as paintbrushes, set to work spreading colour from forty-gallon drums of paint. All the materials had to be scrounged and improvised: sump oil, camouflage nets, cement slurry and tar were all pressed into use. The ingredients they could lay their hands on in Egypt included 'slaked lime, finely ground coloured earths, pigments and ordinary salt, all ground together and mixed in exact proportion according to the formula'. Green paint proved impossible to get hold of and not all paints worked on the runways.

The work was slow: a single airfield could take nearly two months to disguise. Hutton and Maurice Green had to battle with their materials against the elements and the desert. One night a sandstorm hit an airfield that had been made almost invisible. When the storm passed, they flew over to see what damage had been done. To their horror they found that, in a few hours, their work had been destroyed.

In spite of these setbacks, the scheme worked. The optical illusion was so effective that one pilot refused to land. He had a plane full of high-ranking

CAMOUFLAGE TRAINING AND DEVELOPMENT CENTRE R.E. M.E.   Cam Design No. 111a

DECEPTION OF AERODROMES
AND A.L.G's.

Dispersion
Points.

Dispersion
Points.

Runway built
in the pe
of road.

Dummy Aircraft

Dummy Aircraft.

Dispersal Points.

Dummy Aircraft dispersed over
runways of aerodrome. Real
aircraft landing on runways
are taken to dispersal points
via roadways, by this method
no tracks are made leading to
the dispersal points.
Administrative offices should
in the same way be dispersed
away from existing administrative
buildings, thus making existing
buildings decoys.

One of Bill Murray Dixon's (see p. 108) working drawings for airfield camouflage. The schemes were very labour-intensive; nothing was what it seemed and confused even Allied pilots.

officers and insisted that there wasn't a safe place to put down amongst what appeared to him to be a muddle of small buildings, gardens and trees. Hutton also built dummy airfields to attract attention away from the real thing. He recruited local women and children to do the work, a labour force that would unnervingly vanish at midday to cook meals for their menfolk. The dummy airfields came complete with anti-aircraft defences, huts, and the other paraphernalia needed to support an air squadron, all of it conjured from paint, wood and canvas.

*   *   *

Back at GHQ Cairo, Barkas continued to organise his command. At any moment he expected his camoufleurs to be told to put down their paintbrushes, pick up their rifles and do some real soldiering. But somehow he managed to keep his unit intact.

He needed to expand his camoufleurs' reach, organise training courses and find the personnel to run them. Barkas devised two basic courses: one for regimental officers, the other for unit instructors. The Regimental Officers' Course lasted for four days and was designed to teach the basics of camouflage so the officers could return to their units and put the lessons into practice. The course started with a day of lectures explaining the basic principles of camouflage: desert backgrounds and patterns; air reconnaissance, how to annotate 'air photos', and concluded with a lecture on 'Camouflage in Nature'. The next three days looked at types of camouflage, decoys, and choosing the best positions for concealment. Students were told that the German army were trained to put concealability above tactical worth when choosing a military position.

The Unit Instructors' Course lasted six days and was far more comprehensive. Instructors were trained up in order to go back to their units and educate others. Barkas hoped this way the camouflage message would seep by osmosis through the army. Like Buckley at Farnham, he wanted all his students to turn into disciples spreading the gospel of camouflage: conceal or be killed. Both courses were simple and effective.

Barkas needed to develop camouflage strategy from the ground up. For this he required experienced men to work alongside him; but they were few and far between. He had heard that in South Africa there was an experienced camouflage officer named Major Tony Ayrton, the son of Scottish architect Maxwell Ayrton and brother of the painter and sculptor Michael Ayrton. Barkas wanted to get Tony onto his team as soon as possible.

Ayrton was a man in his late twenties with an air of seriousness that seemed at odds with his youth. He was tall, slender and clean-shaven with a square jaw and firm chin, his hair parted low to the side. He wore old-fashioned spectacles with round lenses and thin rims that hid his grey eyes, and always had a briar clenched between his teeth. Ayrton never seemed to hurry, hated bureaucracy and what he described as 'kerfuffle'—the propensity for officialdom to make a meal out of the simplest task. His air of gravity hid a cultured and entertaining man with a very modern outlook.

Ayrton had been instrumental in forming the

105

South African No. 85 Camouflage Company. He was a gifted camoufleur and knew how the army worked. Barkas set about seeing if he could get Ayrton and the South Africans transferred to the desert. With Freddie Beddington's help, he succeeded.

Barkas continued to send out a 'ceaseless stream of appreciations, proposals and pleas'. One of his more querulous papers earned the nickname 'Barkas's Bleat'. An achievement of which he was particularly proud was the production of a booklet with a dramatic black and white cover called 'Concealment in the Field'. Barkas wanted it to stand out from the hundreds of other bits of paper that were being showered on the troops. The design called for the use of dozens of half-tone blocks, beautiful, clear graphics and crisp text. Barkas searched high and low in Cairo looking for block-makers, typesetters as well as paper and material for the covers. The first edition ran to 12,000 copies and was followed by a second run of 34,000 copies. In his rush to get the booklet made, Barkas forgot to get the necessary authorisations.

The bills began to come in and he was called in to explain himself to his bosses, Brigadiers Whitely and Davy, whom Barkas later described as a 'joy to work for, who never issued an order that was not crystal clear, unambiguous and capable of being carried out and backed by the authority and resources needed for its execution'. The brigadiers, Whiteley in particular, were powerful allies. They saw what Barkas was trying to do and shared his view that camouflage could at the very least save many lives, and that its practice should be instilled into a soldier as being as important as looking after his equipment, weapons and ammunition. Whitely

PART ONE

CONCEALMENT IN THE FIELD

"Concealment" is the oldest and the newest weapon in the history of war.

It is not merely a weapon of defence. It is also a powerful weapon of attack.

Successful concealment of armies in the field only becomes possible when it ceases

to be thought of as the business of a few experts, and becomes the personal

and daily concern of every member of the Forces — from front line to base camp."

MIDDLE EAST TRAINING PAMPHLET NUMBER 8
ISSUED BY THE CAMOUFLAGE TRAINING AND DEVELOPMENT CENTRE RE ME
THROUGH M T 1 BRANCH.

Barkas's beautifully designed and produced pamphlet achieved the important status of 'An Operational Requirement'.

107

wrote a minute authorising the outlay. 'There is an operational requirement,' he urged. 'The sooner this book is issued the better.'

Tony Ayrton was seconded to the Camouflage Unit and Barkas made film man Peter Proud 'Camouflage Officer Western Forces', sending him out to oversee the practical work at the front. Proud desperately needed someone to help him. Barkas had heard that there was an ex-Royal College of Art student with the Rifle Brigade somewhere in the vicinity of Tobruk. The hunt was on to find him.

The soldier they were looking for was William Murray Dixon. At the outbreak of war Murray Dixon had joined the Rifle Brigade and was now a sergeant in the 2nd Armoured Division. He proved to be a very capable soldier and had the knack of being able to find his way around the empty wastes of the desert. Dixon had been with Battalion HQ at Sidi Barrani when Rommel attacked. He became separated from his unit and spent the next week dodging Germans, eventually going into the desert to escape them. He was spotted by an Allied reconnaissance plane, which flew over him and dropped a bottle with a message that read: 'Go to Tobruk!'

Murray Dixon wandered for another three days before he staggered into Tobruk. He found Peter Proud, who at first was irritated that Dixon had taken so long to arrive. 'Where have you been?' was his first question. He calmed down when Murray Dixon told him his story.

* * *

On 2 April the first battle between British and German tanks took place and ended in less than an hour, with the British in retreat. For the first time in the desert Rommel used a technique that he was to repeat many times. He sent his tanks forward to get the attention of the Allies, then retreated, luring the British armour onto a concealed screen of lethal anti-tank 88s, which blew the Allied armour to pieces. The Allied tanks did not have the range to return fire.

Against Rommel was Major General Gambier-Parry, whose command, the 2nd Armoured Division, was made up of men recently arrived in Africa, poorly equipped and trained. 'GP' had lost his best men to Greece. He received a signal that a large concentration of enemy tanks was in the vicinity of Msus, where most of his division's petrol was stored. He sent a force to investigate. They found that the Royal Engineers had destroyed the dump to prevent it falling into enemy hands.

Now desperate for supplies, Gambier-Parry fell back to the old Ottoman fort of Mechili, where the British had established a large dump of fuel, food and ammunition. Rommel attacked the fort at dawn on 8 April and took Gambier-Parry and 2,000 of his men prisoner. Rommel also bagged Parry's command vehicle, an armour-plated medium artillery tractor the size of a lorry known as a Dorchester. Inside Rommel found a pair of plastic goggles, which he tried on. A war photographer took a shot of the general with the goggles pushed up on to his cap and, in that instant, created the image of the Desert Fox. Rommel christened the Dorchester 'Max'.

News broke of another, greater disaster involving the capture of irreplaceable senior officers. General Richard O'Connor and Lieutenant General Sir

Philip Neame VC, C-in-C Desert Force and Military Governor of Cyrenaica, had been travelling at night in Neame's car. With them was Lieutenant Colonel Combe, the hero of Beda Fomm. Neame's ADC, Lord 'Dan' Ranfurly, travelled behind in a Ford Mercury van, carrying their baggage. Realising they were lost, Ranfurly stopped and got out of his vehicle: 'It was very dark and we could see nothing. Suddenly a figure loomed out of the blackness and the next thing I knew I had a Tommy gun in my middle. He shouted something incomprehensible and then more figures appeared. They were Germans.' The generals and Combe had run into an *Afrika Korps* reconnaissance patrol. They were taken to Italy as prisoners of war. Rommel had thrown the British out of Libya and deprived them of O'Connor, one of the Allies' most successful and gifted commanders.

Rommel now had to deal with Tobruk, which was far in his rear and a threat to his supply lines. He sent the newly arrived, thirty-five-year-old aristocrat General Heinrich von Prittwitz und Gaffron to attack the port. Rommel thought Tobruk would cave in under his onslaught. What he did not know was that three very tough Australian brigades had fallen back into defensive positions around the town.

On 11 April, Good Friday, just after midday, soldiers defending the perimeter of Tobruk reported that a group of about 300 German vehicles had cut the El Adem–Bardia Road to the east. Three German armoured cars approached the Australians, who opened fire with captured Italian field guns. The cars retreated and their places were taken by tanks that attempted to cross a bridge across a wadi on the Tobruk perimeter. The Australians blew up the bridge and the tanks ground to a halt. Von Prittwitz took matters into his own hands. He ordered his driver to take their staff car across the wadi, straight towards the Australians. He came under fire from a captured 47mm Italian anti-tank gun. The car was destroyed and both the young general and his driver were killed.

Although outnumbered and outgunned, the Australians beat off the attackers. At one point four British tanks rescued Australian infantrymen by driving up behind their position and firing at the enemy directly over the soldiers' heads. Being in close proximity to tanks in action is very disturbing for infantry; the machines are noisy, inhuman and frightening. The Germans withdrew unable to cross the anti-tank ditches. They had lost more than five tanks and a significant number of men at a cost to the Allies of one dead soldier. The siege had begun; it would last for nearly eight months.

Tobruk fortress was surrounded by three German divisions: 35,000 German and Italian troops. Inside, the fortress's commander, Major General Leslie Morshead had 27,000 men, mainly Australians, supported by British Army logistics and the Royal Artillery. They could only be fed and supplied by sea. Churchill decreed that Tobruk should 'be defended to the death without thought of retirement'. Peter Proud and William Murray Dixon were trapped.

German bombers flew over the town, dropping leaflets containing a message from Rommel: 'The General Officer Commanding the German forces in Libya hereby requests that the British troops occupying Tobruk surrender their arms . . . strong

German forces have surrounded Tobruk and it is useless to try and escape. Our dive-bombers and Stukas are awaiting your ships, which are lying in the harbour.'

The official response was unequivocal and succinct.

'**** Off.'

*   *   *

Tobruk came under daily attack: dive-bombers shrieked from the sky and the detonation of shells jangled the nerves of the defenders all their waking hours. Proud immediately saw that there was work he could do to help the garrison survive, and quickly established Fortress Tobruk's own 'school of camouflage'. The programme of camouflage training he established was kept up throughout the siege. Barkas discovered that Peter Proud was a man whose charm and persuasiveness combined to allow him to quietly get his own way.

Proud quickly cobbled together a unit of Australian Royal Engineers, Royal Army Service Corps personnel, a company of Indian pioneers and 'refugees', almost three hundred soldiers who had been separated from their units during the attack and found themselves trapped in the fortress. The usual problems of finding camouflage materials were made much more difficult by the siege conditions. With everything having to travel in by sea, it was obvious that ammunition, food, weapons and reinforcements would take precedence over the wood, netting and wire that the camoufleurs needed. So Proud and his men went on the scrounge. Like rag-and-bone men they rooted through Fortress Tobruk for all the things that nobody else wanted. They assembled mountains of nets, tens of thousands of yards of hessian, as well as wood, woodworking tools, stirrup pumps, nails and screws.

An early success came when Proud was asked if he could change the colour of the paintwork on a large number of vehicles and create the illusion that there was activity on a track that ran near a planned dummy gun emplacement. Proud's solution was clever. He set up a station on the track called the 'Camouflage Service Station', which offered to camouflage lorries and service their camouflage nets while the drivers waited.

The soldiers loved it. Normally each driver was responsible for the camouflage of his own vehicle, a tedious job. The idea of an easy 'while-you-wait' service that painted your vehicle and checked out your netting was irresistible. As there was no paint available, Proud made his own, procuring tens of tons of spoiled flour and thousands of gallons of rancid Worcester Sauce, which he mixed into a disgusting but very adhesive paste. The paste turned out to have many uses: it could be plastered on vehicles, it could dull down steel helmets and it could be painted onto vehicle windscreens to stop them reflecting the sun and attracting enemy fire, a real and lethal problem. It could also be applied to tents and canvas bivouacs. The recipe for Proud's paste went as follows:

1) A double handful of flour mixed to a paste with cold water. Boil one gallon of water, or sea water. When boiling, pour slowly onto the cold flour paste, stirring the whole time.

113

2) *This gives the required thickness of paste for metal surfaces.*
3) *Thin down for fabrics with cold sand of local colour, must be applied immediately, before the paste dries or sinks into the fabric.*
4) *Smooth upper surfaces should be darker and require more texture than the sides. Use coarse sand and thicker application of the paste.*

The instructions ended:

Whatever the shortcomings—if there turn out to be any—it appears more satisfactory than anything so far used . . . Durability will be improved by the addition of a small amount of liquid glue. Supplies of this are expected to be, but are not at present, available.

The scheme was a great success and helped Proud win the trust of both commanders and the commanded, all of whom began to understand the importance of camouflage and that the Camouflage Unit was there to help them survive.

Proud's team achieved their next success with a huge canvas screen behind which they hid a unit of tanks from the enemy. The operational report, written shortly after the event, describes the problem and how it was solved:

REPORT on LARGE NETTING SCREEN
Erected to form false contour of ground
Reference Map TOBRUK DEFENCES—Red
Overprint 1941

114

1 OBJECT
To conceal a section of a reserve brigade defended area and one troop RHA [Royal Horse Artillery] from the view of an enemy OP [Observation Post].

2 FACTORS
The enemy OP was situated on an escarpment (Map ref: RAS EL MEDAUUAR) overlooking the area to be concealed (Map ref: Area 405429), which was being accurately shelled in consequence. Battery could not be withdrawn owing to its A-Tk [Anti-Tank] role.

3 METHOD
Erection of a large netting screen 900 feet long by 58 feet wide, 18 feet high, running across the enemy's line of vision. (Map ref: 4044297 running SOUTH).

To disguise the position the camouflage team used 'fifty-two x thirty-five-foot-square nets; 42,000 yards of hessian garnish; forty-four x twenty-foot posts; 120 smaller posts and 452 small and large pickets for guy rope attachment and net stretching ropes'. It took the 45th Indian Pioneers two days to prepare the nets and a section of thirty-five Royal Engineers 'five working hours' to erect it. Flattened petrol cans were nailed to the tops of the twenty-foot posts to support the nets.

The 42,000 feet of garnish proved a problem: it was standard-issue dark green, completely unsuitable for the desert. Murray Dixon came up with a simple and elegant solution: he bleached it using sea water and slaked lime. The screen did nothing more than hide things while itself remaining visible and was a great success. The operational report concluded:

The enemy expended much effort and ammunition in his efforts to demolish the screen and was prevented from carrying out accurate artillery fire on the concealed guns. The enemy expended approximately 2,000 shells during the next few days in flanking and sweeping the area behind the screen to a depth of about 2,000 yards . . . the shooting was mainly ineffective.

A heavy shoot was carried out on the net with slight damage (i.e. 3 poles down). This was repaired overnight to test the enemy's interest. The following day 15 EA [enemy aircraft] dive-bombed the screen. Due to the 'floppy' nature of the construction only slight damage was caused. Two EA were shot down by our AA during the attack.

To deal with a simple net, which had cost almost nothing to make, and which fewer than a hundred men had taken three days to build and erect, the Germans had wasted over two thousand shells, whilst at the same time tying up support vehicles, observation posts, gunners' time, intelligence work, radio time and fuel. They had also committed to hundreds of Luftwaffe administrative hours, more petrol, bombs and ammunition and lost two expensive dive-bombers and two highly trained pilots. Peter Proud's net was very good value for money.

In June, with the siege into its second month, the screen idea was used in a much more complex decoy operation. The plan was to create a sham, designed to make the enemy think they had spotted Allied activity and to distract their attention from the real fighting. On the night of 13/14, two days before an operation on the Tobruk perimeter was due to start, a diversionary screen was erected across a contour line on another part of the perimeter, far from the planned battle. Wrecked tanks were parked behind the screen and camouflaged, and Bren-gun carriers used to create false tracks. Dummy tank laager and gun positions were set up in the area 1,000 yards behind the screen, but badly camouflaged to attract enemy attention.

Starting at dawn, the Germans shelled the position, destroying some of the dummies and damaging the net. That night the dummies were moved and the net repaired. The next day the Germans shelled the dummies again. At 'zero hour' on 'D-Day' the Camouflage Unit blew up wrecked tanks and created a smokescreen using 300 smoke canisters. At the same time pop-up wooden silhouette figures, which from a distance looked like real men, were revealed to the enemy. The net was allowed to collapse, exposing the devastation created by the German gunners.

Unfortunately, the real operation was cancelled at the last minute, making it impossible to know whether the diversion had worked. Even so, it was estimated that the Germans fired 4,000 shells at the decoy with the accompanying commitment of manpower and supplies. The diversion had required the cooperation of the Army Service Corps' heavy workshops to move the derelict tanks, an Indian Pioneer Group, the 3rd Armoured

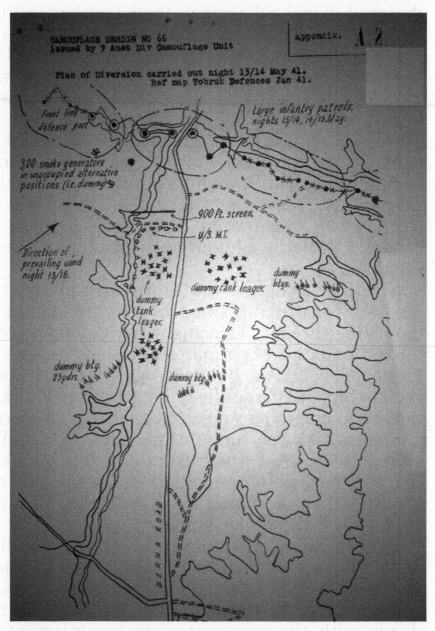

CAMOUFLAGE DESIGN NO 66
Issued by 9 Aust Div Camouflage Unit

Appendix: A 2.

Plan of Diversion carried out night 13/14 May 41.
Ref map Tobruk Defences Jan 41.

Front line
defence post

large infantry patrols.
nights 13/14, 14/15 May.

300 smoke generators
in unoccupied alternative
positions. (i.e. dummy)

900 ft. screen.

u/s. M.T.

Direction of
prevailing wind
night 15/16.

dummy tank leager.

dummy
btys.

dummy
tank
leager.

dummy bty.
25pdrs.

dummy bty.

DERNA ROAD

Sketch for an elaborate diversion scheme in Fortress Tobruk using dummy tanks and a simple hessian screen.

Brigade to provide vehicles to make misleading tracks, the Royal Artillery, the Royal Engineers and the officers of the Camouflage Unit. It was devised and carried out in five days. Peter Proud had turned a screen that had started life as a means of concealment into a workable full-scale deception. It was a major turning point, and the beginning of the concept of the Phantom Army.

Proud camoufleurs also helped the Royal Navy. One of the most important places in Tobruk, and the only means of keeping the garrison supplied, was the port itself. All vessels coming into the port were extremely vulnerable to air attack, including the 'A' lighter flat-bottomed barges that ferried supplies into the port; the gunboat HMS *Gnat,* which provided much-needed artillery support, and the SS *Pass of Balmaha,* a tanker that had to be towed into the harbour after being damaged in an attack out to sea. The crippled tanker was moored in the harbour, with 750 tons of vehicle and aviation fuel on board.

The port itself was full of half-sunk ships, victims of the dive-bombing and shelling. Proud realised that these could form the basis of his naval camouflage work. He used the humble camouflage net on a vast scale to turn the hulks into hiding places. Working at night, booms were rigged, jutting out from the sides of the wrecks; nets were stretched between them, making covers under which the 'A' lighters could shelter as they were being unloaded. The 'A' lighters were met at the harbour mouth and guided to their hiding places. Once moored, they were boarded by Proud's camouflage squads, who covered the open sides with more netting, 'snugly netting them in'.

HMS *Gnat* was hidden in much the same way, but on a far bigger scale. Proud draped a huge net on strung-steel hawsers across a cove under which the gunship could hide. From the air the net looked like an extension of the land and earned the name 'Gnat Cove'. When she wasn't in action, the gunship's topmast and searchlight were removed so she could slink into her camouflaged refuge. The superstructure of *Gnat* itself was also camouflaged. The naval report reads: 'After the sinking of HMS *Ladybird* in Tobruk harbour on 12 May, *Gnat* arrived and needed careful concealment. It was sited by a camouflage officer in a cove. The ship was concealed by painting desert colour and shadows broken up by descending planes of nets fixed to superstructures. Enemy aircraft could be seen searching for this vessel, which eventually left port safely.'

On another occasion the naval officer in command of the harbour noted: 'A raid at 12:30, very high level with sticks of bombs; two sticks probably aimed at two "A" lighters. Another lighter has been well camouflaged and was NOT attacked.'

The camouflage teams hid naval landing craft and stores ships under false dummy jetties and sunken barges. They also hid real jetties under dummy beaches made of pontoons and tubular steel. The Navy's position was summed up after the siege in a signal sent on 26 June 1941 from the naval officer in charge: 'It is requested that all ranks responsible for the operations be informed of the appreciation of the Navy for their work. The prompt and efficient hiding of HMS *Gnat*, SS *Pass of Balmaha* and the "A" lighters has been particularly successful.' The same officer sent personal thanks, writing: 'I am very grateful to Capt. Proud for his most efficient assistance and I have instructed Lt. Laing, my Brigade Camouflage Officer, to cooperate with him.'

*　　　*　　　*

The ferocity of the daily and nightly bombardment of Tobruk was recorded in situation report issued during the long day and night that preceded May Day 1941:

SITREP

MILITARY: No developments except artillery fire and infantry attack after air attack at 19:15. Still in progress. Blenheim shot down, crew dive-bombed and machine gunned.

AIR: Raid at very high level with sticks of very small bombs. 2 sticks probably aimed at two 'A' Lighters. Other lighter has been well camouflaged and was NOT attacked. Coxswain killed and one man wounded in A 12. Similar raid 16:05. One stick of 12 bombs across harbour. Bareham superficial damage and four wounded. Heavy raids at 19:15 on military objectives, dive-bombing and machine-gunning.

NAVAL: 'A' lighters did not make harbour until 08:00 hours. Tanks etc. landed comparatively quickly but loading of vehicles onto them slow. Recommend they only be used for embarking here in case of emergency. CRs light guns and light gear salved from Chakla.

CONCEALMENT OF STORE SHIPS AND MILITARY LANDING CRAFT.

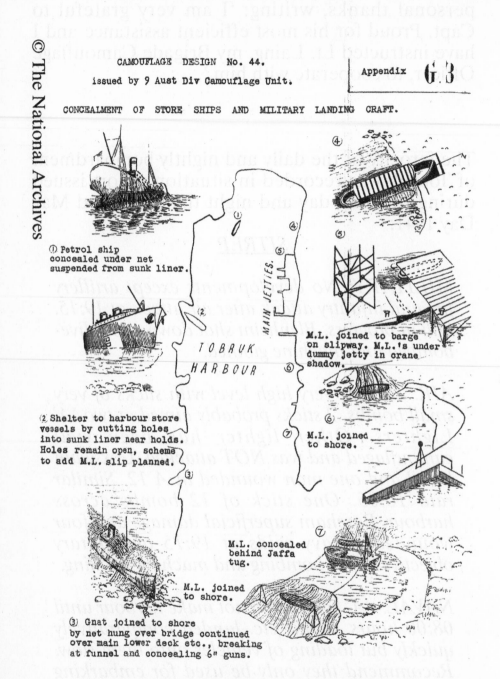

① Petrol ship
concealed under net
suspended from sunk liner.

② Shelter to harbour store
vessels by cutting holes
into sunk liner near holds.
Holes remain open, scheme
to add M.L. slip planned.

③ Gnat joined to shore
by net hung over bridge continued
over main lower deck etc., breaking
at funnel and concealing 6" guns.

MAIN JETTIES.

T O B R U K

H A R B O U R

④ M.L. joined to barge
on slipway. M.L.'s under
dummy jetty in crane
shadow.

⑥ M.L. joined
to shore.

⑦ M.L. concealed
behind Jaffa
tug.

M.L. joined
to shore.

Concealment ideas for Tobruk harbour.

Proud and Murray Dixon were equally ingenious when it came to hiding the fortress's only three Hawker Hurricanes. The planes were of huge importance, not only for their tactical value but also for the morale-boosting sight of them roaring above the town. The RAF was working from an airstrip at Bir el Gubi, well within artillery range of enemy artillery and an obvious target for the Luftwaffe.

Proud hid two of the aircraft by digging hangars in the walls of a wadi, into which the planes could be pushed, and the entrances covered over with netting. The third was disguised by lowering it into a Hurricane-shaped trench. Once underground a lid was placed over it and tents put up above it so as to look like a small encampment. Dummy rocks, made out of petrol tins bashed out of shape and painted the colour of sand with flour paste, were placed on the lid to help disguise it. Proud then built a dummy airfield some way away. Dummy planes and dummy hangars, all made from scrap, completed the illusion. The RAF was able to continue using the landing strip at Bir el Gubi for the duration of the siege.

Proud was delighted when shown some reconnaissance pictures taken from a captured German airman on which his dummies had been marked as real. One ack-ack battery commander reported with satisfaction that he and his men sat in the comparative security of their camouflaged and almost invisible position, watching a flight of ME 109s roar in at low level and attack, with pinpoint accuracy, a gun pit that contained guns made of wood, four stacks of non-existent ammunition and a dummy range-finder. The guns were manned by dummies made of straw and string. The straw men gave their all and were blown to pieces; charred fragments of their bodies drifted over the real gunners, who cheered the German accuracy, knowing that they could have been the victims.

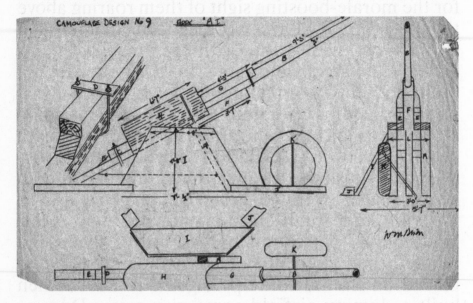

Working drawing for a dummy ack-ack gun.

The team's artificial targets proved too successful for some. One colonel, responsible for a water-supply pipeline, complained to Proud about a fake ack-ack battery that had been put up near his headquarters. 'We have on three occasions had hits aimed at the dummy battery on our pipeline; signals communications also suffer. The dummy battery is certainly a success but has now had so much pasting that it would be the reasonable thing to move it . . . About thirteen lengths of mains were damaged this morning.'

Proud's most dramatic achievement was the deception he created in order to protect Tobruk's desalination plant, which processed 40,000 gallons of sea water a day, essential for the supply of fresh water in the town. Its loss would have been catastrophic and would have led to the surrender of Fortress Tobruk. The building was large and could not be hidden. Proud and Dixon came up with a plan to make the Germans think they had successfully destroyed the plant in a bombing raid. The artist and the film man conspired to create a story for the German reconnaissance cameras. They came up with a scenario in which the plant would look as though it had received a direct hit from a bomb, which had blown a hole in the roof, destroying chimneys and wrecking vehicles parked nearby. The bomb that did the damage was to be one of a stick of three, the other two of which had straddled the building. It was planned to paint black tar onto the roof and wall of the building, giving the impression they had caved in under the blast, making a gaping black hole.

Having worked out their story, Murray Dixon visualised it, drawing a storyboard on thin blue paper. The scheme would have the best chance of working if it could be put into action on the night of a raid, ideally after the plant had suffered a near miss.

First they had to prepare the building. They began by dressing it with all the elements that would be 'destroyed' in the attack. Oil barrels were piled in neat stacks next to the wall and written-off vehicles parked around the building. They took great care to make everything look neat and tidy, as though nothing had happened. Other stores were assembled and concealed in trenches dug near the distillery. Then the unit settled in to wait for the next bombing attack.

When it came, Proud wasted no time getting into action. Murray Dixon remembers 'standing over a sweating clerk, dictating Proud's urgent instructions', which were then typed on the drawings. They read: 'The above sketch shows the camouflage treatment for the building which I hope has not been hit. After the attack this evening it seems now is the time to take action on this scheme. The German recce planes will probably be over tomorrow evening so it is suggested that at least the hole is simulated at once using tar.'

There followed a detailed explanation as to how the rest of the story was to be told. Proud got approval to go ahead at once. His men swarmed onto the site and the neat stacks of oil drums were scattered around as if thrown about by blast. The huge black tar hole was painted to look from the air

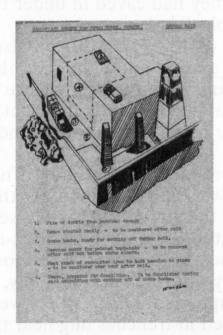

Storyboard describing desalination plant before and after treatment.

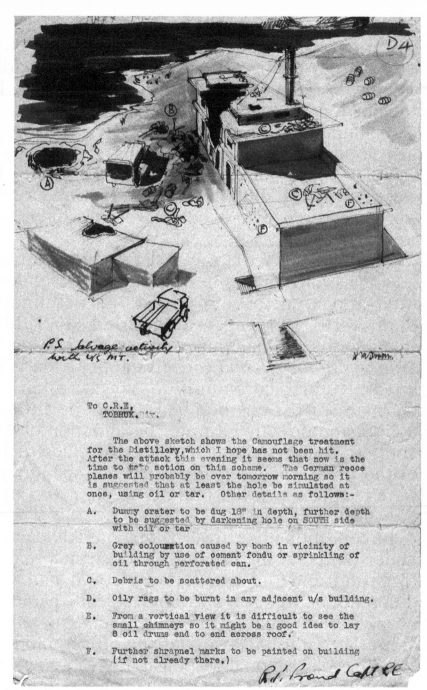

Desalination plant orders. The deception fooled the Germans and was a breakthrough for the Camouflage Unit.

127

like a vast cavity in the ruined roof. They dug craters and painted the sides with more tar to create a perspective effect of depth. A redundant chimney was demolished with pre-set charges. The Indian Pioneers painted shrapnel marks in the walls and chipped off plaster. Piles of oily rags were set light to in all the adjacent building; the written-off vehicles were rolled on their sides, and they too were set alight. Finally cement dust and rubble were scattered everywhere, creating pulverised stonework.

The trick worked perfectly. German reconnaissance planes flew over, taking pictures of what appeared to be a devastated desalination plant, still burning, surrounded by rubble, smouldering buildings and vehicles. On 17 May, the *Sydney Morning Herald* carried the news that: 'The latest ROME communiqué says: Italian and German formations bombed enemy positions at Sollum and directly hit water desalination plant at Tobruk.' Reports about the successful destruction of the plant appeared in Italian newspapers and were broadcast on the radio. The plant was never directly bombed again.

In conditions like this, troops quickly came to understand that the camouflage doctrine preached by Proud and the camoufleurs could make the difference between an uncomfortable life and death or mutilation. Thanks to Proud, every company at Tobruk had a trained camouflage officer and every soldier took personal responsibility to understand how the nets should be positioned and garnished.

The siege dragged on. Towards the end, Barkas summoned Proud and Murray Dixon back to GHQ Cairo. A weary Peter Proud handed over command to the commercial artist Edwin Galligan, who came in at night by a destroyer that conveyed Proud and Murray Dixon to Egypt. When Proud reported to Grey Pillars, he found a delighted Barkas gloating over a pile of reports, sketches and photographs that had filtered through to his office from the beleaguered port.

Especially satisfying were some captured German reports. One dated 11 June 1941 ran: 'At 08:00 hours we reached the gap held by the enemy. On our approach he opened fire from well-camouflaged posts, all these concentrating their fire on our tanks passing through the narrow opening. Before beginning the three attacks, the regiment had not the slightest information about the excellently constructed enemy positions, an enormous quantity of anti-tank guns. The presence of heavy tanks was also not known.'

Another read: 'The Australian is unquestionably superior to the German soldier in . . . the use of ground camouflage and every means of taking us by surprise, e.g. posts held strongly, sometimes weakly and possible only feigning to hold them, forward batteries firing from an artificial dust cloud made by motor transport. The enemy allows isolated individuals to come right up to his positions before firing.'

A captured German pamphlet issued to troops as a briefing document described the British use of ground camouflage as 'outstandingly good, not visible from the air'. Barkas also had reports from his own side detailing the bombing of fake positions and the destruction of straw men: 'At 10:30 hours on 15 May, one enemy battery engaged the dummy positions with air observation from a Heinkel.

When ranging was complete, the position was engaged by troops and the real positions were untouched.' While on 23 May, a 'JU 87 dive-bombed the position using 100lb bombs. One dummy gun-pit hit, one dummy shelter burnt out. Four dummy figures blown over and hit. At least three bombs fell in the middle of the dummy position.'

Perhaps most satisfying was this signal from the colonel of the 1st Battalion the Royal Northumberland Fusiliers who, on 17 June, had signalled to complain of 'a dummy petrol dump, composed of large numbers of used petrol tins, located immediately east of my unit HQ. The dump increases daily in size and is now within 200 yards of my HQ. During the past few nights this dump has amply fulfilled its purpose, having attracted enemy bombers, and it has been bombed four times during the last week with varying degrees of accuracy. I should be most grateful if further extension of this dump, if intended, should be continued in the opposite direction to my HQ.'

Peter Proud was especially keen to commend the unsung heroes of the siege, the 45th Indian Pioneer Group, whose work had proved invaluable to the realisation of the various camouflage schemes. His report read: 'Engaged in the more tedious work of garnishing nets and treating vehicles, they have worked tirelessly and efficiently. They have also carried out artillery camouflage and decoy work under shellfire with great cheerfulness and pride. It is hoped that their great aptitude for this work may be considered in future, and that small camouflage units will have the benefit of a recognised claim on their excellent services.'

Barkas summed up the problems Proud had faced at the beginning of the siege of Tobruk: 'At the outset it was found that troops were quite untrained in concealment. The Camouflage Officer found that materials issued, palpably the wrong tone for the locality, were being jettisoned or incorrectly used. A Camouflage Unit was hastily organised and roadside demonstrations for training were given . . . An immediate improvement was noticed in concealment as soon as troops understood the basic principles and the importance of the air view.'

A general appreciation written by Barkas declared with good reason: 'It is likely that the use of deceit has never before been exploited on such an active scale by a Camouflage Unit. It has proved that the use of decoys of all kinds is an integral part of surprise in attack or defence, and points to a definite operational role for all Camouflage Officers.' He went on: 'All branches of the Services soon realised the necessity for concealment. The service of the Camouflage Officer [Proud] and his assistants were in constant demand.'

At last Barkas was getting somewhere with his work. Tobruk had been a large-scale audition in which Peter Proud and William Murray Dixon had proved that the Camouflage Unit could punch its weight in the tightest corner.

6

OPERATION CRUSADER

Churchill's Greek expedition was not going well. Axis forces invaded the mainland at dawn on 6 April 1941 and the Allied position quickly deteriorated. By the thirteenth, Wavell warned his commanders that they would not receive any more reinforcements and authorised Major General Freddie de Guingand to start making evacuation plans to get the 62,000 Lustre Force troops out of the country.

By 16 April the operation had begun, with the Allies evacuating their forces on ships operating from Volos in Thessaly, and from the harbour at Piraeus. On 21 April, Wavell formally ordered all Commonwealth forces to be moved to Crete and Egypt, and six days later the first German troops entered Athens, capturing huge quantities of petroleum. That evening the swastika was flying over the Acropolis. By 30 April, 50,000 of the original Lustre Force had been evacuated, but there were still 8,000 troops waiting on the beach at Kalamata for rescue by the Royal Navy, among them Blair Hughes-Stanton and Garrett Clough.

Hughes-Stanton had made it onto the beach and collapsed, exhausted, into a ditch. He woke to find a German soldier prodding him with a bayonet. He was dragged to his feet and, with Clough and thousands of others, marched to temporary barbed-

132

wire POW cages. There they were kept, short of food and water, while the Germans worked out what to do with them.

At some point a Greek peasant approached the wire barrier with a few scraps of food for sale. Hughes-Stanton went towards him, holding out his hand. A German guard, thinking that Hughes-Stanton was trying to escape, panicked and swung his sub-machine gun, squeezing the trigger. The bullets knocked Hughes-Stanton off his feet. He hit the ground, blood pouring from his head. The blast had caught the winner of the Venice Biennale International Prize for Engraving, and the man who had pioneered techniques for making the most intricate carving in wood, full in the face, badly injuring him and permanently damaging his eyes. His life was saved by members of a New Zealand field hospital who had been captured with the rest of the members of Lustre Force. They dressed his wounds and nursed him as best they could. Over the next two years Blair was moved from POW camp to POW camp in Nazi Europe, and came close to death, but somehow the medics kept him going. Eventually he returned to England. His injuries severely affected his three-dimensional vision and he would never work as a woodcutter and engraver again.

*   *   *

Churchill now looked for a success to redeem his position and set his sights on Rommel. He demanded from Wavell: 'A victory in the Western Desert to destroy Rommel's army. This would at least save our situation in Egypt from the wreck.'

133

Wavell told him that the Axis forces in Africa were now very much superior to the Allied Western Desert Force. Churchill reacted by sending assorted tanks and Hurricane fighters to Alexandria, ordering that they go the short way round, through the dangerous waters of the Mediterranean, in order to save forty days' sailing time.

Convoy WS 58, codenamed Tiger, arrived in Alexandria on 12 May. It carried 238 tanks and forty-three Hurricanes. On the way, one of its number, the *Empire Song*, was sunk with the loss of a quarter of the convoy's tanks and Hurricanes. After taking such a risk, Churchill expected results and asked Wavell when the remaining equipment would be committed to battle. The prime minister was made the more frantic when he received an Ultra report telling him that Rommel had been ordered to stop and hold his position. One thrust, Churchill thought, and the battle would be done. So was born Operation Battleaxe, a plan to raise the siege of Tobruk and push Rommel's army out of Cyrenaica.

Battleaxe was drawn up in a hurry by General Beresford-Peirse, helped by Brigadiers Hardinge and Galloway. All three men had served under General O'Connor, commanding in O'Connor's once-victorious XIII Corps. One element of the force was the 7th Armoured Division, now a sad ghost of the force that, the year before, had fought so valiantly at Bardia and raced to cut off the Italians at Tobruk. Seventh Armoured had been a well-trained, beautifully equipped and well-run unit but was now disorganised, badly trained and short of transport and spares. The three planners were themselves not clear where Rommel was.

Beresford-Pierse, who had never commanded armour, now proposed a full-frontal assault on an enemy over whom he lacked superiority of men, air support and artillery.

The attack began on 15 June and by the end of the day some, but not all, of the Battleaxe objectives had been gained. The cost to British armour was high. At one point Beresford-Peirse ordered the 4th Armoured Brigade to 'rally forward' and move in front of the infantry and guns. The brigade's commander, Alexander Gatehouse, queried the order, wondering whether Beresford-Peirse meant the more common command 'forward rally', an order to move behind the protection of the supporting infantry and guns. Beresford-Peirse lost his temper and snapped: 'You have your orders, Gatehouse—carry them out.' Gatehouse did so, and lost 99 of his 104 tanks.

The next day things did not go any better. By the middle of the afternoon Rommel was confident that within twenty-four hours he would be able to encircle and defeat his opponents. He began his advance at 04:30 on the seventeenth. Less than seven hours later the British began to withdraw and by late afternoon Rommel had won the battle. The road to Cairo was open to him, although Tobruk, still under siege, continued to pose a threat to his supply lines and a drain on his reserves. Battleaxe was a dismal failure, the victim of bad and hurried planning.

Churchill was furious at the lack of success and impatient for victory. It was the end of Wavell's command in North Africa. Churchill needed a scapegoat and fired him, appointing General Auchinleck in his place. In September the Western

135

Desert Force was renamed the Eighth Army. Auchinleck's task was to destroy Rommel's armour, push him back to Benghazi, and relieve Tobruk on the way. He demanded time to prepare. Reluctantly, Churchill agreed, giving him until 1 November to put the scheme, codenamed Crusader, into operation. Comparative quiet descended on the battlefield as both sides drew breath.

* * *

All through the spring and summer of 1941, Geoffrey Barkas had struggled with the structure of the Camouflage Unit and its place in the British Army's hierarchy. Starting from scratch, the unit had grown very quickly. It had acquired and deployed large amounts of material, innovated camouflage ideas suitable for the desert wilderness and started to train the fighting troops to think in terms of camouflage. Barkas had issued a summary of the role of the camouflage officer. It included studying the terrain from the air and the ground, establishing what local materials could be obtained, reconnoitring specific military works, preparing schemes for their camouflage and feeding back schemes to GHQ Cairo.

Another Barkas initiative was to form and send out Camouflage Training Units, small groups comprising an officer, sergeant, a draughtsman and a driver plus vehicle, in order to give camouflage instruction in the field. But Barkas still struggled to find a workable internal administrative structure that meshed with the British Army's own, long-established systems. He recognised that one of his problems was that he had no trained staff officers:

his men were civilians who, while they might be inspired camoufleurs, knew nothing of the military way of doing things.

For its part, the British Army struggled to accommodate the Camouflage Unit and fit it into the overall pattern of command. The training of camouflage officers proved especially demanding of resources, and for a while, in the mid-summer of 1941, this dominated the thinking of Barkas and the army. Several administrative structures were tried, none of which worked. Eventually it was decided that all forms of 'visual deception' would be concentrated in a new branch of the general staff at GHQ Cairo and that this would be reflected in all commands and formations in the Middle East. The new 'Camouflage Branch' would, by the end of the year, be placed under the control of Colonel R. A. Bagnold OBE, founder of the reconnaissance and raiding unit, the Long Range Desert Group. It was hoped that the Camouflage Branch would be able to coordinate the work of the Camouflage Unit with the other branches of deception, such as activities behind enemy lines, sabotage and counter-intelligence.

In less than a year Barkas's organisation grew from being a small technical advisory service to a separate organisation coordinating all aspects of deception and working closely with the operational planning staff. In order to do this properly, Barkas had to make sure that he had adequate vehicles, clerks, draughtsmen and other administrative staff to service the unit, though he would always be short of personnel and fighting for more. John Morton, a carpenter and model-maker who was serving as a sergeant with the Searchlight Regiment, was recruited by Barkas to work in the Camouflage Unit's drawing office at Grey Pillars. He remembers his interview with Barkas at GHQ, which provides a glimpse of the colonel's style. Barkas greeted him with the words: 'Good afternoon, how very nice of you to come.'

On 1 January 1941 the Camouflage Unit was authorised to have twenty-two officers and eighteen other ranks serviced by four vehicles; this core organisation was supplemented by labour taken from military or local sources. By June, Barkas's establishment stood at twenty-six officers and twenty-nine other ranks; by November the numbers had risen to thirty-nine officers and 103 other ranks. Not a lot of men but, nevertheless, the Camouflage Unit now had a place in the army hierarchy, its status raised by the successes at Tobruk. Barkas and his men had achieved a great deal.

*　　*　　*

While Barkas struggled to solve his staff and logistical problems, Jasper Maskelyne provided a minor diversion when he asked permission to demonstrate what he called 'Fire Cream'. He was certain that it could save the lives of tank and air crews, whose greatest fear was to be trapped and burned to death in their vehicles. Barkas agreed to let him stage a public demonstration. More than a hundred people from all arms were invited and most accepted, with a particularly large contingent from the RAF and the Royal Tank Regiment.

A section of Royal Engineers, acting as Maskelyne's assistants, piled parts of an old Spitfire fuselage in the centre of an arena about the size of half a football pitch. To one side stood a fireman in a fireproof suit; other firemen ran hoses out from a water bowser, and a bench had been set up with fire-fighting equipment, blowlamps, asbestos gloves and matches. The crowd gathered in a large semicircle to watch the action. A fireman wearing a silver asbestos, flame-resistant suit marched into the arena like a robot.

Maskelyne stood in front of them in tank-crew overalls and a pair of gloves. He started proceedings by announcing that the clothes he was wearing were ordinary, standard-issue kit. He explained to the crowd that the same went for his 'assistant', at which point two of the Royal Engineers came forward carrying a dummy dressed in the same overalls and gloves. The audience laughed. Maskelyne continued with his introduction while the engineers strapped the dummy to a chair and poured the contents of a four-gallon petrol can over it.

As they worked, Maskelyne described the horrors experienced by the crew of a tank that has been hit by an armour-piercing round. In a fraction of a second after impact a patch of the armour inside the turret will glow white hot, bending in like rubber; an instant later the round itself will burst through; for the crew the ordeal will be over before they even know what is happening. Thousands of shards of the searing metal will bounce around the interior at supersonic speed; the temperature will soar, causing the ammunition stored in the tank to explode with colossal force, sometimes sending even the five-ton turret spinning in the air. By the time it crashes back to ground, what had been a fighting armoured vehicle will be a burning, blistered hulk inhabited by 'scorched and shrivelled crows who were once fathers, brothers, sons. If, on the other hand, the tank is not destroyed but merely catches fire . . .'. Maskelyne let his voice tail off as the silver-suited fireman threw a match at the dummy assistant, which burst into flames. Maskelyne let it burn for several minutes before signalling to the firemen to put the blaze out. The smoking dummy sat charred and black, a tankman or a pilot's nightmare.

He then announced that he had been working on a cream that could make the terrible fate of burning to death a thing of the past. The engineers produced a large zinc bath into which Maskelyne climbed. They then poured buckets of creamy paste over his head; the effect was deliberately comic and got the desired laugh. More buckets of paste were produced and poured over him. One of the firemen walked towards him holding a flaming blowlamp. Maskelyne stood and held his arms up and the firemen played the flame all the magician's body. It had no effect, he was unharmed. Maskelyne announced that he was now about to embark on the most dangerous part of the experiment.

At these words the orderlies opened the rear doors of their ambulance and pulled out a stretcher. A medical officer broke away from the crowd and crossed the arena to join them. Firemen moved forward, dramatically unrolling more water hoses. Maskelyne soaked a long, heavy cloth in the pasty liquid and wrapped it round his face; finally he put on a pair of goggles. The crowd looked on with rapt attention. The fireman in the flameproof suit lumbered over and took up a position to one side

140

of the Spitfire fuselage, hose at the ready. Several of the Royal Engineers ran to the wreck and emptied can after can of petrol over it. The air thickened with sickly fumes.

Maskelyne asked the crowd to imagine that here was an Allied aircraft, crippled by enemy action. The pilot has managed to crash land and the aircraft is about to burst into flames. 'Maskelyne's Cream, fire resistant, patent for the use of . . .' the showman declared, would save the pilot from the flames.

Then Maskelyne raised his hand, ready to signal that the fire be lit. The crowd fell silent. He stood stock still, arm in the air, white paste dripping on the ground, letting the tension build. The crowd was eating out of his hand. Then his arm dropped, an engineer stripped the striker from the side of a thunderflash, dragged it across the fuse and lobbed the fizzing pyrotechnic into the plane. There was a huge *whoomph* as the fuse ignited the petrol, followed by a very large explosion. The crowd backed away as waves of heat rolled out from the pile of burning metal.

Photographs taken at the time show a tall, slightly comic figure soaked in white liquid walking bravely into the wreck of a blazing aircraft followed by Fireman Kelly in a primitive silver asbestos suit. The two men disappeared into the flames; a desert wind fanned the fire, which roared and flared. For a second the crowd glimpsed the figure of Maskelyne, silhouetted, right in the centre the blaze. A minute passed, the flames began to die and Maskelyne appeared from the wreck, moving fast; Kelly lumbering several feet behind him.

Suddenly Kelly staggered and sank to his knees

then fell forward onto the sand. The other firemen pulled their hoses forward and soaked him with a powerful spray. The medical orderlies cut open the fireproof suit and freed Kelly's head from the helmet. Kelly stirred and opened his eyes. He was not injured, but had been overcome by the heat, which had penetrated his suit. The ambulance rolled forward. Kelly was put on a stretcher and placed inside to be taken to the nearest hospital, where he made a full recovery. Thanks in part to Fireman Kelly, Maskelyne's Fire Cream demonstration had been a dramatic success.

Secretly, Barkas wondered whether the Fire Cream could ever have any practical use, but he was pleased to accept the handshakes and congratulations from the visiting dignitaries. It was all good publicity for his Camouflage Unit.

In a letter written to his wife, Maskelyne described his invention and his hopes for it. 'I am including a few pictures that I think may interest you. I've invented a Fireproof Cream which has cut out the asbestos suit. Any chump can make it! With a boiler suit dripped in it and a wet towel round your head you can walk right into a burning aeroplane and rescue the crew. I have walked into several burning planes, two wrecked fighters and a big bomber. If I had not been in the army I could have sold the idea to the WO [War Office] for £50,000!! Still, such is life!! Anyway I have been recommended for a reward after the war—about £1,000 I'm told?! So if you have news of a new Fireproof Cream—it's mine. It's very cheap to make—10d per gallon.'

Luckily, Maskelyne's cream was never used: one of the ingredients was shredded asbestos.

Back in his headquarters office, Barkas knew that the work in Tobruk had shown that the Camouflage Unit's strengths lay as much in deception as concealment. He wanted to be able to create, at very short notice, whatever illusion a commander needed to help win a battle. Barkas and Proud described their ambitions as 'film production on a grand scale', and that was the snag: the grand scale was colossal, far bigger than anything they had attempted at Tobruk. Camouflaging the widely spread out Eighth Army was going to demand vast resources.

Barkas calculated the amount of material his unit required for the coming year. The figures amazed him. They would need wire, fabrics, nets, mild steel, rush matting, locally made hurdles, paint and distemper, gauze, brushes, tallow, fireproofing materials, spun yarn, shellac, even gelatine wafers. The quantities were eye-watering: 8,000 tons of paint; nearly 2.5 million fathoms of cordage; 125,000 nets made of anything they could lay their hands on—cotton string, sisal and any other sort of fibre; 2.5 million square feet of rabbit wire; 5 million square yards of white fabric; 125 million yards of three-inch cotton strip, to be dyed and woven into the camouflage nets as garnish. Where was it all going to come from?

He had recently commandeered half-a-million square yards of unbleached calico, which had many applications: dyed black it could be laid in strips on the ground to look from the air like slit trenches; it could also be used as dressing on fake gun-pits to create artificial shadows that made a two-dimensional

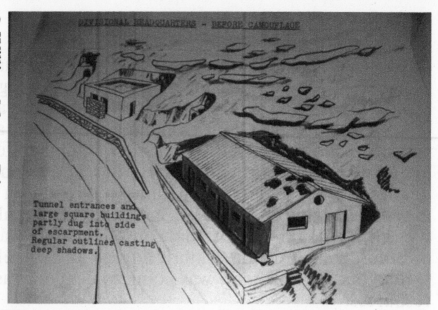

DIVISIONAL HEADQUARTERS - BEFORE CAMOUFLAGE

Tunnel entrances and
large square buildings
partly dug into side
of escarpment.
Regular outlines casting
deep shadows.

DIVISIONAL HEADQUARTERS - AFTER CAMOUFLAGE

Large nets, rock pattern,
stretched tightly from
escarpment over buildings
and picketed down, then
forced up out of shape
with petrol tin posts
supporting.

Hiding large structures. Storyboard for the camouflage of a divisional HQ using nets and local materials. Some of the rocks were made from crushed four-gallon petrol cans.

144

object look as though it was a solid three-dimensional artillery position. Unbleached calico was used mainly by the lower classes in Egypt. The *Egyptian Mail* ran a story claiming that 'Unbleached calico had almost disappeared from the market'. Barkas sent the clipping to his immediate superior, Hindley. Signing himself 'Director of Decency', Hindley replied with a piece of doggerel:

> *Debagged beside his native Nile*
> *Stark naked 'neath the sun he smarts,*
> *With nothing left except his smile*
> *To Camouflage his private parts.*

Barkas's search for more manpower brought him into conflict with the army's inherent conservatism and bureaucracy. His main adversary was the War Establishment Committee. Regulations required that every unit of the British Army had to have two documents, a War Establishment (WE) and a G1098. These two pieces of paper set out in minute detail who and what any unit could have on its strength. It was the Establishment Committee that approved the issue and content of the WE and G1098 and Barkas spent many hours sitting in front of them pleading the case for new equipment and personnel.

The committee was manned by senior officers who sat in almost permanent session at a long table in a room at Grey Pillars. On one occasion a brigadier had asked Barkas about the duties of a proposed sergeant:

'He will be required to design and produce models, sir.'

'For what purpose?'

145

'Training, Brigadier.'

'But there's nothing especially difficult about that. I could do it myself quite easily—anyone could.'

'In that case, sir, I will willingly forego the sergeant if I can replace him with you.'

At this point the chairman intervened: 'I think we had better keep Brigadier Cox on the committee, if you don't mind, Major Barkas. In any case, I don't see how we can pass this Establishment as it stands.'

'Why is that sir?'

'It has no resemblance to any other unit I've come across!'

'With respect, sir,' replied Barkas, 'in the Camouflage Unit our whole mission in life is to make the army behave and look as much unlike an army as we possibly can.'

There was a long pause; the chairman muttered to his colleagues. Barkas could not make out what they were saying and wondered whether his cheek had ruined his chances. Finally the chairman gathered his papers and said: 'We are going to approve your Establishment, not because we understand it. We don't.' He smiled wryly. 'You are the first sponsor to present us with an argument that none of us has heard before.'

*   *   *

In spite of his frustrations and battles with the bureaucracy, Barkas's empire continued to grow. He looked around at the Camouflage Unit's bustle of young officers, sergeants, corporals, sappers and privates that surrounded him. In peacetime they

146

had been clerks, model-makers, draughtsmen, photographers, craftsmen of all sorts; he had kidnapped them from every part of the army.

In the early autumn Barkas was promoted to Director of Camouflage, and placed under the Director of Military Operations, his old ally, 'Jock' Whitely, now a brigadier general. Barkas's establishment was given a name: The Camouflage Development and Training Centre, the twin of the organisation at Farnham. A short time later he received a request for a General Staff Officer, Grade 2 Camouflage (Major) to be posted to the headquarters of the Eighth Army, an important opportunity. No Grade 2 Camouflage Staff Officer had ever been appointed to an army formation before. Whoever he chose would have to have energy, enthusiasm and an understanding of camouflage as a tactical weapon of war. The new officer would need the confidence and initiative to make things up as he went along and be able to beg borrow or steal men, materials and equipment. Peter Proud was an obvious choice, but he was too valuable at Grey Pillars.

Then he remembered Sykes, the sometime graduate of the Royal College of Art and veteran of Calais. Barkas had recently described Sykes as 'an excellent camouflage officer technically and one who thinks about camouflage in terms of battle'. He called in his clerk and instructed him to find Captain Sykes.

They found him in hospital in Jerusalem, where he had been taken with another bout of malaria, languishing among young cavalry officers suffering from broken bones, cuts and abrasions incurred in the transition from horses to armoured cars. By his own admission, Sykes's career in the desert had started badly. Soon after arriving, he and the other camouflage officers from the *Samaria* had overflown the Canal Zone to get a perspective on the desert. The pilot took the aircraft into the sky and as he did so the temperature inside the unpressurised cabin dropped, making the interior very cold. Sykes began to shiver and feel nauseous until, somewhere over Port Said, he began to throw up. He wrote in his diary that everyone was very sympathetic but it took him a long while to live the incident down.

Sykes was then sent to Palestine to help prepare defences against a possible attack by the Vichy French. His boss there was Captain Patrick E. 'Pep' Phillips. Sykes found himself overseeing the disguise of the hundreds of pillboxes and advising on the camouflage of Port Haifa. But he continued to get into scrapes. One wet morning, in a steep gorge on the road to the Horns of Hattin—where in 1187, Saladin routed the Crusaders—Sykes's truck lost traction and went into a 'long relentless skid'. He braced himself for the end, the truck hit something and spun round, slithering between the precipice on one side and the rock face on the other, coming to rest in a ditch. Shaking, Sykes went back to see what had happened. Two black skid marks showed that the front wheels of the truck had gone over the edge. He had been saved by a heavy stone bollard that had clipped the rear wheels, slewing the vehicle round, knocking it back onto the road.

Later, driving along the coast road to Sidon, Sykes looked out to sea and saw a French warship flying a giant tricolour from its stern. He was bewitched by the sight and as he drove little flashes twinkled along the ship's side. Sykes idly wondered what they were until, fractions of a second later, the sound of heavy gunfire rumbled across the water, followed by thudding explosions as shells began to detonate on the road ahead. He swerved into an olive grove, looking for cover. When it was safe he drove on to Sidon, where he sat in a café listening to artillery in action in the north and watching soldiers trying to catch fish by firing their rifles into the water.

Between escapades Sykes the artist found time to draw and paint the rock roses, sage, pyramid orchids, tiny blue irises, pink flax and other wild flowers that carpeted the Palestinian hillsides. One night he threw a wild and raucous party on the roof of his apartment and invited an assortment of guests: military, civilian, Jews and Arabs. They drank lavishly on a balmy night under a full moon to the sound of a sapper swing band. Soon after the party he fell ill with another bout of malaria.

By October, Sykes was well enough to report to Colonel Barkas at GHQ. He wrote in his diary: 'Six months since last in Cairo, same smells.' After a short period of leave and further recuperation, Sykes was installed as Camouflage Staff Officer at the Eighth Army HQ, Sidi Bagush, on his shoulders the pips of his new rank of major.

After two days settling in, Sykes's commanding officer, Colonel David Belchem, an amiable but overworked man, told him to report immediately to the office of Brigadier Robertson, the Assistant Quarter Master General. An important conference about the railhead at Misheifa had started and Camouflage had been ordered to attend. Sykes hurried off in a panic.

He scuttled through a maze of underground tunnels trying to find the meeting. Eventually he located a door leading to Robertson's office. He could hear the murmur of voices and, peering through a crack in the door, saw a flash of red tabs, which he assumed to be those of the brigadier. The conference had already started. They were discussing Crusader, Eighth Army's forthcoming operation. Most arms were represented by senior men, gunners and sappers, plus Medical Corps and Service Corps. Through the crack Sykes could see another door through which he thought he might squeeze without attracting too much attention. He found it, gently pushed it open, slipped in and arrived just as the brigadier was going round each person in the room asking: 'Gunners, any questions, sappers—OK? Medical—any problems?'

His gaze then fell on Sykes. 'Who the hell are you?'

'Camouflage, sir.'

On the wall was a large board with a plan of the huge, newly constructed rail complex at Misheifa, comprising a depot, marshalling yard, sidings for all services, vehicle recovery and ambulance train sidings, locomotive facilities, watering and coaling. Robertson swept his hand in a circle that encompassed the whole site. 'How are you going to hide this lot then?'

Sykes had no idea. He had not yet had a chance to visit the site, but he knew the railhead was too big to hide. He blurted out: 'The only thing I can suggest, Sir, is to make a decoy railhead.' To his amazement Robertson liked the idea and ordered him to come back after the meeting to explain his thoughts in detail.

Back in Cairo, the 85th Camouflage Company of the South African Engineer Corps, which Tony Ayrton had helped set up, was disembarking at Suez with orders to join the new Camouflage Training and Development Centre. This was very good news: the 85th were the first unit of their kind in the British and Commonwealth forces, especially trained in camouflage and, even more importantly, supplied with the right equipment, vehicles and men for the job. The Company had three elements: headquarters, a mobile section that could work independently in the field, and a factory and experimental section. The latter was sent to join Jasper Maskelyne's Experimental Unit. The 85th were led by Major Derek von Berg MC, who in peacetime had been an architect in Johannesburg. Von Berg was a smart and efficient soldier, ideally suited, thought Barkas, to the work in hand. He and Barkas hit it off at once.

*　　*　　*

Sykes now focused on the conundrum of the dummy railhead. He approached the New Zealand army's specialist engineers, the Railway Construction and Maintenance Group, and found that its commander, Colonel Anderson, was a veteran of camouflage from the First World War. At their first meeting Anderson described with great enthusiasm how he had disguised a Vickers machine gun in a brickworks that overlooked the enemy. He painted the gun's metal shield to look like brick and then, at night, positioned it among

151

the stacks of bricks. The gun was invisible and the next day opened up with devastating effect. For Sykes the story opened the door to a creative and productive partnership.

Sykes wanted to make a tank delivery spur stretching six miles from the railhead at Mesheifa. The spur had two functions: to act as a diversion and, while it was under construction, to fool the enemy into thinking that the British were not planning to attack until it was finished. The two men quickly got down to practicalities. Anderson offered to extend the existing railway line by laying his surplus rails along the dummy route.

Next they persuaded the RAF to fly them over the real thing to see what other buildings they would have to mock up. From the air they saw that they would need to create the illusion of locomotives, tank delivery trucks, tanks, dumps, anti-aircraft defences, installation buildings and tented accommodation—a very big undertaking. Sykes christened the scheme 'No. 2 Depot'. Soon John Baker, an architect, joined them. Baker was hard working, good company and unflappable, an ideal man to deal with all the detail the project required and he quickly set to work making the mass of working drawings for the scheme. As usual for the camoufleurs, there were not enough men or materials for the job. Sykes had been assigned one platoon of Indian pioneers arranged through XIII Corps and one mobile detachment of the South African 85th Camouflage Company, supervised by an officer, two European NCOs, and eight European other ranks. The British XXX Corps had agreed to provide a further platoon if necessary.

Sykes now met Captain Simpson, the 85th's

second-in-command, and the officer assigned to supervise the South African contingent. Sykes was worried that Simpson and his men had underestimated the difficulty of getting materials by lorry from Alexandria and Cairo. For their part, the South Africans were dubious that the dummy railhead would work at all. They did not believe that something made of such flimsy and fragile materials would fool anyone. Sykes explained that it would only have to bear scrutiny from the air, above 500 feet, or from a great distance. Through the heat haze even a wily observer with binoculars would find it difficult to see the installations as anything more than railway- and train-shaped structures.

Soon they were experimenting with ways to build the dummy train and exploring how to make the most of the construction materials available. At the start of the scheme they had 5,000 feet of timber. They doubled the amount of wood available by splitting the timber lengthways. However there were no power tools and therefore the splitting, or 'ripping', had to be done by hand, and took a very long time. As usual, the camoufleurs went on the scrounge, looking for anything they could salvage to help with the build. Cookhouse stoves were requisitioned and adapted to make realistic, smoke-belching fireboxes for the locomotives.

Thousands of feet of steel rails were supplied by Anderson's New Zealand Railway Construction Group, but Sykes calculated that they still did not have enough material to construct all of No. 2 Depot at full scale. They would have to scale down. Sykes decided to reduce the size of everything to two-thirds of the original. The final track width

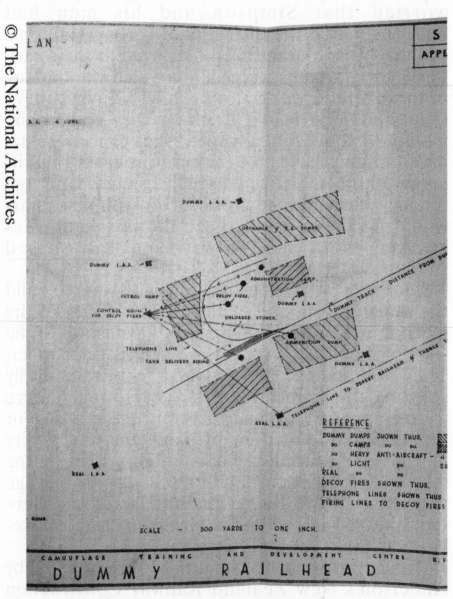

Working drawing for dummy railhead
('No. 2 Depot').

over the course of a mile was just three foot eight inches. Von Berg, who was based in Cairo but keeping a close eye on his unit's first important project, was convinced that the subterfuge would be invisible from the air, and repeated aerial checks confirmed this as the line grew. A reconnaissance flight carried out near completion reported that everything worked well at heights of 1,000 feet and higher. At lower levels imperfections in the points and the use of straight rails on curved sections became apparent. The pilot of the reconnaissance plane thought that this would not be noticed by a pilot flying in the face of ack-ack fire, or who had not been given reason to be suspicious. He did, however, point out that the lines lacked shine.

To the shortage of steel rails Sykes found a solution in the almost limitless supply of empty four-gallon petrol tins. The flimsy metal containers that were hopeless for carrying petrol had many other uses: they could be cut up and used for cooking stoves, shower heads, in-trays, wastepaper baskets, even metal 'sandbags' for lining trenches. At a huge desert crossing nicknamed Piccadilly Circus, the engineers had even used the cans to make a giant sculpture of Eros.

Sykes instructed his men to cut the cans open and beat them into hollow railway-line sections, using the real thing as formers. Then the short sections were welded together to make twenty-foot lengths. Dummy locomotives and rolling stock were made out of wood and canvas. Native hurdles made of palm fronds were used to make dummy tanks, which would be placed on dummy rail transporters. The rolling stock was made out of hessian, slid along wires and anchored at either end to posts; in this way it was hoped to alter, fairly easily, the shape of the cars and hence the composition of the train. The sides of the cars were stretched between split canes, sprayed with water dyed red, and braced strongly against the high winds that were a feature of the desert in autumn.

The train itself was made up of thirty-three box wagons, one tank wagon, three Hungarian cars, fifteen flat cars, a locomotive and a tender. The components for the train were built in the army's camouflage workshops at Sidi Haneish and brought to the real railhead at Misheifa by train. From there they were transported by lorry to the fake depot.

To add authenticity, a dummy headquarters, complete with tents, mess huts, kitchens and straw figures, was set up near No. 2 Depot, where there was real accommodation for the workers on the real railhead. Lorries drove between the two locations, deliberately creating tracks, adding to the impression of reality. The railway crept across the desert, protected by dummy Bofors guns manned by men of straw who hung around dummy cookhouses waiting for dummy tea that would never appear. A few real gunner volunteers were positioned among the fakes to bring the enormous stage set to life. Sykes instructed the gunners to use two real Bofors anti-aircraft guns to fire very real shells at the enemy. As a finishing touch, Sykes positioned cans containing waste petrol that could be detonated electronically to simulate the fall of bombs and confuse enemy aircraft. Wrecked vehicles were towed in to bulk up the appearance of motor activity.

All was ready and in position by the night of 17/18 November, the eve of Operation Crusader,

The Phantom Army standing by.

Like many artists, Edward Wadsworth found 'Dazzle' camouflage a creative inspiration. This is his painting *Liverpool Shipping*, 1918.

A

B

C

This analysis by Roland Penrose of the zebra's stripes illustrates the importance of matching camouflage to background.

Jasper Maskelyne and his wife Evelyn just before he sold their car to raise money to send Evelyn and their two sons to New Zealand.

Steven Sykes and Jean Judd on their wedding day. A few weeks later Sykes was sheltering from dive-bombers on the quay at Calais.

Camouflage officers on the Andes heading for Cairo. (From left to right: John Hutton, Geoffrey Barkas, P. E. 'Pep' Phillips and Blair Hughes Stanton.)

Two painters and a film set designer just after the siege of Tobruk. (*Left to right*: Edwin Galligan, Steven Sykes, Fred Pusey.)

Photograph taken by Fred Pusey: the officer on the right is believed to be Tony Ayrton, who became Barkas's right-hand man during Operation Bertram.

Codenamed 'Diamond', the dummy pipeline's construction was timed to obscure the start date of the Battle of Alamein.

To reconnaissance aircraft flying above 500 feet these mock-ups looked exactly like real petrol stores.

Whether entertaining at the British Embassy or demonstrating his fire cream, Maskelyne was happiest playing to the crowd.

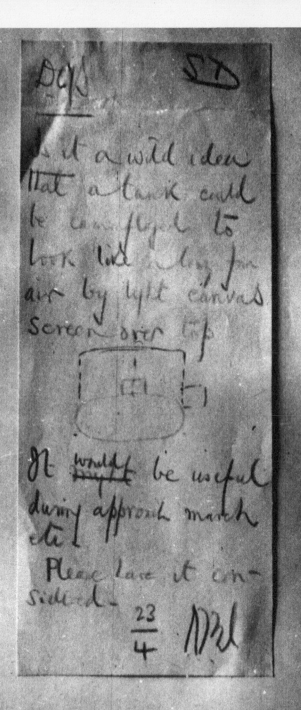

NOTE FROM C-in-C MIDDLE EAST

Wavell's first thought about disguising tanks as lorries. The general had been interested in deception since the First World War. This sketch contains the idea for the 'Sunshield', an essential element in Operation Bertram.

Tanks turned into lorries and string and hessian turned into tanks.

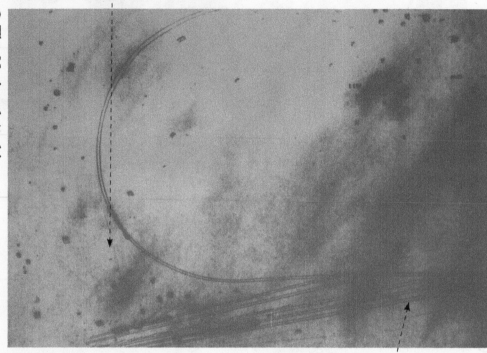

Depot No. 2, which looks real when seen from 1,000 feet in the air. The arrows show where the dummy trains are standing and the pictures show how unrealistic the trains are when viewed close up. The figure by the train in the upper picture indicates the extent of the 'scaling down' to make the materials go further.

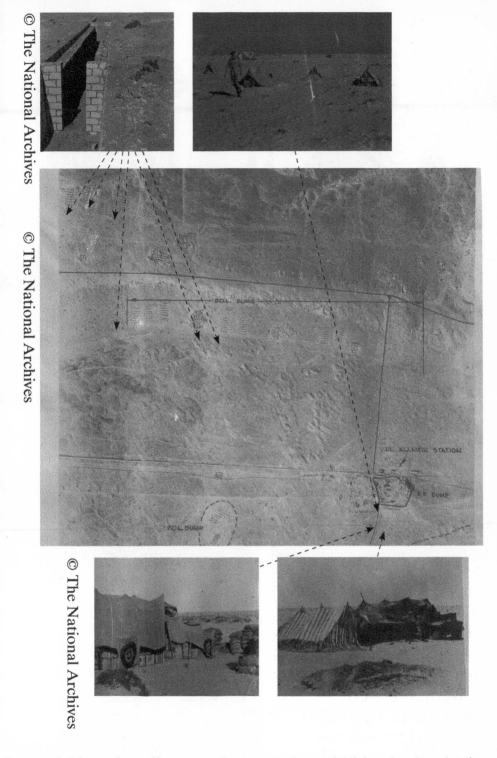

Around Alamein railway station petrol was hidden in the shadows of pre-constructed trenches which had been built a year before and never used. Other stores were disguised as tents and lorries.

General Sir Richard O'Connor KT, GCB, DSO, MC, ADC (right), was one of the most gifted generals to command in the Western Desert. Unlike Monty (top right) or Rommel, he was not obsessed with his image.

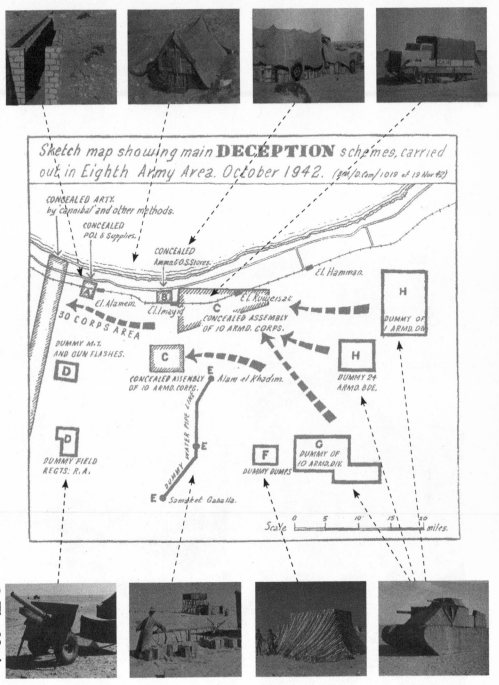

Hey presto! In the south, dummy stores and the pipeline; in the north, real stores hidden among harmless lorries; to the east and too far away to be a danger, the tanks. Overnight the lorries became tanks that still look like lorries, while in the east the tanks don't appear to have moved.

Alamein: the battle starts and the Phantom Army stands down
The fighting turns into a vicious slogging match in which th
Allied troops pay dearly for every yard of ground but, in the end
they defeat the German–Italian Panzer Army.

Real War. Thirteen thousand Allied troops were killed or wounded in the fighting at Alamein.

when disaster struck. A storm tore half of the fake tank delivery siding to shreds. While they were patching it up, Operation Crusader started. Twenty-eight-year-old Bainbridge Copnall, the sculptor, who was working with Fred Pusey at XIII Corps' forward positions, marked the occasion by sending a signal: 'Battle joined, all Camouflage Officers in action!' This caused some hilarity, as soldiers imagined the camoufleurs chasing the enemy with their camo nets, trying to capture them like butterflies. Depot No. 2 was repaired but would not be fully 'operational' until late November.

*   *   *

Operation Crusader started under the command of General Alan Cunningham, Dick O'Connor's replacement, who had made his name by beating the Italians in Somaliland and seeing to it that Haile Selassie regained the throne taken from him in 1936.

Cunningham arrived in Cairo in August 1941 and had very little time to organise his command or train his troops. He found his task overwhelming: he had never handled armour and was disorientated by the desert. One historian describes him as being like the 'successful owner of a village shop suddenly put in charge of a London department store'. Cunningham started the battle after much disagreement about tactics and strategy but with more tanks than the Axis alliance. His force included 126 new American Stuarts. Known as 'Honeys', they were faster than any other tank in Africa, but undergunned, thinly armoured and prone to 'brew up'—to burst into flames if hit—

157

because of their petrol-driven Pratt and Whitney aero engines.

The same torrential rain and storms that had threatened to completely wreck Sykes's railhead made it impossible for the Desert Air Force to fly the planned missions against the Luftwaffe's airfields ahead of the land assault. However, before dawn on the morning of the eighteenth, the Eighth Army rumbled out of its positions at Mersa Matruh to launch its surprise attack across the Libyan border. Churchill sent them a message wishing them God speed, and saying: 'The Desert Army may add a page to history which will rank with Blenheim and Waterloo. The eyes of all nations are upon you. All our hearts are with you. May God hold the right!'

The battle proper started on 18 November when General Gatehouse (who had lost nearly all his tanks 'rallying forward' in Operation Battleaxe) was attacked by the 15th Panzer Korps led by *Leutnant General* Ludwig Crüwell. Gatehouse's force, re-equipped though it was with over a hundred new Stuarts, was soon outnumbered and in trouble. Speed, it appeared, was not enough. The Panzers knocked out Stuart after Stuart, many of which burst into flames, incinerating the crews and demoralising comrades in other tanks. Rommel then decided to concentrate his 15th and 21st Panzer Divisions in a move on Sidi Rezegh, south of Tobruk. The British commanders interpreted this as a German retreat, the first of many mistakes the Allies were to make during the next six weeks.

At the dummy railhead site, Sykes waited for proof that his ruse had worked. He wanted to be bombed. A special telephone line was laid between the real railhead and No. 2 Depot to help warn of the approach of enemy aircraft. A small company of sappers had been stationed with the two real Bofors anti-aircraft guns; their job was to detonate the decoy explosions and fires. They were to do this if the installation came under attack, and they were understandably nervous. For three days nothing happened. Then, on 28 November, the fake railhead was attacked by aircraft flying at about 5,000 feet. The sapper officer froze. Sykes shouted at him: 'For God's sake, do something!' The flustered officer detonated all the charges, simulating more explosions and fires than there had been bombs.

The site was regularly attacked for the next fortnight. Nearly a hundred bombs were dropped on it that would otherwise have fallen on the vital railhead at Misheifa. On 1 December an enemy map was captured and on it the six-mile extension of the line and No. 2 Depot were marked as genuine targets. The dummy railhead ruse was nearly discovered when, on the night of 1 December, a convoy of box trucks containing enemy prisoners was parked under guard at the Misheifa railhead. An air raid started and it was decided, on humanitarian grounds, to release the prisoners. In the darkness and confusion some of them escaped and went westwards to their own front, using the railway line as a guide. Sykes worried that they would realise what he had been up to. But in their panic to escape through the night, the fugitives discovered nothing.

The fighting raged on. Rommel counterattacked and the British generals became more confused. One afternoon, film designer Fred Pusey found himself driving parallel to a convoy of mixed armour and soft-skinned supply vehicles, dust churning everywhere. It slowly dawned on him that they were German; discreetly, he swung away from the column and escaped into the desert.

Crusader was a long and unpleasant battle that lasted until the end of the year. At one point the ill-fated General Gatehouse lost his headquarters and was seen directing his troops from an armchair tied to the top of his tank, a tartan rug slung across his lap against the bitter cold of the desert winter dawn. Tragically, over a thousand 3.7-inch British anti-aircraft guns sat idle, defending Suez and Cairo from air raids that never materialised, despite pleas that they should be redeployed in an anti-tank role in which they would have been as lethal as the feared German 88mm. One of the most vicious and confused tank battles of the war was fought at Sidi Rezegh. On one occasion a small company of 88s took just twenty-five minutes to knock out fifty-two tanks, a whole regiment. In the fighting, three VCs were won, two of them posthumous.

Cunningham, who had exhausted himself in the run-up to the battle, could not cope, and Auchinleck relieved him of his command, replacing him with a younger man, Lieutenant General Neil Ritchie, former Deputy Chief of the General Staff in Cairo. 'The Auk' handed Ritchie the sword of command at one of the most difficult and complex moments in the Desert War. Four years earlier Ritchie had been a major and had never commanded anything bigger than a company. Now, in the middle of a battle, he had to manoeuvre an army of more than 100,000 men, 700 tanks and as many aircraft. Like Cunningham he found it a daunting prospect. Slowly, the tide turned in the

Allies' favour. Rommel began to withdraw. On 30 November the siege of Tobruk ended. It had lasted for 242 days.

On Christmas Eve 1941, as Jasper Maskelyne gave a gala performance of conjuring tricks to dignitaries at the British embassy in Cairo, the Eighth Army entered Benghazi. Crusader was all but over. Against the odds the British had won. Rommel was back to square one. Steven Sykes received the following signal from the Commander-in-Chief:

Most Secret

To G 2 Cam: Will you please convey to all those concerned in the construction and maintenance of the Dummy RH [railhead] my congratulations on the success which the scheme has achieved. The very considerable organisation, labour and artistry employed in the No. 2 Depot Scheme have proved well worthwhile and the results achieved are a very excellent reward.

I would like a report in the greatest detail with photographs including a diary of enemy action against it so that the scheme can be tried in other places in future.
Neil Ritchie
Lt. Gen.
GOC-in-C Eighth Army

Ritchie's signal was exactly what Barkas had been working for: acknowledgement from the highest level of command. The Camouflage Unit had arrived.

7

THE NO. 1 DECEPTION UNIT

By the end of 1941, the Camouflage Development and Training Centre had established new premises at Helwan, near Cairo, in what was known as 'E' Camp. The site included sixty huts, modified to provide lecture halls, workshops, offices, cookhouses, mess huts for all ranks and living accommodation for the staff and 150 students. The new accommodation housed permanent large-scale models, essential for instruction, some of which were up to 150 feet long and showed camouflage schemes for whole battalions, even ports. Best of all it came with a patch of desert, a camoufleurs' playground, measuring about a mile by a mile and a half. The area contained a cross-section of features that were found in the desert, and offered the perfect testing ground in miniature for ideas developed in the workshops. On it instructors could set up examples of good and bad camouflage, and demonstrate how to conceal artillery positions, defence lines, oil boxes, headquarters, company positions and other military installations.

A regular soldier, Major J. Sholto Douglas of the Royal Scots, became the camp's first commandant, while Hugh Cott was drafted in from Farnham as the centre's chief instructor. Peter Proud was put in charge of the direction and control of camouflage training. Barkas and his staff went to work

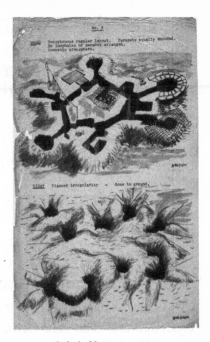

Instructions for siting and hiding
a fire position.

procuring 'indispensable items', including cameras
and dark-room equipment, projection facilities,
duplicating equipment and tools for model-making.

But Helwan came with a headache: Jasper
Maskelyne. Von Berg's 85th South African
Camouflage Company, complete with headquarters,
mobile, factory and experimental sections, had
stolen the thunder from Maskelyne's small
Camouflage Experimental Unit. Barkas had started
the section on an ad hoc basis, using as his model
the shortlived Camouflage Unit set up by Freddie
Beddington with the BEF in France. In reviewing
the situation, Barkas listed Maskelyne's
achievements. He had come up with the vital
Sunshields used to disguise tanks; he and Morrison
had taken the idea further, producing a very useful,
lightweight dummy tank, which two men could erect

and nine of which could be packed into a three-ton truck. The Fireproof Cream had made for an entertaining demonstration but, so far, no one had been able to use it in the field—it was impractical to expect the crew of a burning tank or crashing airplane to start pouring the paste onto themselves, even if it could be stored in the limited space on board.

Then there was the 'Dazzle Light', which had become something of an obsession with Maskelyne. He had put a great deal of effort into designing a searchlight powerful enough to disorientate enemy pilots. He thought that with it he could protect the port at Alexandria and even use it to hide the Suez Canal. So far he had built a prototype, using a modified 90mm searchlight with a set of spinning mirrors fixed to it. The light was expensive and used up labour that Barkas could ill afford. Even if it could be made to work, which was doubtful, it was too expensive to produce in sufficient quantities to have any operational use.

Camouflage was now comparatively big business and had outgrown Maskelyne's small department based in two huts at Wingate Barracks. Barkas decided there was nothing for it: the Camouflage Experimental Unit would have to go. He would merge it with his newly formed Development Wing, which was already doing sterling work under its commandant, Captain A. E. Upfold. Working with the South African 85th Company Factory and Experimental, the unit was already coming up with designs for easily transported, flat-packed tanks; field artillery; ack-ack guns and other military installations. Barkas broke the bad news to Maskelyne in person.

After the interview Maskelyne took himself off to the Army Entertainment Branch, who offered him a job. The affair had upset and humiliated him. He wrote home to his family saying: 'I have also invented a thing for dealing with the night bombers [the Dazzle Light]. The army gave me a grant of £200 [about £7,500 today]. It covers the cost of my experiment in connection with it. There are also other little things I have done that I cannot tell you about . . . But I am very sad as I've been told that my section is to be moved very shortly to a very rotten part of the country, an officer whom I don't like is to be placed above me. They have told me that by this arrangement I can't get any more promotion. I was terribly fed up about this as I've worked so hard to get my section going and now it's all going to be messed up. So I went to see the Army Entertainment Branch (nothing to do with ENSA) and they offered me the post as Welfare Officer for the whole of the Cairo area!! A marvellous job! I shall take it. I'll be a staff captain & have my own car and driver! I am building a theatre to seat 6,000 in the garrison! I shall open at Christmas with a panto! This is work after my own heart. I shall also draw staff pay £6.10d a day.'

Barkas willingly agreed to the transfer and met Maskelyne to thank him for all he had done. Maskelyne asked him what would happen to the Dazzle Lights, and Barkas replied diplomatically that now the Desert Air Force had command of the air, the threat from the Luftwaffe to the Suez Canal had gone away. The two men shook hands: 'Cheerio Jasper, good luck.' 'Cheerio Geoffrey, thanks for everything.' Maskelyne saluted and went back to what he loved best—performing on a stage in front of hundreds of people.

There is film footage, taken in the summer of 1942, of Maskelyne entertaining a large garden party at the British embassy. He wears his dashing major's uniform—a tall, handsome figure twirling magic hoops round his arms and flirting with the pretty female guests in their summer frocks. He is obviously enjoying himself and so is his audience. Maskelyne was back in his element. While his former camouflage colleagues prepared for Operation Bertram and El Alamein, he rehearsed his 'Eastern and Western Magic Show—Two and a Half Hours of Music, Mirth and Mystery'. It opened at the Empire, Cairo's largest open-air cinema, on 7 September 1942.

* * *

Barkas now moved the bulk of his operation to Helwan camp, but kept his headquarters office at Grey Pillars, where he and Captain Peter Proud worked to make sure that the training curriculum at Helwan was as realistic and battleworthy as possible.

Word of Steven Sykes's success with the dummy railway spread fast, and staff officers were keen to see what other schemes could be started using deception. Just before Christmas 1941, Sykes was ordered to report to John 'Jock' Whitely, who was now no less a person than Brigadier General Staff. After adding his congratulations on the success of the Depot No. 2 scheme, Whitely went on to talk about the threat to the newly liberated ports of Derna, Tobruk and Benghazi. All three installations had been badly damaged and were still vulnerable to attack from the air. He asked Sykes if there was anything the Camouflage Unit could do to take the pressure off these harbours. Stunned to be asked to give advice to such a senior officer, Sykes asked for some time to think.

In two days Sykes worked out a plan for a decoy port installation, which he described to his Eighth Army boss Colonel Belchem. He wanted to build a fake, specialised, 'high-priority' port for the disembarkation of tanks, fuel and ammunition. Like the dummy railhead, the proposed port would encourage the Germans to waste time and bombs on an apparently vulnerable new target, and distract them from the real ports. The plan was approved on the spot and Belchem gave Sykes the use of a captured enemy Ford truck that the Germans had kitted out as a mobile workshop, complete with shelving and lockers. Belchem christened the scheme Operation Belsea and congratulated Sykes on his new command for the project: the No. 1 Deception Unit.

The unit's first task was to find a location for the dummy installation somewhere between Tobruk and Benghazi. Wherever they chose had to be plausible as a site for a port. Sykes needed expert help from the Navy before he could set about reconnoitring for his location. He was sent to see the Senior Officer Inshore Squadron who listened very carefully to what was required and appointed Lieutenant Commander Harris of the Royal South African Navy as his naval liaison officer. Harris was a friendly, cheery man. With Harris's help, Sykes made some preliminary sketches of how he thought the port should look.

Sykes had also managed to co-opt the tall and affable Fred Pusey, who joined the No. 1 Deception Unit on Boxing Day. Pusey was the talented art director who had worked on *Things to Come* and had spent part of 1940 working again for the Korda brothers on the lavish Technicolor fantasy movie, *The Thief of Baghdad*. Harris briefed them that the site they were looking for had to have water deep enough to be realistic as a port. He had charts that he had marked up with possible locations.

The team of eight set off for the Gazala area, men and equipment piled into a Chevrolet pick-up, the Ford mobile workshop, and Sykes, Harris and Pusey in a large, comfortable Humber staff car, which their driver, Rifleman York, had mysteriously acquired. York was a silent type, given to rare and odd pronouncements. One day they were making good progress, travelling at speed along a desert road. Even in the car they were tormented by flies. Sykes asked: 'How do these damned flies keep up with us?'

After a pause York replied: 'Oh them, they've no sense of gravity.'

The team had saved their best festive rations for the trip, including (tinned) Christmas puddings soaked in whisky, bought from the NAAFI, which they ate on a beach in Gazala. Their first recce was to Jebel Akhdar, the 'Green Hills'. This was an area that Mussolini had tried to colonise with Italian peasants and they passed through small coastal settlements with names such as Giovanni Berta and D'Annunzio, Italianate places with colonial buildings and churches interspersed with white colonists' villas. Drawing a blank, they turned north towards Cyrene with its famous beautiful ruins, the

Mediterranean sparkling tantalisingly in the distance, but still had no luck.

In the afternoon they found a deserted Italian supply depot from which they were able to take food and drink to add to the monotonous corned beef and hard tack they carried with them. Eventually they found themselves on a steep, dangerous road with sharp bends and deep drops interspersed with narrow bridges and culverts. The sun was setting and in the fading light they decided to stop and spend the night in a deserted Italian café. Outside the wind rose and heavy rain began to fall. They ate their supper and talked about the possibility that they might be ambushed by one of the isolated pockets of Germans or Italians who had been cut off during the confusion of Operation Crusader. Eventually they slept, taking it in turns to mount guard in pairs. The rain rattled on the iron roof, the wind howled through the ruined windows, and Sykes wondered if he was the only one to feel lonely and afraid in the creaky, smashed building.

The next day they drove along a twisting road that finally curved through a beautifully engineered tunnel down a hill to a small sandy beach called Ras Al Hilal. They were at the most northerly point of Cyrenaica, at a place where Mussolini had planned to build a splendid port to welcome newly arrived colonist families. The vehicles crunched to a halt and the men got out, stretching in the warm sun. Sykes, Harris and Pusey stood by their Humber and looked around, squinting against the glare from the sea. In front of them, heading into the sea, was a partially demolished jetty. Behind them there was a mosque, shops, offices and a piazza surrounded by open arcading. A road led from the harbour into another tunnel that had been half demolished.

Apart from the jetty, there was nothing to indicate that it was a harbour, no cranes or other unloading equipment—in fact, no equipment of any kind. The whole place was surrounded by steep, rocky cliffs. Sykes thought the silent, deserted little harbour was more like an empty film set than a real town. He asked how quickly they could get men down on site and working. They had found their port. Operation Belsea was on the road. Before they drove back to report on their find, No. 1 Deception Unit lined up in front of the vehicles and Fred Pusey took a team photograph.

Work started in early January 1942. The area was cordoned off, heavy security established and a construction camp set up. Lorries arrived with stores to be unloaded onto the jetty. The men worked hard, and during breaks sunbathed and swam in the warm sea. Stripped to their shorts, they ate their meals with their legs dangling over the jetty. They all agreed they could be on holiday.

While the team got on with the site work, Sykes dealt with the plans and the admin, travelling back and forth between Eighth Army headquarters and the Belsea site. The long hours and long drives were taking their toll on his health. The malaria that he had contracted in 1940 continued to dog him. One night he wrote in his diary: 'First year from home today. Bad night with fever or something.' When the symptoms of fever began to ease, he developed a very unpleasant boil on his forearm.

Sykes's plan was ambitious. He wanted to make the jetty look as though it were in heavy use. His

170

story included dummy ships disembarking tanks and realistic oil storage tanks just inland of the port. The ships were to be moved about to create the illusion of life and activity. He needed to create a similar illusion by the quay and on the cliffs above the harbour. Engineers from the 85th Camouflage Company, under the command of two officers called Newdigate and Allen, were brought in to repair the Italian jetty and prepare the oil tanks. By 18 January they had built the first oil storage tank, a huge structure made of wood, tubing and hessian, using the same techniques they'd employed at No. 2 Depot. Protecting it from the elements proved to be very difficult and the work harder than they had anticipated, but somehow they remained more or less on schedule.

Pusey undertook the job of making the part-destroyed tunnel look as though it was in working order. Using what is known in the film business as a 'painted cloth', he hung a massive canvas over the wrecked entrance and on it created a giant perspective picture of the repaired tunnel. This was a very big job, but Pusey had a lot of experience painting backcloths at the studios at Lime Grove and Pinewood. First he made a large colour drawing, about two feet square, of what he wanted the tunnel to look like. He then drew a grid on the picture and a scaled-up grid on the cloth, which was hung on scaffolding over the tunnel, weighed down with stones to keep it taut. The grid squares on the drawing had numbers and these were reproduced much larger on the giant canvas. The art director began to paint, matching each giant square on the canvas to its equivalent on the picture. Pusey worked quickly, balancing on the precarious scaffolding, cigarette in mouth, round glasses balanced on his nose, shouting down to the engineers of the 85th Company when he wanted more paint or brushes to be handed up to him.

Encouraged by the way things were going, Steven Sykes made more ambitious plans. He drew up a scheme to make a ship superstructure that didn't float, but could be hung from the side of the jetty. Through Harris he persuaded the Royal Navy to start sending some real shipping into the harbour to add to the effect. One day a German plane flew over, very high, circling the site. Sykes hoped his work would stand up to the scrutiny of the camera that would inevitably be on board.

As the site grew, security became more of a concern. A contingent of Poles from the Carpathian Brigade helped the Rifle Brigade keep the area sealed off, but even so Bedouin Arabs in long camel trains still managed to file through the area, close enough to spot the fake work. Sykes saw Pusey trying to stop a caravan, screaming at them in English while they screamed back in Arabic. In the end the Poles were augmented by a detachment of the Libyan Arab Force. Sykes enjoyed the fact that his first command had taken on in international flavour, with British, Polish, Libyan, Arab and South African pioneers. He even got GHQ to once more lend him a detachment of Bofors anti-aircraft gunners. They brought with them a desert rarity, a loaf of bread, something Sykes and his team had not tasted since leaving headquarters.

One of the camoufleurs, Lieutenant David Jeffries, a former tea planter serving with the West African Rifles, made it his work to equip the captured German workshop with pyrotechnics, flares, high explosives and loudspeakers, a mobile sonic warfare unit. Sykes did not know how the vehicle would be deployed, but humoured Jeffries and let him carry on with his fantasy scheme.

By 23 January the second oil tank was in place and a dummy bridge-span, made from wire and steel cannibalised from Italian vehicles destroyed by Operation Crusader, was stretched across the harbour. At the end of the month the Royal Navy deployed a floating boom to regularly divert real ships in and out of the imaginary port. Soon Sykes would be able to give the appearance that dummy ships had started unloading armoured vehicles and heavy stores onto the quay. His big, ambitious scheme was almost ready. To Sykes it was the obvious time to throw a party.

*　　　*　　　*

At the same moment Rommel, recovering in El Agheila from the battering he had received during Crusader, thought it was time to test the strength of the Allies' positions. Although they had pushed him back nearly five hundred miles, he knew their success gave them the problem of very long supply lines. His intelligence also told him that front-line Allied troops had been pulled back to work building up supply dumps and lines of communication in preparation for a further advance towards 'Tripolitania'. The *Afrika Korps* had been strengthened by reinforcements in the form of armour and troops that had been brought in by sea at Tripoli. On 21 January, Rommel sent out a tactical reconnaissance of three armoured columns. They probed and found that there was only a thin skin of Allied troops to stop an advance. Rommel seized the opportunity and prepared to unleash 179 German and 79 Italian tanks. Ahead of him lay the 150 armoured fighting vehicles of the British 1st Armoured Division.

On the evening of 25 January, in the unreal, film-set-like atmosphere of the dummy port, Steven Sykes's party was underway. Halfway through a riotous evening they heard somebody thumping at the door. Sykes opened it to reveal a figure, half-hidden in the darkness. The figure clicked his heels and at first Sykes thought he was German; then, in a very thick accent, he asked: 'You *Mayor Sikkis*?' Sykes recognised him as Lieutenant Michaelovsky, a Polish officer who was part of the Carpathian Brigade guarding the installation. Michaelovsky handed Sykes a signal ordering him to pull out immediately. Operation Belsea had been cancelled. Rommel had turned his reconnaissance into a full-scale assault and was advancing on Benghazi. If they did not move at once, there was a danger they would be trapped in the port, taken prisoner or killed.

Sykes knew that it was the end of his grand scheme, and glumly ordered all plans and the dummy port to be destroyed. The engineers blew up the oil storage tanks, which collapsed into two huge piles of flaming wood and canvas. Everything else, including the dummy boats and Pusey's tunnel artwork, was burned. Reflected light from the destruction of the harbour masterpiece glowed red on the water. The captured German workshop vehicle was pushed over the cliff into the sea. By the light of the burning harbour, Sykes watched the vehicles towing the Bofors guns crawl up the hill

174

and disappear into the night, heading back to their units. Worse, three camoufleurs, Jeffries, Phillip Cornish and Sergeant Rolf, had not returned from a trip to pick up wood at Msus, a hundred miles away and right in the path of Rommel's advance.

Sykes climbed into a three-tonner with Pusey at the wheel and led No. 1 Deception Unit back to Eighth Army HQ. The coast road was choked with vehicles travelling eastwards away from Rommel's forces. They arrived the next day at headquarters in a sandstorm.

Sykes scribbled in his diary: 'News scarce and general depression.'

RETREAT: THE GAZALA STAKES

On 21 January, Rommel wrote to his wife: 'Dearest Lou, two hours from now the army will launch its counterattack. After thoroughly weighing the pros and cons I have decided to risk it.' It was a calculated risk based on intelligence.

At the American embassy in Cairo, the US military attaché, Brevet Colonel Frank Fellers, no admirer of the British, sent nightly messages to Washington describing what the British were planning. Fellers had the complete trust of the British; they told him everything and let him visit the front. He said later: 'If I was going to be a good observer and write good reports, I'd better report what I saw myself. It wasn't difficult to learn a good deal.'

What he did not know was that his embassy's 'Black Code', the cipher used to transmit his signals across the Atlantic, was being read by the Germans and the Italians. Rommel had access to Fellers' reports within hours of their being written. A security leak at the US embassy meant that Rommel knew on an almost hourly basis what the British were up to. British intelligence at GHQ, on the other hand, knew very little about what Rommel was planning. They were certain that he would not be able to mount a counterattack for several months and were unaware that a convoy had delivered tanks, men and supplies onto the quayside at Tripoli.

Shortly after Rommel sealed the letter to his wife, a specially prepared Heinkel made a round trip of 1,600 miles to bomb the Free French-controlled Fort Lamy airfield, destroying eight new Hawker Hurricanes and 80,000 gallons of fuel. At the same time Rommel's tanks fell on and destroyed the 2nd Armoured Brigade, newly arrived from England and inadequately trained. Next the anti-tank guns, artillery, mounted troops and tanks of Panzer Regiment 8 turned on the 1st Armoured Division, who retreated. Very quickly things fell apart. The retreat turned into a stampede. Rommel took a chance and chased after them. His intelligence officer, Colonel F. W. von Mellenthin, wrote later: 'The pursuit attained a speed of fifteen miles an hour and the British fled madly over the desert in one of the most extraordinary routs of the war.' Rear echelon vehicles, including kitchens, mobile workshops, signals trucks, office trucks and trucks loaded with headquarters company furniture fled headlong east to safety. The Royal Army Service Corps got a new meaning to their acronym RASC—Run Away, Someone's Coming. A British cavalry officer likened it to 'a hunting field'. Rommel's pursuit was so fast that sometimes he found himself behind enemy lines. On one occasion he came across a New Zealand Army field hospital and asked the bewildered staff if they needed anything; he left promising to send them medical supplies, a promise he kept.

Blitzkrieg was not the only trick up Rommel's sleeve. He had another, which one of his officers called *Fingerspitzengefühl*, a sort of sixth sense, an uncanny instinctive ability to read the battlefield, as if through his 'fingertips'. He would appear at the decisive moment in the fight, pull a rabbit out of the military hat and then disappear, like a magician. This unnerving and seemingly supernatural ability was a powerful force in the creation of the legend that Rommel was unbeatable.

On 1 February 1942, in a lame attempt to stop the Rommel myth in its tracks, Auchinleck issued an Order of the Day that stated: 'Rommel is becoming a kind of magician or bogeyman to our troops, we are talking far too much about him . . . Even if he were a superman, it would still be highly undesirable that our men should credit him with supernatural powers. I wish you to dispel by all possible means the idea that Rommel represents something more than an ordinary German general . . . P.S. I am *not* jealous of Rommel.'

In the end it wasn't the British that stopped Rommel, it was lack of fuel. In nine days he had taken back almost all the ground won in Crusader. His spoils included thirty brand new Valentine tanks, 1,300 lorries in perfect working order, huge quantities of stores and ammunition that Auchinleck was stockpiling for his own attack, plus the town of Benghazi. He complained: 'I have never had victory so nearly within my grasp as I have today . . . Once more they are disorganised. Once more they are wandering about in the desert ready for the *coup de grâce*.' But without petrol, there was nothing that even Rommel could do about it.

*   *   *

The camoufleurs were swept up in the Allied exodus east. Sykes got separated from the rest of No. 1 Deception Unit and Fred Pusey got lost, and in the dark drove in to what he thought was a makeshift British camp. He pulled up and heard voices shouting orders in German. He decided that retreat was the better part of valour, spun his wheel and accelerated out. He and most of his unit were reunited. But Phillip Cornish, David Jeffries and Sergeant Rolf were still missing, as was Bainbridge Copnall.

Slowly the camoufleurs emerged from the desert. After a few days a disintegrating Chevrolet appeared, its windscreen shattered, its springs sagging and steam pouring from the engine. In it were Jeffries, Cornish, Rolf and Bainbridge Copnall, all looking battered and exhausted. The wood-collecting camoufleurs had managed to meet up with Bainbridge Copnall in Benghazi. Jeffries' lorry had broken down and for a while Copnall towed it with his own vehicle. This had led to a great deal of argument, as Copnall wanted to abandon it. They got back to Ras Al Hilal to find the abandoned ruins of the dummy port. Jeffries had been particularly upset to see his 'sonic warfare vehicle' lying wrecked in the sea. They followed the coast road back to HQ, one of the last vehicles to do so. Sykes celebrated the men's return with a 'gloomy reunion party, playing increasingly rude drawing games and drinking a lot of captured Italian plonk'.

*   *   *

The Eighth Army and the *Panzerarmee Afrika* each settled down for a period of reinforcement and training that lasted from February to May. Ritchie's army held a line that stretched fifty miles from

Gazala on the coast, south to Bir Hacheim in the desert. Along this, the Gazala line, they established a series of huge defended squares known as 'boxes', gigantic versions of nineteenth-century infantry squares. Each box held a brigade of men. The Allies waited, stringing out miles of barbed wire and sowing vast minefields in front of the boxes, hoping they would stop the next German advance. One British officer later described the boxes as 'useless' during the battle.

During the battle, one of Ritchie's commanders, Lieutenant General Godwin-Austen, had asked to be relieved of his command, claiming that Ritchie 'had displayed a lack of confidence in him by issuing orders directly to his subordinate commanders'. Auchinleck sent his clever Deputy Chief of Staff, Dorman-Smith, to snoop about and find out what was going on. Chink was seen by some as a malign, Rasputin-like figure with dark powers of control over Auchinleck, his Commander-in-Chief, luring him down paths strewn with crackpot ideas. At a private picnic by the waters of Lake Fayoum, Godwin-Austen had told Chink that in his opinion, Ritchie was not 'sufficiently quick-witted or imaginative enough for the command'. Dorman-Smith interviewed other divisional commanders and returned to report that, in his opinion, Ritchie was repellent, patronising, limited in his ability to command and overassured. He claimed that every divisional commander he had spoken to agreed, including Jock Campbell, who had recently won a VC at Sidi Rezegh, and 'Strafer' Gott, who rarely had a bad word to say about anyone. Dorman-Smith recommended that Ritchie be replaced.

Auchinleck prevaricated, uneasy about whom Churchill might foist on him in Ritchie's place. He argued: 'I have sacked one army commander. To sack another within three months would have effects on morale,' adding that the commander needed time to settle in, something Ritchie had not, so far, enjoyed. Auchinleck decided that the Eighth Army commander should stay. It was to prove a deplorable decision.

*　　　*　　　*

Rommel went home to be fêted by his countryman and was again promoted, this time to *Generaloberst*, by his Führer. In Africa his *Panzergruppe* became the *Panzerarmee* and received a reinforcements, but nothing like enough to please Rommel, who grumbled that: 'The strengthening of my army by just a few more divisions and adequate supplies would have been enough to ensure the complete defeat of the British armed forces in the Near East.' Hitler refused to send any more troops; he needed all his manpower on the Russian Front. The desert troops on both sides kicked their heels, obsessed about killing flies and succumbed to exhaustion, jaundice and dysentery. Spring came and Rommel was spotted near his headquarters at El Agheila filming wild flowers and almond blossom with an 8mm home-movie camera.

*　　　*　　　*

During the lull, Sykes continued to command in the field. Geoffrey Barkas ran things from Cairo, getting into the desert as often as he could. One day, on a visit to a box known as 'Knightsbridge', Barkas sat in his car with a new driver, a regular soldier on secondment from the Rifle Brigade. A military policeman waved them down to let a convoy of heavily armed vehicles cross their path. The driver apologised for the delay, and explained that what they were looking at was a 'Jock Column' on its way to patrol the no-man's land that lay between the boxes and the German army. The column roared by. Barkas estimated it was nearly two miles long: Bren-gun carriers, jeeps bristling with guns, lorries packed with jolting infantrymen; they looked like pirates sailing out onto the desert seas. The troops wore improvised uniforms, coloured scarves, Arab headdresses, long hair blowing in the wind with eyes hidden behind dark glasses. In their own slang they were 'off into the Blue to swan about spying on the enemy and, given half a chance, shoot him up'. The last vehicle clattered by, a carrier with a soldier on the back swinging ostentatiously on twin-mounted Lewis guns.

Barkas remembered that in his day you marched, ate, slept and fought as a battalion and knew the commanding officer, and his horse, by sight. The regulations about dress, haircuts and ceremonial were strictly observed. In this new army he found that the troops had gone native. In the vast open areas of the desert men found it difficult to relate to anything but their immediate environment, thinking of themselves less as members of a unit and more as part-owners of a motor truck. The Eighth Army wore its hair long, its shirts outside its trousers, and drill had become a thing of the past. Barkas wondered if he was just being old-fashioned.

Barkas was right to be uneasy about the new way of doing things. Standards of military dress are more than official pedantry. European armies are not made up of guerrillas, mercenaries or special forces, and cannot work as detachments of freelance fighters. Soldiers fight and risk their lives not for abstract ideals like 'country', or 'freedom', but for the man next to them. The kit and uniform helps give him a sense of belonging, pride and unit discipline. None of this is epitomised better than in the soldier's cap badge, the most sacred symbol of belonging. Montgomery understood this, which is why, when he first appeared, he tried to wear the cap badge of every unit under his command, a way of showing that he, too, was one of them, a comrade, if not exactly a mate. The importance of the cap badge is underlined by the reaction of the commander of the Rifle Brigade, Lt Col Vic Turner, to Monty's request for a badge. Turner refused to supply one, saying that Monty was not entitled to wear it.

Sykes set up his new headquarters at a camp called El Adem, next to an airfield, which he hated because of the noise and dust kicked up by the aircraft. He got hold of another captured vehicle and spent the next few weeks journeying around the desert trying to get the camouflage training units back up and running. The process wore him down. In his diary he wrote: 'Bivvy, have scrap meal, bully and biscuits, have usual trouble with primus stove.' 'Leave 1.30 for Buq Buq and have to stop for dark. Most uncomfortable and cheerless meal—biscuits and Marmite. No tea, primus bust. Getting cold and feeling thoroughly miserable and tired.' 'Buq Buq, leave without breakfast. Spring gone on Ford PU—over 650 miles since 4 February on bad surfaces.'

He had one very strange encounter with a staff officer called Colonel Clarke, the importance of which neither he nor Barkas realised, because the true nature of Clarke's work remained secret until after the war. Sykes, who was twenty-seven, described Clarke as 'an elderly Staff Officer, always immaculately dressed in a beautifully cut British camel-hair coat'. Clarke instructed Sykes to disguise the tanks of 437 Royal Tank Regiment as Bedouin tents, and then disappeared. Clarke struck Sykes as a shadowy figure who seemed to wield vast power through a network of 'agents' controlled over the radio, which is exactly what he was.

His full name was Lieutenant Colonel Dudley Wrangel Clarke and he was one of nature's freelancers. A contemporary described him as being able to enter a room silently without anyone knowing he had come in. He had come up with the idea of the Royal Marine Commandos, lost part of an ear in their first raid, and devised the name for 'the Special Air Service'. He was the brains behind Operations Copperhead—the deployment of a lookalike Montgomery—and Mincemeat, a ruse in which a corpse was floated ashore in Spain carrying forged documents indicating an Allied landing at Greece rather than Sicily. His most extraordinary escapade was to be photographed in a Spanish police cell dressed as a woman.

No one has ever really worked out why the colonel had chosen to wear such a disguise. Clarke was in the Middle East at the invitation of Wavell who, in 1940, had ordered him to Cairo to set up a 'special section of intelligence for deception'.

Clarke's organisation was known as 'A Force'. In the coming year Clarke was to play a very important part in the life of the Camouflage Unit and would be behind two of their biggest deception schemes, Sentinel and Bertram, even though neither Sykes nor anybody else from the unit ever knew who he was.

* * *

In an attempt to cheer people up, Barkas published a cyclostyled magazine called *The Fortnightly Fleur*. In the introduction to the April 1942 edition he wrote: 'In this war of lonely groups of scattered tents and trucks it must be hard enough for the men of a battery or battalion to capture and hold that warming sense of belonging to a corps or regiment with a story, a tradition and comradeship of its own. One might think it even harder for the still more widely scattered "Camo-fleurs" of the Middle East to keep that feeling of community. And yet I think we do. For some reason or other I think the job demands—or does it create ?—a quite extraordinary enthusiasm and a faith. There perhaps is the comradeship of camouflage. We do not seem to have lost it. It is profoundly to be hoped we never shall.'

In his endless search for more labour, Barkas asked Peter Proud if he could think of a way to persuade the Establishment Committee to increase the official number for their unit. The question sent Proud into a brilliant flight of fancy. He conjured an essential new unit with satellites from India, South Africa, Australia and New Zealand, all revolving around Barkas's central headquarters and

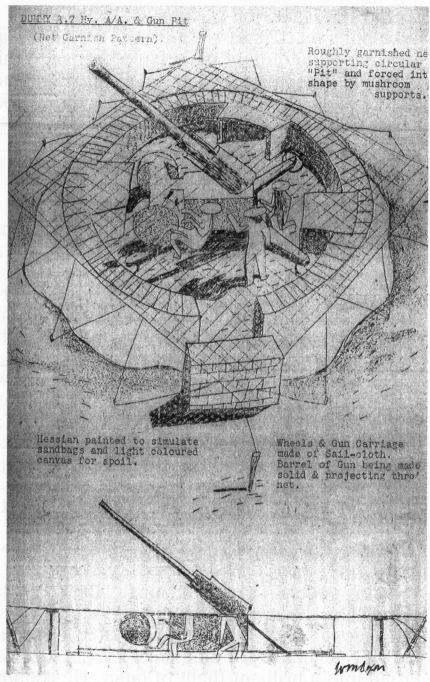

DUMMY 3.7 Hy. A/A. & Gun Pit
(Net Garnish Pattern).

Roughly garnished ne
supporting circular
"Pit" and forced int
shape by mushroom
supports.

Hessian painted to simulate
sandbags and light coloured
canvas for spoil.

Wheels & Gun Carriage
made of Sail-cloth.
Barrel of Gun being made
solid & projecting thro'
net.

Working drawings for Peter Proud's 'net gun-pits'.
Many types of gun were dummied up like this.

all providing muscle for the pick and shovel parties, without which the Camouflage Unit could not work. Proud suddenly broke off, leapt up and left the room saying: 'Sorry, I've got an idea that's worth jotting down before it evaporates.' He returned minutes later with a sketch for guns to be made out of camouflage netting—'net gun-pits'—ingenious illusions made of nets, sticks and squares of dark cloth. He envisaged nets stretched into the circular shape of a gun-pit; he wanted to stitch panels of dark cloth onto the nets in carefully worked-out patterns, creating the illusion of the black shadows and depth created by the emplacements. The trick was completed by a piece of pipe simulating the ack-ack barrel of a gun, elevated in the anti-Stuka dive-bomber position.

The next day they had a mock-up ready and a plane to fly over it. The illusion worked: from the air they looked exactly like gun positions. The 'net gun-pits' went into production. A fifteen-hundredweight lorry could carry nine of them and they could all be deployed in an hour.

At Grey Pillars two regular staff officers were appointed to run matters on a professional army basis. They were called G1 Deception Colonel Goff and G2 Deception Major Gregson. Neither understood what the camoufleurs could and could not do. Barkas found they would come back from planning meetings having agreed to undertake deception schemes without really understanding the practical difficulties, committing the unit to schemes that it did not have the labour or the material resources to complete, or which were impossible to design. Barkas worried that this recklessness was undermining the credibility of the Camouflage Unit.

187

Meanwhile, General Ritchie was becoming almost entirely defensive in his thinking and had turned the Gazala line into a desert version of the Western Front in the First World War. Infantry and guns were crammed into the boxes with tanks deployed behind in reserve; they only ventured out on patrol or skirmishing 'Jock Columns'. His plans had little to do with mobile, motor-driven warfare or the demands of the desert. The flexibility of manoeuvre that had been O'Connor's strength had gone, as had the cooperation between the artillery, the infantry and the armour. Auchinleck grew more and more uneasy about Ritchie's disposition of forces and wrote to him with advice that was ignored.

The lull came to an end on 26 May 1942, when elements of the 1st South African Division at the north end of the Gazala line saw a huge cloud of sand slowly approaching, possibly tanks. It was a hoax. Rommel had ordered that aircraft engines be mounted on lorries to create enormous dust clouds that looked as though the entire *Panzerarmee* was attacking. The real attack came further south and was reported by a scout car whose signals were overheard by Lieutenant David Parry, a gunnery officer:

Scout: 'There is a cloud of dust to the south. It has the appearance of a military formation.'
HQ: 'There are no, repeat no, troops to your south.'

The argument went on until Major John 'Shan' Hackett of the 8th King's Royal Irish Hussars went

188

out to see for himself: 'There in front of me was the whole bloody German army, as far as I could see, coming my way.'

Rommel's army was heavily outnumbered. He attacked with 320 tanks, 50 of which were the obsolete Panzer IIs. The British fielded 900 tanks, which included 200 of the brand new American 'Grants'. But the Desert Fox moved fast and was backed up by tightly organised staff officers who had been trained to react quickly and change plans as the battle dictated. General Ritchie, on the other hand, ran an army controlled by a cumbersome, slow-responding staff that hated change and didn't trust him.

Edward Tomkins, a British liaison officer with the Free French, saw the difference between the two styles of command with his own eyes. After a conference, Tomkins, who spoke German, had got lost in a sandstorm and was captured. He was taken to Rommel's HQ where he found that, 'Rommel had two signal vehicles, one presumably for outgoing messages and the other for incoming. He was sitting between them in some kind of scout car barking out orders or writing notes, then handing them to people to deliver to his wireless operators, and dashing off to lead from the front when he judged the situation to be critical [while] at Ritchie's headquarters there were some thirty ADCs dancing about, and an awful lot of paperwork.'

The fighting went on for nearly a month. Rommel's troops were shocked by the new Allied Grants, which were making their first appearance in the desert. On a plateau overlooking the Knightsbridge box, 115 *Panzergrenadier* Regiment was dug in ready to support the Mark III and Mark IV Panzers. The Grant tanks appeared and were fired at by the 50mm gun of one of the Mark IVs. To the astonishment of the German troops, the round just bounced off the enemy tank's hull. The Grants returned fire, hitting one of the Mark IVs, blowing it to pieces and severely wounding 115 Panzer's commander, who was forced to hand over to his second-in-command.

In spite of his advantages in numbers and firepower, Ritchie's campaign turned into a series of last-ditch stands. First he lost his 150th Infantry Brigade at Got-el-Ualeb, which left an enormous hole in the Gazala line. Then he came up with a plan called Operation Aberdeen, which started at night with an artillery barrage that, had it been aimed at the enemy, would have been very effective. Faulty intelligence ensured that the Allied shells landed on empty ground and only succeeded in alerting the enemy to what was happening. Ritchie let his Grant, Crusader and Matilda tanks go forward without covering artillery fire. They advanced face-on into the muzzles of waiting German 88s. One officer, Rea Leakey MC, describes what happened next: 'In the first seconds we must have received at least four direct hits from armour-piercing shells. The engine was knocked out, a track was broken and one shell hit the barrel of the 75mm gun and broke it . . . Almost every tank in the battle met with the same treatment and the whole line was halted on the crest of a small ridge.'

This happened over and over again as Ritchie failed to concentrate his armour and sent them forward piecemeal. Rommel could not believe that a commander could be so incompetent and wrote in his diary: 'What is the advantage of enjoying overall superiority if you allow your enemy to smash your formations one after the other?'

Having wrecked Ritchie's Operation Aberdeen, Rommel now turned his attention to the Free French in their box at Bir Hacheim, on the southern end of the Gazala line. He sent the defenders an ultimatum: 'Any further resistance will only serve to shed more useless blood. You will suffer the same fate as the two British brigades which were exterminated at Got-el-Ualeb two days ago . . . We shall cease fire when you raise the white flag and come towards us without arms. Rommel.'

The French general Koenig declined the invitation and fought on, surrounded by the German infantry, enduring days of shelling and dive-bombing. The Free French held out for twelve days. On 9 June they were ordered to withdraw, which they did in the darkness of the night of the tenth and escorted by the Rifle Brigade. General Koenig's driver was also his mistress, an English woman called Sue Travers, who drove through gaps in the minefields surrounding the box with 'shells falling round us like rain and sudden, violent explosions tore the night, showering our car with burning metal . . . The wounded who could walk were ordered to get out and continue on foot to lessen the weight of the vehicles picking their way through minefields . . . it had become a shambolic flight.' Over 2,400 men made it out, leaving behind 500, some dead, but mostly wounded.

Nevertheless, Ritchie thought he had the Desert Fox on the run. Rommel now turned to the Knightsbridge box, where the Allied troops held on for just over three days. Exhausted German soldiers battered at even more exhausted Allied soldiers. There were many acts of bravery, but after four days the Allies were defeated. Rommel had destroyed 230 of Ritchie's 300 tanks and on Saturday 13 June, a day that became known throughout the Eighth Army as 'Black Saturday', Knightsbridge was abandoned. A German soldier moving into the box said: 'It was like a naughty child had had a tantrum and thrown his toys all over the room. There were upturned guns, trucks and tanks everywhere, a lot of them burning.' Another soldier commented: 'I had never seen so many dead Englishmen before.'

*   *   *

On 22 June, after the fall of Tobruk, Rommel was made *Generalfeldmarshal,* the youngest German soldier to hold that rank. He held a short celebration, drinking a small glass of whisky and eating a can of tinned pineapple. He said: 'Hitler has made me a field marshal. I would much rather he had given me one more division.'

The Gazala line had collapsed. Shocked and defeated Allied troops began to pour back across the desert towards Cairo and for the second time in six months, retreat turned into rout. The soldiers christened it 'The Gazala Stakes'. The only men not on the run were the defenders of Fortress Tobruk, whose commander Major General Bernard Koppler had written to GHQ in Cairo on 16 June, blithely declaring: 'Things are going very well here, spirits are high and I don't think morale could be better. We are all looking forward to a good stand.'

The defence of Tobruk had been a source of damaging conflict between Auchinleck and Churchill. The Auk sent London an Operation Instruction stating: 'It is NOT my intention to hold, permanently, Tobruk or any other locality west of the frontier.' Churchill's Chief of the Imperial General Staff, Alan Brooke, wrote: 'In my opinion it would be right to avoid such detachments in future.' Churchill must have known about this correspondence. On 15 June, Churchill, feigning ignorance of Auchinleck's earlier signal, wrote to him saying: 'We are glad to have your assurance that you have no intention of giving up Tobruk.' The prime minister's meddling was about to precipitate the second biggest disaster in the Middle East after the decision to send troops to Greece.

*   *   *

The defences of Tobruk had been allowed to deteriorate since the last siege had been raised. The vital tank ditch had silted up in places and Peter Proud's camouflage initiatives had been forgotten. Vehicles, trenches and artillery were now, in many places, visible for the enemy to see. Rommel was determined that there would be no second siege. At 15:20 hours on 20 June his Stukas began their howling attack, accompanied by conventional bombers. Rommel led the armour in himself, battering his way into the town. Leading from the front, he was heard to shout at the commander of an 88mm gun: 'Shoot, man, shoot. You can almost spit into the harbour.'

A day later, on 21 June, Auchinleck's fifty-eighth birthday, Tobruk fell and 35,000 Allied troops and supporting personnel were taken prisoner. The spoils included nearly 1.5 million gallons of petrol, over 120,000 rounds of artillery and a warehouse full of Löwenbrau beer, brewed under a pre-war licence in Egypt.

Among the POWs was Colonel Mainwaring, who had just taken over from Goff as regular commanding officer of the Camouflage Unit. An expert on the Tobruk defence system, Mainwaring had gone into the town to advise and became trapped. He spent the rest of the war as a prisoner. A gunner, W. A. Lewis, summed up the feelings of the defeated troops: 'Bodies lay everywhere. At what was once the town square we found thousands of prisoners. My God, the humiliation of it all.'

Churchill heard the news while staying with President Roosevelt in Washington. He later wrote: 'This was one of the heaviest blows I can recall during the war. Not only were its military effects grievous, but it had affected the reputation of the British armies. At Singapore 85,000 men had surrendered to inferior numbers of Japanese. Now in Tobruk a garrison of 33,000 seasoned soldiers had lain down their arms to perhaps half their number. If this was typical of the morale of the Desert Army, no measure could be put upon the disasters which impended in North East Africa. I did not attempt to hide from the President the shock I had received. It was a bitter moment. Defeat is one thing: disgrace is another.'

Rommel signalled to his army, 'Soldiers of the *Panzerarmee Afrika*, now we must utterly destroy the enemy! During the coming days I shall be making great demands on you once more so that we may reach our goal [the Suez Canal].'

The news of Rommel's victories caused panic in Cairo. Arrangements were made to evacuate women and children from the city. Defence trenches were dug around Grey Pillars. At Helwan, the Camouflage Development and Training Centre received instructions to prepare to burn all secret documents. Steven Sykes was ordered to destroy his latest dummy railhead, Depot No. 3, and pull up the fake track before the Germans discovered the ruse. Once more the Camouflage Unit was scattered and once more Sykes tried to pull them all together, an almost impossible task. 'Things were altogether chaotic,' he wrote; the next few days were full of 'uncertainty, indecision and unsuccessful attempts to get guidance or instructions.' It did not help that his vehicle had been commandeered by Colonel Mainwaring and was now in German hands.

On 24 June, Barkas got permission to go into the desert to offer any help he could. He set off in his staff car, a Chevrolet driven by Driver Jack Ashman RASC, a stolid twenty-eight-year-old Yorkshireman. They headed out along the Ghiza road, past the Pyramids towards Alexandria and the left turn onto the now all-too-familiar road, into the sand. They immediately found it choked with retreating vehicles, carriers, tanks, jeeps, mobile workshops, ambulances, lorries; some stacked high with useless office equipment and luxuries that had been seen as essential to life in the desert. The jam stretched nose-to-tail to the horizon. The Gazala Stakes was in full gallop, with German and Allied units racing in the same direction, east towards Cairo.

Eventually Barkas found the forward battle HQ, a sprawling cluster of tents, marquees, office trucks, lorries and staff cars parked among the dunes. A captured German Fieseler Storch reconnaissance aircraft buzzed overhead. Barkas met Sykes and was shocked at how tired he looked. Auchinleck arrived and disappeared into a marquee. Eventually they were summoned into his presence. The C-in-C told them: 'Collect all the dummy guns you can at Alamein. South of the main box astride the road there is a wide stretch of open desert. It is good going for tanks and there is not much to stop them. We are trying to cover it but there are not enough guns for the job. Anything that will look like batteries may persuade the enemy to pause and regroup. A pause of any kind will help. See what you can do. But there is not much time, twenty-four hours, thirty-six at the most.'

Allied planes roared overhead and Barkas considered, not for the first time, how much worse the situation would be without the RAF in control of the skies. As they drove, Barkas asked his driver what he thought. After a long and reflective pause Ashman replied in his broad Yorkshire accent: 'Well sir, it's not properly for me to express an opinion, but since you've asked me, I'd say the arrangements wasn't very good.'

Along the road Barkas found a telephone and got clearance to make a priority call to the Camouflage School at Helwan. He got through to Major R. J. 'Tony' Southron, who had recently joined the Camouflage Unit from the Royal Tank Unit, and told him to organise a convoy of a dozen three-tonners, and to put every experienced man onto the job, from the school, the Development Wing, anywhere; it didn't matter. Then he asked Southron if he could pull the dummy gun batteries out of stores and get them to Alamein within the next twelve hours. Southron had been to the Territorial Army version of Staff College. He was a big clever, soft-spoken man who knew how to work the army system. Barkas thought that if anybody could pull this last-minute effort together, it was Southron. He told the major to call him back as soon as possible.

An agonising three hours later Barkas got his answer. Southron had the men, he had the dummy batteries, but he had no transport of any kind and movement to the front was impossible: the roads westwards out of the city were choked. It was a crushing disappointment for Barkas. The equipment was so near and yet so far that it might as well have been on the moon. He went back to the Eighth Army HQ to confess that his efforts had been a washout and offered to at least camouflage the forward gun positions. The offer was met with a pitying smile and the comment that a few truck loads of ammunition, petrol, food and water would be more to the point but 'thanks all the same'.

*　　　*　　　*

On 22 June, Ritchie told Auchinleck that he proposed to withdraw, very quickly, to Mersa Matruh to fight a last-ditch stand. Auchinleck agreed to this plan and by so doing started another 'Gazala Gallop'. Rommel pushed on, past Sidi Barrani to the coast. Twenty-four hours and a hundred miles later he had the Eighth Army on the ropes. They had lost nearly 80,000 men, mostly to prison camps. As darkness fell on the twenty-fifth, he was outside Mersa. Ritchie braced himself for a final cataclysmic battle. His force, in a confused state of ruin, would fight, and if necessary die, where they stood. If they died the battle would be over and Rommel would control Egypt. The Eighth Army would pay dear for its freelance ways, the uncoordinated Jock Columns and the swanning about in the Blue.

The next day, 26 June, Auchinleck visited Ritchie and relieved him of his command. In spite of what Dorman-Smith had concluded, Ritchie was liked by his subordinates, whose feelings were summed up by General Messervy, commander of 7th Armoured Division during the Gazala battles: 'He was an absolutely honest, downright soldier who was put in a position which at the same time was beyond his capacity. Although he had leadership and powers of command, he was thrown into a very difficult position before he had had time to develop methods of command.'

For the Allies things went from bad to worse. The Commander of the Mediterranean Fleet, Admiral Harwood, decided to move the ships from the harbour at Alexandria to other, safer ports. Overnight and with no warning, the port emptied. In Cairo, Harwood's action triggered 'The Flap', an unprecedented panic by the army, Navy and European civilian population. The BBC compounded the problem by broadcasting bulletins announcing that the Germans had superior tactics and weapons, and calling the fighting 'The Battle for Egypt', which emphasised the desperate nature of events. Vice Admiral Sir Gerard Wells, in charge of the Ports and Lighthouses Administration of Egypt, deserted his post.

In the embassies and at GHQ, officials began

burning files. British civilians left the city; the railway station quickly became packed with women and children frantic to get a place on the dwindling number of trains. Others loaded cars with all their possessions, tied mattresses to the roofs as protection against being strafed and joined the flight into the Delta. Plans were drawn up to destroy power stations, equipment, vehicles and anything else that would have to be left behind. Six million Egyptian pounds were printed in case the supplies of unissued notes ran out. A scheme was put together to flood the cultivated areas of the Nile.

From the west, thousands of vehicles full of defeated Allied troops poured into Cairo, further clogging the streets. The city waited for German parachutists to appear in the sky. Officers were ordered to carry revolvers at all times. Jewish businessmen, remembering what had happened in Poland, sold their businesses at knock-down prices, and there was a run on the banks. Cecil Beaton, who, weeks before, had been taking artistic shots of soldiers and their equipment, wrote that Cairo was 'in the most dreadful state of unrest . . . "Flap" is the word of the moment'.

By 29 June it was rumoured that the biggest enemy airborne invasion since Crete was imminent and that Rommel would be in Cairo within twenty-four hours. The same day Mussolini piloted himself to Derna. His plane touched down, followed by a huge transporter. On board was a magnificent white charger chosen to carry *Il Duce* in triumph through the gates of Cairo, where Italian women were organising committees to welcome him.

In scarcely a week, Rommel's troops had

199

advanced 400 miles, fought two major battles and nearly forty skirmishes. But there was a price: they were exhausted and running out of ammunition, food and fuel. On 1 July the Germans stopped in order to regroup. They were just sixty miles from Alexandria. Eight hundred yards ahead of them they could see the lonely and heavily defended railway halt called El Alamein. Rommel was down to a few worn-out Mark III Panzers; some of his divisions had been reduced to the size of a small infantry brigade, barely a thousand men. The Allies, cowering before the German advance, could field 500 tanks and 100,000 men and fresh troops were arriving all the time. Rommel knew he would never win a set-piece battle. He had to break through immediately.

On 5 July, the German commander launched his last real attempt to reach Cairo. The same day the air over the packed streets of the city swirled with burnt paper, like black snow; traders used some of the charred, top-secret documents to wrap their goods. The day was christened 'Ash Wednesday'. A rumour went round that Rommel had booked the best rooms at Shepheard's. Locals joked that only the service in the hotel could slow the Desert Fox up.

After four days of fighting, Rommel was forced to go on the defensive, ordering his men to dig in and to wait for the supplies that were en route from Germany. Rommel had so nearly pulled it off. By force of his personality and reputation he had convinced the Allies that he was invincible and this psychological advantage had nearly won him the Suez Canal.

* * *

Barkas established his HQ next to the sea, some miles to the east of the Alamein line. The Eighth Army waited for Rommel to make his next move, expecting him to attack at any moment. Barkas and Sykes reconnoitred the length of the front, travelling from Alamein on the coast south to the Qattara Depression, the vast sand sea that was impassable to tanks and that protected the southern flank in the same way as the real sea fifty miles north. They found the line fragmented and incomplete. All they could do was send out trained camouflage officers equipped with ready-made devices, like the net gun-pits; those and advice for the fighting units were all they could offer.

Sykes was clearly exhausted and Barkas decided to take him out of the field. (Sykes wrote: 'Although I was worn out I did not really want to go, but the last few weeks had not really been much fun.') On 17 July, Sykes handed in his faithful pick-up and was upset when he learned it was to be scrapped. After the excitement of the desert he found Cairo a strange place and was shocked at the way some of his colleagues at GHQ would knock off in the late afternoon to pursue their social lives. After another bout of malaria, Barkas sent a 'very feverish and ill' Sykes to Baghdad. He saw him off in a flying boat at four in the morning. Just before he left, Barkas told Sykes that he had been promoted to General Staff Officer Grade 2, with more pay. His place was taken by Tony Ayrton.

Sykes's contribution had been enormous. He had helped change the notion that the desert was a hopeless place for camouflage, where the only thing to be done was to disperse vehicles. His deception schemes, especially the dummy railhead, had made the authorities realise that the rock and sand of the desert wasteland was a theatre where the enemy could be deceived by the substitution of the real for the false and vice versa.

Sykes was not the only one to collapse under the strain. John Hutton had been working non-stop, building false tank traps in Damascus. His health was worn down by the long journeys, long hours, irregular meals and the intense atmosphere of crisis. He fell ill and was admitted to hospital in Cairo. He wrote home to his wife Nell: 'This is no more than a damn nuisance and only limits my spheres of distraction since I can't smoke or drink much. It is terribly hot here.' His health did not improve and after a long argument with the authorities, Hutton was sent home.

Barkas realised that in Hutton he had lost one of his best men. He confided to Sykes: 'My besetting sin in life has always been trying to do everything myself, telling the other chaps what to do and interfering with them. I think Hutton has mastered better than any of us the secret of getting things done with the greatest economy of time, effort, paper and spiritual wear and tear. He has a quality which you also possess in equal degree—namely, a good hard common sense approach and a critical aversion to schemes which are showy at the expense of practicality.'

*   *   *

Fighting continued along the Alamein line and the spectre of Rommel hovered over the battlefield. The British could not believe that he wasn't going make another major attempt at breaking through. But Rommel, too, was in crisis. His own morale had been ground down by the lack of support from Berlin, which meant that he lacked everything he needed to bring the campaign to a successful end. On 17 July he told Lou: 'It is going pretty badly for me.' The next day he wrote: 'It cannot go on much longer or the front is lost. Militarily these are the worst days I have lived through.'

The battle had ended in stalemate; both sides were exhausted. Rommel may have gone on the defensive, but he had not gone away. The Eighth Army still felt vulnerable to attack and was in a state of deep chaos. Damaged tanks and equipment clogged the workshops; new tanks had been ordered from America but were still en route somewhere in the Atlantic. A new division, the 51st, was on its way from England, but it wouldn't arrive for several weeks.

*   *   *

There was nothing the Camouflage Unit could do about these big tactical problems. However, it was managing to establish a fine reputation with all ranks and was trusted by the high command. Odd and unmilitary as it was, Barkas's unit built their reputation on solid rock, not shifting desert sands. Lt Gen. 'Jock' Whiteley, the director of military operations (DMO), called Barkas for an urgent conference. He said that GHQ wanted to persuade Rommel that the Eighth Army was in much better shape than it really was. If Rommel could be made to think that large forces were building up between the *Panzerarmee* and the Suez Canal, he might be persuaded to pause and wait for reinforcements before going back on the offensive.

The bigger the build-up Barkas could fake, the longer the time the Allies might buy. The more time Barkas could win, the bigger the real build-up. Barkas should offer the enemy's eyes and cameras all possible signs to suggest that behind the Eighth Army's thinly held positions in front of Alamein there were substantial mobile reserves and formidable 'hedgehogs' of defence. The DMO promised that the army would provide all the labour, stores and transport. He said that at GHQ, staff were already working on the size of force they

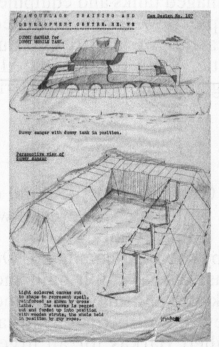

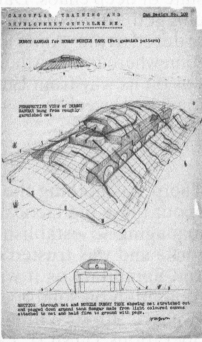

Sometimes dummy equipment was treated as though it were real. Here is a scheme to camouflage dummy tanks in real blast pits. As a double bluff the tank might be 'accidentally' revealed; even the fact that it was a dummy might be let slip.

wanted to create and how quickly it should appear to muster. The scheme was to be called Operation Sentinel. Then he spoke the magic words: he was going to give the Camouflage Unit 'operational priority'. This meant the scheme was an important part of the staff plan for battle and would be given the resources it wanted without argument. Barkas had been working towards this moment from the second he arrived in Egypt. The Phantom Army would be deployed on an equal footing with its comrades in the real army.

Sentinel was the brainchild of Dudley Clarke. He had been asked by Ritchie's replacement, Montgomery, to devise a scheme to delay Rommel's attempted breakthrough at Alamein for a fortnight. Clarke came up with the idea of a dummy build-up and embellished it by inventing a story that the Allies were planning to lure Rommel onto their minefields, where he would be destroyed by hidden anti-tank guns. This tale was transmitted to Athens via a radio network codenamed 'Cheese'.

Sentinel took a huge amount of detailed staff work. Lists of fictitious equipment, dummy timetables and estimates of required man hours began to flow out of Grey Pillars. Southron, who had been a regular tank officer and knew the intricacies of staff work, came into his own. On the dusty plains north of Cairo, the Phantom Army gathered for battle. Tented camps sprang up, smoke rose from cookhouses and incinerators; huge dust clouds were created to draw attention to the black-tarred roads under construction to connect the growing camps; lorries full of Peter Proud's net gun-pits rumbled out to reinforce real gun positions. A phantom Light Armoured Brigade rallied to fill a real gap in the front line. Huge phantom supply dumps appeared, ready to service the growing volume of trucks, guns and light tanks flooding in to reinforce Barkas's command.

To make a dummy 200,000-gallon petrol dump required over a thousand empty cans, salvaged from wherever they could be found (which was everywhere), six three-ton trucks and forty labourers. A thirty-yard-square dump could be set up quite easily in twelve hours. They could be used as decoys in other places to get the enemy to waste his ordnance on empty, useless old cans. The dumps could be made more real by the use of wrecked vehicles, positioned to add life and looking from the air like perfectly serviceable lorries or fighting vehicles. After three weeks back-breaking

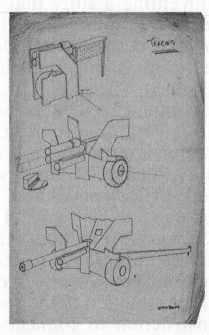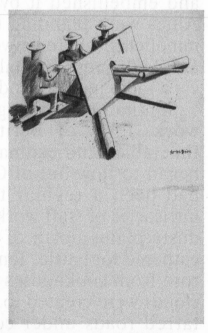

Assembly plan and storyboard for 'flat pack' artillery. These dummies were very easy to move around and deploy from three-ton lorries.

206

work, it looked from a reconnaissance aircraft flying as low as 600 feet as if two brand-new motorised divisions were in being held close reserve, ready to be brought into action at short notice. Nothing gave away that the canvas-and-wood weapons were manned by scarecrows, old uniforms stuffed with rubbish. Mobile camouflage units toured the battlefield advising where items should go, how they should be set up and strictly monitoring concealment. More workshops sprang up at Helwan to churn out more dummy tanks, lorries, fake twenty-five-pounders and miles of specially garnished netting almost faster than they could be deployed.

In the real world, 300 Sherman tanks and over 10,000 new lorries disembarked at Suez and were soon moving into places kept warm for them by Barkas's ghosts. By the end of August order had been restored in the Eighth Army and the Phantoms were stood down.

*   *   *

It was now the turn of General Auchinleck to feel the force of the prime minister. In Britain, Churchill's stock as leader of the coalition government was very low. In June, at a by-election in Maldon, the voters had turned on the coalition, throwing them out and stripping them of a huge majority. In the Commons, Churchill was attacked with a motion that read 'This House . . . has no confidence in the central direction of the war.' The British Army in the Far East had virtually handed Singapore to the Japanese on a plate. Churchill took the fall of Tobruk as a personal humiliation.

He looked for a scapegoat and found it in Auchinleck. Churchill set off for Egypt and metaphorically cantered into Cairo, riding the whirlwind of history.

Churchill arrived at Eighth Army HQ, Ruweisat Ridge, sweating in a siren suit, topee on his head and cigar clamped between his teeth. He was driven in an open car past a thin line of troops who received his 'Victory V' sign with little enthusiasm. Afterwards the prime minister disappeared into Auchinleck's stuffy caravan for a conference.

The Auk offered breakfast in what Churchill described as: 'A wire-netted cube full of flies and important military personages.' These included Dorman-Smith and Freddie de Guingand, Auchinleck's staff brigadier. The meal was a humble affair. The Commander-in-Chief served the same rations that his men were eating that morning. Auchinleck and Dorman-Smith both argued that no full-scale attack could be mounted before mid-September. De Guingand said, 'I remember noticing that the prime minister did not like this attitude.'

Churchill then moved on to RAF headquarters at Borg-el-Arab, where he was entertained to luncheon by Air Vice Marshal Arthur Tedder. There, in the shade of a tent set up on the sands by the sparkling blue Mediterranean, they enjoyed food and wine flown in from the Shepheard's Hotel. Mess stewards, immaculate in dazzling white coats, hovered in attendance; silver cutlery and cut glass glittered on snow-white napkins and tablecloths. The sixty-eight-year-old prime minister thought it was 'a gay occasion in the midst of care, a real oasis in a very large desert'.

Auchinlick's fate was sealed. In the evening Churchill wrote a memorandum to Deputy Prime Minister Attlee saying: 'I have come to the conclusion that a drastic and immediate change is needed in the high command . . . I have no doubt that the changes will impart a new vigorous impulse to the Army and restore confidence in the command which I regret does not exist at the present time.' On 6 August, Auchinleck received a visit from Colonel Ian Jacob, who handed him Churchill's letter, telling him that he had been relieved of his command. Jacob described his task as: 'Like going to murder an unsuspecting friend . . . I handed the C-in-C the letter. He opened it and read it two or three times in silence. He did not move a muscle and remained outwardly calm and in control of himself.' Churchill described his own part in the sacking as 'like killing a magnificent stag'.

Auchinleck was replaced as C-in-C Middle East by Lieutenant General Harold Alexander. To the position of GOC (General Officer in Command) of the Eighth Army, Churchill at first appointed Lieutenant General William 'Strafer' Gott MC, DSO, but on his way to take up command, Gott's Bristol Bombay aircraft was attacked and shot down. The pilot, nineteen-year-old Sergeant 'Jimmy' James, crashed and managed to escape. A door had buckled, trapping his passengers inside the blazing aircraft. James watched in horror as the camouflage paint on the fuselage began to blister and blacken from the heat inside.

But another, more flamboyant and controversial personality was waiting in the wings: Gott's substitute. On the evening of 12 August a plane landed in Cairo. It taxied to a halt; the cabin door opened to reveal the new boss of the Eighth Army, Lieutenant General Bernard Law Montgomery.

9

MONTY

A few days later, two young camouflage officers were supervising the unloading of dummy Valentine tanks at the southern end of the Alamein line. The real Valentine was winning a reputation as a reliable and well-armoured tank, though cramped and under-gunned. The two men were both captains. One, twenty-eight-year-old Richard 'Pippin' Heseltine, was a small, red-faced Charterhouse-educated man with long hair and, by his own admission, entirely ignorant of all military matters. The other was Stanley 'Corker' Crocker, a fiery Welshman with a ginger moustache and a graduate of the Royal College of Art. The two men had become friends when they took a camel tour of the Pyramids and Crocker had developed a bad crush on an ENSA girl who had joined them on the trip.

They were in charge of a mixed company of Middle Europeans, many of whom were Jews who had escaped the Nazis and were terrified of being captured. As the workers unloaded and erected the fake Valentines, Heseltine charged around in a real tank, making tracks for the dummies and sending up huge clouds of dust. A Humber staff car appeared and pulled up a few hundred yards away. Noticing that the car was unescorted, Heseltine became suspicious. He ordered his driver to pull up near the Humber and keep the tank's machine gun trained on the strangers. The great beast lumbered forward, turret swivelling, holding the staff car in its sights. The driver braked and killed the engine. In the sudden silence the car and the tank confronted each other, surrounded by billowing sand, dust and buzzing flies. The car door opened and a middle-aged man, casually dressed in khaki slacks and a roll-neck airforce-type sweater, got out. He carried a map of the desert.

Heseltine heaved himself out of the turret and jumped to the ground, where he stood staring at the intruder, who stared back with unflinching, piercing blue eyes. The older man asked if Heseltine knew where to find the headquarters of the Light Armoured Brigade.

'Yes, they are at Samaket Gaballa.'

'How do I get there?'

'Well, not the way you are going, you are heading straight for Jerry. Have you got a protractor?'

'No, why?'

'God, man, you're not desert-worthy, I'll show you.'

Heseltine took the map, spread it out on the hot metal plates of the tank, and set his protractor on it. He found the bearing and verified it with his heavy brass, army-issue compass. As he did so a second man got out of the car, tall and debonair and covered in the red tabs and crossed swords of a staff officer general. Heseltine immediately saluted.

The two strangers began to interrogate the camoufleurs. What were they up to?

Heseltine explained. The general asked what they would do if they were attacked. Crocker said they could dismantle and withdraw very quickly.

212

Their orders were to make sure that under no circumstances were the dummy vehicles to be captured or even detected.

The general and his companion listened intently, then climbed back into the Humber and drove off on the bearing that Heseltine had given them. The camouflage officers found this all very odd: what were these men, one a very senior officer, doing travelling alone together very near the front line? If they were spies, Heseltine had given away the position of the Light Armoured Brigade. They debated whether perhaps they should chase after the Humber and arrest them.

Their talk was interrupted by the wireless operator, who had received an urgent signal. There was a panic on: the unit was ordered to pack up the dummies and return to brigade headquarters immediately. General Auchinleck had gone, and had been replaced by a new commander called Montgomery, whom nobody had heard of.

The next day Heseltine and his colleagues were summoned to meet their new chief. They stood in a large group around Montgomery's armoured command vehicle. Heseltine was at the foot of the vehicle's ladder as Monty emerged and climbed down wearing his full uniform. The new commanding officer stepped onto the sand and looked Heseltine full in the face. It was the same man he had seen yesterday in the slacks and jumper. Heseltine blurted out: 'Glad you got here, sir.'

Monty replied: 'Thank you captain, your directions were very accurate and helpful. I will make sure we have a protractor next time.'

*   *   *

Bernard Montgomery was a complicated man. At fifty-four he was much older than most of the senior men under his command. He came from a family that could trace their ancestry back to one of William the Conqueror's knights, Roger de Montgomeri, and which had settled in Ireland in the seventeenth century. His mother, Maud, married his father when she was sixteen. Bernard was her third and possibly least-liked child. Even Monty described himself as having been a 'dreadful little boy'. In the end, he cut off all contact with his mother and, when she died, he refused to go to her funeral. In his memoirs he stated: 'She made me afraid of her . . . Certainly, I can say that my childhood was unhappy.'

Montgomery's relationship with women could be distant and difficult. Nevertheless, aged thirty-nine, he married Betty Carver, a widowed mother of two who was about to start at the Slade School of Art. They had one son together, David. Ten years later Betty died of septicaemia. Bernard nursed her through her last agonising months and she died in his arms. After her death Monty wrote to his stepson, Richard: 'Life is very black at the moment. I do not know what I shall do without her. It will be very hard for you to bear . . . Mummy looks very peaceful now. There is a look of complete calm and rest on her face.' After losing Betty, Monty devoted himself entirely to his work.

At Sandhurst, Montgomery had been considered a cad and a bully. In the First World War he was shot through the lung by a sniper. The sergeant who ran up to give him first aid was shot dead and fell on top of him. For three hours Montgomery lay in the mud, under fire from the sniper, protected by the body of the dead medical man. He was then hit a second time, in the knee. He survived and lived through some of the worst battles, including the Somme, Arras and Passchendaele. He ended the war with a reputation as an excellent staff officer.

In 1940, at Dunkirk, Monty's was one of the few formations in the BEF that did not fall apart. On the beaches he and his boss Harold Alexander were in charge of a corps each and both were models of cool, effective leadership. He was described as being 'clever, energetic, ambitious and a very gifted instructor', but also as someone who, on the other hand, had to cultivate 'tact, tolerance and discretion'. He favoured those with 'grip' and loathed those without it.

An Order of the Day he issued in November 1941 to Southeast Command was typical of the way Montgomery thought: 'The powers of endurance of all ranks will be brought to the highest pitch. Every officer and other ranks must be able and mentally wishful to take part in a real rough-house lasting for weeks. They must be one hundred per cent enthusiastic for battle and must possess one hundred per cent Binge.'

Nobody could define 'Binge' but everybody knew you wouldn't go far without it if Monty was your boss.

Montgomery arrived at Eighth Army HQ on 12 August 1942, two days before he was to take over. He did not like what he found there, saying it was 'enough to lower anyone's morale . . . no mess tents, work done mostly in trucks or the open air, in the hot sun. Flies everywhere. I asked where Auchinleck used to sleep; I was told that he slept on the ground outside his caravan. Tents were forbidden in the Eighth Army; everyone was to be as uncomfortable as possible, so they wouldn't be more comfortable than the men. All officers' messes were in the open air, where, of course, they attracted flies . . . The whole atmosphere was dismal and dreary.'

Things were going to change very rapidly. Montgomery, a perfectionist with a penchant for self-publicity, the man who loved drill, sport and physical activity, who was overbearing and obsessed with punctuality, and whose men had christened him 'the Mad General', was going to see to that.

*   *   *

At Helwan, Colonel Barkas waited at the gates for the arrival of the new C-in-C Middle East. General Alexander, Monty's boss, the man in the red tabs whom Heseltine had suspected of being a spy, was coming to inspect them. Alex's car and escort sped along the road from Cairo, following the route of the Nile, which was in flood, transforming the dusty flat plains into a shallow lake. Overhead the trees formed a green vault, studded with blood-red blossom. On the Nile huge lateen-rigged feluccas sailed serenely by, while on the banks of the river, boats unloaded thousands of fragrant melons to be taken into the city by camel, truck, donkey and pushcart. They passed through mud villages, and along the roads, goats and buffalo grazed, surrounded by innumerable offspring.

Alexander was fifty-one years old, an aristocrat with a love of painting, Classical history and culture, who at one time had considered leaving the army to become an artist. He was not clever and saw himself as a man of action; in 1911 he had been commissioned into the Irish Guards. Famous for his self-possession and the fact that, however bad the situation, he never flapped, he was the perfect foil to Montgomery. Some people, especially those jealous of his meteoric rise, put this down to a lack of imagination. He was wounded four times in the First World War but later described the period as 'the happiest years of my life'.

At the age of twenty-four he had been one of the army's youngest battalion commanders fighting in the trenches, where he won an MC, a DSO and the *Legion d'honneur*. The *New York Times* correspondent Walter Duranty described Alexander as 'the most charming and picturesque person I have ever met, and one of the two soldiers I have known who derived a strong and permanent exhilaration from the worst of danger'. His style was typified by a report that at the Battle of Loos in 1915 he had requested that he 'would be greatly obliged if they would kindly send more men up and with speed'. The citation for his DSO described him as being 'the life and soul of the attack, and throughout the day led forward not only his own men but men of all regiments. He held the trenches gained in spite of heavy machine-gun fire.'

Inside the Dunkirk perimeter Alexander had ordered that all his personal kit be destroyed, saying later: 'Thus my sole-surviving possessions for the remainder of the battle were my revolver, my field glasses and my briefcase.' Churchill gave him permission to surrender but he quietly stated that he would 'at all costs extricate his command and not surrender any part of it'. He considered that the perimeter could not be defended past the night of the 1/2 June 1940 and told his French counterparts that he had decided to embark 'without delay'. As a last resort he piloted a small boat to search the beach line, shouting in French and English: 'Is anybody there?' There was no reply.

Alexander got things done. He was an expert at making the system work for him and he had already ensured that supplies of the new Grant tank were on their way to the Middle East. Kipling said that Alexander's 'subordinates loved him, even when he fell upon them blisteringly for their shortcomings'. He had spent the days since his arrival in the Middle East trying to get the sprawling bureaucratic nightmare that was GHQ to understand that it existed to serve the needs of the troops slogging it out in the blazing heat of the desert.

Montgomery had been Alex's instructor at Staff College, where, ironically, Monty judged his future boss to be 'an empty vessel'. Alexander knew that Montgomery could be vain, bombastic, high-handed, egotistical and a showman who would put his commander in the shade. But he also knew that Montgomery could deliver victory, and so long as he did that, he, Alexander, would play second fiddle and protect him from whatever Churchill threw at him. If Alex disagreed with Monty, he said so, calming his prima donna subordinate. When Monty wanted to sack Major General Gatehouse, calling him 'useless', Alex replied: 'I think he is a borderline case. There is no doubt that he is slow and stupid ... Against this he has more experience of actually fighting armour than anyone else.'

Alex and Monty, for all their differences of personality, could rival each other in Binge, the magic quality that Montgomery had invented.

Alexander's staff car pulled up at Helwan, the driver leapt out to open the door and the senior members of the Camouflage Unit—painters, sculptors, set designers and artists of all sorts—came to attention and saluted in the most military manner they could manage. They were surprised when out of the Humber stepped a man with film-star good looks, wearing an immaculate uniform.

Alexander paused for a moment before returning the camoufleurs' salutes with a languid grace. Then he shook Barkas's hand and, with exquisite good manners, asked how he was and if the inspection might begin. Barkas led the way into the gloomy workshops. He was shown the dummy tanks and was given a demonstration of the special Fire Cream, though without Maskelyne to heighten the drama it was a tame affair involving just a dummy and a blowlamp. Alexander looked at the burnt dummy and asked how the cream could be deployed. Barkas admitted that no practical use had so far been found for it. Next they proudly exhibited the net gun-pits. Alex did not seem impressed; he didn't think they were that realistic. Barkas pulled out a file of aerial photographs and spread them in front of the general, who stared at them very intently, said nothing, and moved on.

The only time the general came alive was in the woodworking shop. He chatted at length to the sergeant in charge, examining the spokeshaves, planes, bradawls, saws, augers, chisels, rasps and all the other specialised carpentry tools in minute detail; nearby, the iron glue pot bubbled its black, strong-smelling contents made from horse skin, bone and hooves.

Next Alexander was introduced to the unit's chief instructor, Hugh Cott, who they found in a tent looking lost and surrounded by empty petrol cans that had been sawn in half to house Cott's collection of snakes, beetles and lizards. Even the desert and the war could not stop Cott the zoologist from carrying on with his research.

The inspection ended. Alexander walked back to the staff car in silence. With almost comic courtesy he thanked Barkas and his men for their trouble. At the last minute he asked if the Fire Cream was worth going on with. Barkas replied that it probably wasn't. Barkas watched the big Humber Super Snipe disappear into the shimmering heat, then walked back to his office, through his string and canvas world of illusion.

Barkas might have been disappointed that the new C-in-C showed so little enthusiasm for the work of his unit, but he did not know that Alexander was checking to confirm that the camoufleurs would be able to pull off the biggest military conjuring trick ever attempted. Alex was in the first stages of planning for the battle of Alamein and its huge deception counterpart, Operation Bertram.

* * *

Barkas's search for recruits never stopped. The Camouflage Unit was always short of personnel at every level, from senior officers to labourers. Barkas had heard that there was an illustrator named Brian Robb serving somewhere in the desert as a private soldier. So he went in search of him.

He found Robb sitting bored and disconsolate in the Sinai Desert with No. 27 Searchlight Unit.

Barkas learned that Robb had trained at the Slade and Chelsea School of Art, drawn cartoons for *Punch*, designed posters for London Transport and worked for Jack Beddington at Shell. He was a short, bald, slightly tubby man. He told Barkas he was frustrated: manning the searchlight didn't feel like real soldiering, and the closest he got to doing anything creative was drawing sketches of the men in the platoon.

Barkas went back to Grey Pillars and talked to Tony Ayrton about the problem. Very soon Brian Robb was transferred to GHQ and elevated to the rank of lieutenant with the Camouflage Unit. His life was transformed. Robb loved the work and his character, a mixture of shyness and bubbling good humour, made him a popular member of the team. He had a flair for detail, dealing with the endless tables of statistics that had to be assembled in any bid for manpower and the numerous lists of materials and equipment. The work was not remotely creative but the environment was. Barkas decided to team up the cartoonist with Ayrton who, having taken on Sykes's workload, needed help. They worked well together and soon struck up a strong friendship. Barkas patted himself on the back for this clever piece of team building.

*   *   *

Montgomery was late, something he hated. He was due to address his staff officers for the first time and the officer charged with escorting him to the meeting had driven them into a minefield. They

221

had been forced to back out, following their own tyre tracks. The mistake had cost Montgomery half an hour and the escorting officer his job.

At last he stood on the steps of Auchinleck's old trailer and stared at the assembled officers, all standing at attention. The men fidgeted; they had heard too many pep talks and had had too many new commanders for them to feel anything but bored and cynical. This curious, beaky-nosed, white-kneed little officer was the opposite of the tall, confident, handsome Auchinleck; this one looked more like an admin clerk than a commander. The rumour was that he had never commanded armour, had no large-scale battlefield experience and had never fought in the desert. He told them to stand easy and began to speak, his voice high-pitched, unmodulated and squeaky, with unmilitary crushed 'R's. He used no notes; to one side a clerk sat at a table, recording in shorthand what was said.

'I want first of all to introduce myself to you. You do not know me and I do not know you, but we have to work together.' He could have been a civil servant addressing a housing committee. Then he went on. 'Here we will stand and here we will fight; there will be no further withdrawal. I have ordered that all plans and instructions dealing with further withdrawal are to be burnt, and at once . . . if we can't stay here alive, then let us stay here dead . . . Now I understand that Rommel is expected to attack here at any moment. Excellent. Let him attack. I would sooner it didn't come for a few weeks, just to give me time to sort things out . . . Rommel can attack as soon as he likes after that and I hope he does . . . It will be the beginning of a new campaign to hit Rommel

222

for six out of Africa . . . He is definitely a nuisance. Therefore we will hit a crack and finish with him.'

The message was clear: no surrender. The audience was transformed. Freddie de Guingand, Montgomery's new Chief of Staff, summed up their feelings: 'Brilliant, absolutely brilliant.'

BERTRAM STEALS THE SHOW

By August, Rommel was poised for battle: an attack on Alam el Halfa. For two months his men had endured constant bombardment from the Allied artillery and Desert Air Force, while at sea the Royal Navy sent two-thirds of his resupply to the bottom of the Mediterranean. His reconnaissance pilots reported that the enemy was building up supplies and equipment and appeared to be getting stronger by the day. Initially this effect had been achieved by the Camouflage Unit's efforts to deploy dummies in accordance with their orders for Operation Sentinel. By mid-August it wasn't straw and hessian dummies that stood ready for Rommel; it was 760 armour-plated tanks (to Rommel's 440) and every division had the new six-pounder anti-tank gun, a match for the German 88mm.

Rommel had been promised 6,000 tons of fuel, but by 27 August, three days before his battle was due to begin, only 1,800 tons had arrived. Rommel himself was ill. His doctor reported that he could only 'command the battle under constant medical attention' and that it was 'essential to have a replacement on the spot'.

Nevertheless, on 30 August, he went back on the offensive, personally leading a night attack, an armoured hook to the south towards the Alam el Halfa Ridge. His first obstacle was a British minefield, which he needed to get his troops across in sixty minutes. He had reckoned without the RAF, who dropped dozens of parachute flares, creating artificial daylight. Stripped of the cover of darkness, his tanks became easy targets for the bombs that followed. When the sun rose, Rommel's armour was still creeping through the minefields, jammed nose to tail and vulnerable to everything the Allies could throw at them.

Rommel took his command vehicles forward into the inferno. He drove through the smoke, past blazing Panzers while Allied bombs and shells crashed around him with terrifying effect. Seven of his close staff were killed and he narrowly escaped mutilation when an eight-inch sliver of red-hot shrapnel thumped into the leather seat beside him. Other senior men died or were wounded in the deluge of fire. The forty-year-old General Georg von Bismarck, buccaneering holder of two Iron Crosses, who liked to play his men into battle with military bands, was killed by a mortar bomb while leading his tanks through the minefield on his motorbike. The *Afrika Korps'* commander, General Nehring, was wounded by a bomb blast.

The next night, Montgomery gave orders that German soft-skinned vehicles were to be especially targeted. The lorries could do no damage, but they carried petrol supplies, ammunition, food and water, without which Rommel could not operate.

Bombing and artillery fire continued through the first day of September. Rommel was forced to stop and take cover six times in two hours; he later described 'vast numbers of low-flying fighter bombers' coming in the wake of the heavy bombers higher overhead, leaving 'huge numbers of vehicles burning in the desert'.

On the third day Rommel had had enough, and gave the order to withdraw. The Allies had been too well dug in and his own supply chain let him down. He had lost 3,000 men—killed, wounded, captured or missing—along with hundreds of tons of supplies, and 49 tanks, 36 aircraft, 60 guns and 400 assorted trucks. The Allies lost 1,750 men and 67 tanks.

Montgomery, the general with no desert experience, had been well prepared. He knew Rommel would beat him in a battle of manoeuvre, so he had ordered his tank commanders to stay put. By 3 August, Rommel's army had never been more vulnerable or more disorganised. A great 'what if' of the Desert War is the question: what would have happened if Montgomery had seized the initiative and hit Rommel with a devastating counterattack, which he was well able to do? Would the *Panzerarmee* have thrown in the towel? Could the war have been stopped in its tracks with no need for more fighting? But this was not Monty's way. He didn't like the unexpected; for the next few days he proceeded with great caution and then regrouped, giving the Germans time to retreat.

By 6 September, Rommel had pulled his army out of danger back behind the minefields. His position included the hill of Himeimat. This feature was to prove a very useful vantage point from which Rommel's troops were able to observe the Camouflage Unit preparing for the coming of Bertram. In their memoirs both Generals Montgomery and Horrocks claim that this was a deliberate Allied ploy.

Alam el Halfa left Rommel exhausted and demoralised. His old vitality had vanished; a stomach complaint made him constantly nauseous. The field doctors told him he had problems with his liver; he also had sinusitis, a sore throat and a constant headache. The Desert Fox was reported to be only capable of dragging himself from his bed to the chair by the side of his map desk, where he would study strength tables, charts and plans. It became clear that he would have to leave the desert to recuperate.

Rommel's replacement was General Georg Stumme, a small man full of good intentions with a big paunch and a lot of energy. He was a comic opera figure whose soldiers nicknamed him 'The Italian'. On his first recce he drove from position to position calling his troops 'old fellow'. His last posting had been on the Eastern Front, where he had been court-martialled for allowing the enemy to capture not only his chief of intelligence but also the plans for the battle of Stalingrad. He was freed from his five-year prison sentence by the intervention of his commander, Field Marshal von Bock.

Rommel tried to brief Stumme, who just waved his hands about, saying, 'No problem. The position is a good one and the men are firm. The British will break their teeth on it.' Rommel gave up, leaving Stumme with a yellow envelope containing written orders as to what he should do when Montgomery attacked.

The *Panzerarmee* had retreated to a formidable defensive position. The tank corps troops were a mixture of German and Italian armour and their positions stretched for twenty miles from the sea to the impassable Qattara Depression. In the north, 15th Panzer was supported by the Italian Trieste and Littorio Armoured Divisions and in the south, 21st Panzer had the Italian Ariete and Bologna Divisions. The area between the two forces contained the artillery and an ad hoc body of elite paratroopers, the Ramcke Brigade, named after their commander Hermann-Bernhard Ramcke, a tough veteran of the airborne invasion of Crete. Ramcke had won his parachute wings at the age of fifty-one. Between the tanks and the mines were what remained of the dreaded 88s. In front of the positions were four million mines, sown in belts nearly five miles deep, as well as miles of barbed wire that could wrap itself round the drive wheels of a tank and immobilise it. Rommel called the minefields the 'Devil's Garden'.

Rommel's last act before going on leave was to pull back some of his Italian troops to Fuka, forty miles behind the front. He wanted them to act as a reserve in depth. Finally he deepened his minefields, ordering that a million more mines be buried. On his way back to the Fatherland, Rommel stopped in Rome and had an interview with Mussolini. At home he was reunited with his son Manfred and his wife Lucie, and was given a hero's welcome in Berlin. He told a press conference that he would soon be in Alexandria and the Suez Canal would be his for the taking. The Mediterranean would become Hitler's private pond.

Montgomery did not agree. He told his staff that Rommel's presence in Berlin meant that the Axis powers could not mount another offensive and that 'Egypt has been saved'. It was around this time that Montgomery began to morph into 'Monty'. He knew that his soldiers were not soldiers but newspaper-reading civilians in uniform. He said: 'It seemed to me that to command such men demanded not only a guiding mind, but a point of focus . . . And I deliberately set out fulfilling this second requirement. It helped, I felt sure, for them to recognise as a person . . . the man who was putting them into battle.'

In spite of their very different outward appearances and different backgrounds, Montgomery and Rommel had many qualities in common. Both men were conscious of the importance of image and went to lengths to control the way they looked. Monty's style was homespun: baggy cords and a comfortable cardigan; he could have been mistaken for a don or a well-to-do farmer relaxing at the weekend. Rommel took the glamour route, looking like a film-star soldier. He shared the Nazi obsession with leather and wore short leather tunics or long leather trench coats worn over breeches and jackboots. One of the few times Monty wore leather was in France in 1940 when he wore a fleece-lined flying jacket. It did not make him look like a fighter pilot, more like an uncle whose young nephew had lent him the garment to keep him warm.

Both men were showmen, and liked their props. Monty went to great lengths to achieve the right look with his headgear. As soon as he arrived in the desert he took to wearing an Australian bush hat, decorated with the badges of the regiments under his command. The hat often came off in the wind and his driver, frustrated at having to keep stopping to retrieve it, offered the general his own little oil-stained beret. To everyone's amazement Monty put the beret on and it became his preferred form of headgear. He claimed later that 'what started as a private joke . . . became in the end the means by which I was recognised'.

Rommel had his famous peaked cap and desert goggles. He travelled in Gambier-Parry's captured command vehicle, which he had renamed 'Max', plus a dashing open-topped Mercedes staff car. Not to be outdone, Monty acquired a modified Grant tank, the barrel of which was removed and replaced with a wooden one, making room inside the turret for an extra map table while preserving the vehicle's war-like profile. Both men cultivated the press and gave photographers plenty of picture opportunities, sometimes carefully posing for the defining shot. Montgomery, the leader, standing in the turret of his command vehicle, binoculars in hand, staring into the distance, his face bearing the rapt concentration of 'The Commander', a master tactician whose only thought was how to beat the enemy. He had the words 'Monty' painted in two-foot-high Gothic letters on its armour plate.

Rommel would be shot in close-up, trademark cap and goggles on his head, or shown studying a map pointing towards new conquests, surrounded by admiring and respectful subordinates. The images of both men flashed around the world. 'Monty' was how Montgomery was known to the world. *Panzerarmee Afrika* troops universally referred to their general as 'Rommel', even when talking to a superior. Both men were single-minded and ruthless in pursuit of their aims. They were masters of their professions and intolerant of others. Rommel disobeyed orders to gain an advantage over the enemy and Montgomery too often pushed his luck. (When he arrived in the desert he took charge two days earlier than he should have. He later said that when he went to bed that night: 'It was with an insubordinate smile that I fell asleep.') In France in 1944, Eisenhower had to remind Monty on more than one occasion that he, Eisenhower, was the boss, not the other way round.

They had both served in the First World War and been badly wounded. Both men were born leaders and made it quite clear that they were in charge. They knew that close cooperation between the different service arms was vital to success and understood the importance of intensive training and realistic battle rehearsal. But whereas Rommel loved mobility and could wheel and manoeuvre his army with great *élan*, risking his arm and pushing forward when it was dangerous to do so, Montgomery relied on overwhelming superiority of numbers; he was cautious and reluctant to change his meticulously prepared battle plans. This caution meant that at Alam el Halfa he passed up the chance to wipe out the *Panzerarmee*. He would do the same again with the Germans in Normandy, at the Falaise Gap.

*   *   *

Preparations for the coming battle were very intense, physically and mentally. Montgomery's aim was to get his soldiers into a state of bloodlust. At one meeting he insisted that the troops 'must be worked up into that state which will make them want to go into battle and kill Germans'. Even the padres were encouraged to join the slaughter: 'One on weekdays and two on Sundays.' The joke brought the house down, but Monty was deadly serious.

Monty thought the troops had spent too much time sitting in trenches and being driven about in lorries. He was a fitness fanatic and often quoted Kipling's lines that 'nations . . . fell because their peoples were not fit'. The soldiers were given a new regime. At 06:00 hours every day they staggered out of bed, pulled on gym kit and clambered into lorries. They were then driven for five miles and told to run back. One commanding officer who fell by the wayside was sent home to England and never seen again. Montgomery's reply to a medical officer who complained that a particular colonel might die if he continued was, 'Let him die . . . much better to die now rather than in the midst of battle when it might be awkward to find a replacement.'

Monty planned to start the battle of Alamein with a night attack, a challenging manoeuvre: any operation in the dark would take two or three times longer than in in daylight. The Germans were not good at large-scale night assaults and Rommel was said to be very impressed with the way the Allies pulled them off. Montgomery made his army practise realistic battle exercises. The infantry learned to clear the minefields while walking behind a terrifying creeping barrage of twenty-five-pounder shells, maintaining radio discipline and cooperating closely with the huge, bellowing tanks.

On 16 September, Montgomery's corps and divisional commanders gathered in his headquarters at Borg-el-Arab, where for the first time he was to brief them on his plan to beat Rommel.

* * *

On the same day, Barkas and Ayrton were also on their way to Borg-el-Arab, summoned by Freddie de Guingand, Monty's trusted right-hand man.

They drove towards the huge camp set in a tangle of blinding-white sand dunes about thirty-five miles to the east of El Alamein. At the gates they were stopped by the military police, who examined their passes and waved them through into the small town of tents, marquees and stores. Staff cars, jeeps, radio trucks, Royal Army Service Corps lorries and vehicles of all sorts were parked everywhere. They drove past signallers rigging power and telephone cables, some attached to poles, others trailing on the ground; linesmen ran out more and more wire to add to the complex cat's cradle. Despatch riders came and went, roaring up and down the picket lines. The headquarters had been widely dispersed to minimise the damage that would be caused in the unlikely event of an air attack. The Tactical Air Force was based on the airfield next door and fighters and bombers roared over their heads, flying round the clock to batter the Germans.

Barkas and Ayrton, who had arrived early, passed the time sitting on the burning sand near de Guingand's tent, chatting and smoking. Around them, staff and regimental officers hurried towards the large marquee where Montgomery was to give his briefing. Barkas hoped that they might catch a glimpse of the great man himself.

Barkas noticed that in the last few weeks shirt tails had been tucked back in and long hair had vanished. It suddenly became usual to see large units of men parading in perfect order by the roadside, waiting to be inspected by the new boss. Barkas found a strange satisfaction from hearing the drill sergeants bellowing commands that floated through the air followed by the crunch of hundreds of steel-studded boots slamming onto the gravelled rock in perfect unison. The freelance days were over, 'Jock Columns' had been abolished and nobody swanned about in the Blue looking for private fights. Even 'bellyaching', the soldiers' favourite pastime, was now an offence. Monty had unleashed a new energy. 'Binge' was everywhere.

Monty walked onto the stage; the audience stiffened to attention. Behind him were large-scale maps of the Alamein line. Clear acetate sheets hung over the maps with the Allied and Axis positions marked in coloured chinagraph pencil. This time there was no fidgeting, only deep, concentrated silence. Montgomery told the men to sit at ease, and then he began.

The battle would start with two simultaneous attacks: the real one in the north, and the other, a feint, in the south. He went on to describe his scheme in detail.

Dead on time, Barkas and Ayrton were summoned into the caravan that was Brigadier de Guingand's field headquarters. Inside the ordered, precisely arranged vehicle, were two men: de Guingand seated behind a desk and, standing next to him, Colonel Charles Richardson. Freddie de Guingand, a product of Ampleforth and Sandhurst, was a neat, solidly built man with gappy teeth and a humorous sparkle in his eyes that counterbalanced his otherwise stern face. When Monty arrived in Egypt, one of his first acts was to summon his old friend de Guingand to meet and discuss the possibility that he might become Chief of Staff. Montgomery later wrote: 'I [needed] someone to help me, a man with a quick and clear brain, who would accept responsibility, and who would work out the details and leave me free to concentrate on the major issues—I decided that de Guingand was the man . . . I never regretted the decision.'

Richardson was thirty-four and joined the Royal Engineers after getting an honours degree at Clare College Cambridge. He had seen action in France and was a veteran of Dunkirk. He had spent a year with the Special Operations Executive in Cairo working for Dudley Clarke's 'A' Force, where he was tasked with inventing ideas to defeat the enemy by means other than brute strength. Richardson would be implementing the deception element in Montgomery's plan.

De Guingand warned the camoufleurs that what he was going to tell them was top secret. He explained that General Alexander had been very impressed by his visit to the workshops at Helwan. Now, not only did he have a very special job for them, he also wanted their advice as to how it should be put into action. He turned to Colonel Richardson.

Richardson outlined the problem. He told them that preparations were in hand for an offensive to see off Rommel once and for all. He outlined Monty's idea for a two-pronged attack, the real one in the north and the feint in the south. 'D-Day' would be 23 October, but they were to make the Germans think it would be at least a week to ten days later.

Then Richardson went into detail, describing a plan, already underway, to assemble a huge numbers of tanks, artillery, ammunition and stores in four large areas about forty miles behind the front line. These would have to be hidden. The chief engineer had already started bulldozing access roads from the assembly points up to the front, which, like the assembly points, would have to be concealed.

Richardson finished and de Guingand continued: 'We're calling it Operation Bertram. We want to know what your chaps can do to make it all happen.'

Geoffrey Barkas was flabbergasted. Richardson had just described the largest battle yet planned in the desert, possibly the largest ever attempted in the Western hemisphere, and his Camouflage Unit was being asked to play a major part. The field of operations covered 1,500 square miles of desert. He needed time to think. 'How many soft-skinned vehicles will there be sir?' he asked.

'I'm not sure, at least 700.'

'And how long will it take the armour to move up to their battle positions from the forming-up positions?'

'Two days.'

'So while the tanks are waiting to move forward, the enemy will know that the offensive can't happen for at least two, possibly three days.'

'Correct.'

'Sir, I need to discuss this with Captain Ayrton here.' De Guingand dismissed them, saying he wanted some ideas by the end of the afternoon.

Absent, but in the shadows, stood Dudley Clarke, the originator of the Bertram idea. He had been called to Washington to help with the planning for Torch, the invasion of Sicily, leaving Richardson in charge of the final design and execution of Bertram. Barkas and Ayrton would never have any idea of the top-level machinations behind the plan.

Clarke had come up with two parallel schemes to back up Operation Bertram, codenamed Treatment and Canwell. Treatment was a strategic deception ruse to make the Germans think that the British were planning to invade Crete and perhaps mount a minor desert attack in November. Operation Canwell consisted of twenty-five radio transmitters pretending to be the Eighth Army Tactical Headquarters and the headquarters of a corps, two divisions and five brigades. The radios would transmit signals from the Phantom Army, messages from the men of straw.

* * *

In the marquee Monty concluded his briefing. The battle would be 'a real rough-house' and the turning point in the war. 'There will be no tip-and-run tactics in this battle,' he said. 'It will be a killing match. The German soldier is a good soldier and the only way to beat him is to kill him in battle.'

As Barkas and Ayrton left the caravan, hordes of officers began to pour out of Monty's briefing, bustling about, talking, lighting up cigarettes, and looking for their drivers. The two camoufleurs jostled through the crowd and headed out across the dunes, searching for somewhere to talk without being overheard. Their eyes were dazzled by the glare of the light that bounced between the sea and the white sand. Behind them the sounds of slamming doors, revving car engines and despatch riders kicking their BSA bikes into life, ready to tear off into the desert with urgent new orders, slowly died away.

On the beach they sat down against some

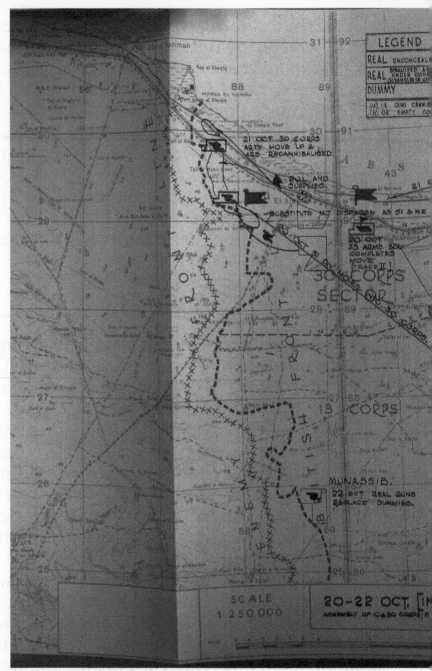

Most secret. An operational map showing the code-named build-up areas and the complex logistics to be undertaken on the eve of the battle of Alamein. This was the climax of Operation Bertram and Colonel Geoffrey Barkas's finest hour.

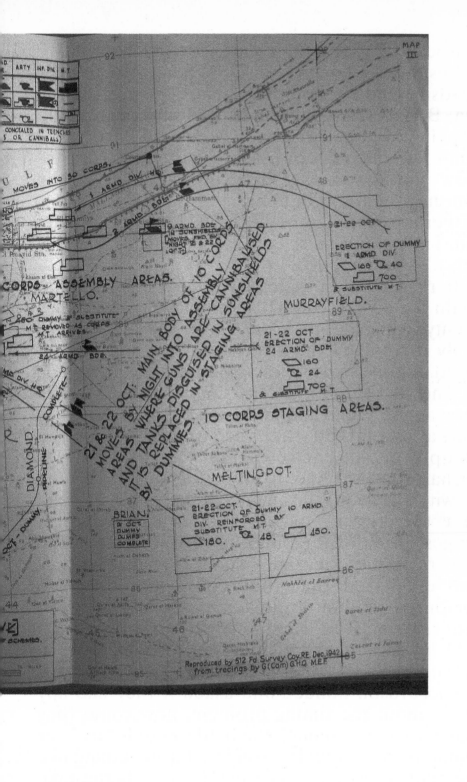

MAP III

CONCEALED IN TRENCHES
S OR CANNIBALS)

MOVES INTO 30 CORPS.

1 ARMD DIV HQ

2 ARMD BDE

9 ARMD BDE
(9 SUNSHIELDS
(MOVES FWD BY
NIGHT 21 & 22
OCT.)

9 21-22 OCT

ERECTION OF DUMMY
1 ARMD DIV
⬡ 168 ⬡ 40
700
& SUBSTITUTE M.T.

CORPS ASSEMBLY AREAS.

MARTELLO.

DUMMY & SUBSTITUTE
M.T. REMOVED AS CORPS
M.T. ARRIVES.

MURRAYFIELD.

21-22 OCT
ERECTION OF DUMMY
24 ARMD BDE
⬡ 160
⬡ 24
& SUBSTITUTE M.T. 700

24 ARMD BDE.

21 & 22 OCT: MAIN BODY OF 10 CORPS
MOVES BY NIGHT INTO ASSEMBLY
AREAS WHERE GUNS ARE CANNIBALISED
AND TANKS DISGUISED IN SUNSHIELDS
IT IS REPLACED IN STAGING AREAS
BY DUMMIES.

10 CORPS STAGING AREAS.

MELTINGPOT.

DIAMOND

PIPELINE

COMPLETE

BRIAN.
21 OCT
DUMMY
DUMPS
COMPLETE

21-22 OCT.
ERECTION OF DUMMY 10 ARMD.
DIV. REINFORCED BY
SUBSTITUTE M.T.
⬡ 180. ⬡ 48. 450.

Nakhlet el Barre

Qaret el Abd

Zabrat el Faires

Reproduced by 512 Fd Survey Coy. R.E. Dec. 1942
from tracings by G (Cam) G.H.Q. M.E.F.

tussocks of grass, their backs to the land, their voices drowned by the noise of the water and their heads cooled by the breeze that blew in from the sea. Barkas started: 'You know Tony, I can't help thinking of poor old Jasper. We could have asked him to do one of his vanishing tricks. Hey presto! Now you see them. Now you don't. The lady vanishes—that sort of thing.'

'Perhaps that's exactly the way to go, use the Sunshields to disguise the tanks as lorries and vice versa,' Ayrton replied.

Barkas looked puzzled: 'Would you say all that again for an old colonel? Remember, I'm nearly twenty years older than you.'

By the end of the afternoon they had a plan, typed out on a typewriter scrounged from the back of one of the many office lorries. Back in the caravan, de Guingand and Richardson listened as Barkas explained that, provided he had the manpower, he believed they could deliver Richardson's scheme. Even better, they had come up with a few embellishments of their own. He said that the key to its success was the careful orchestration of the build-up of vehicles and the construction of the road system. He said that they had estimated that they could simulate two armoured brigade groups, roughly 350 vehicles, tanks, armoured cars and attendant support vehicles and infantry. These would be deployed in the south.

Richardson nodded and asked if they had any ideas about the timing problem, how could they make it seem as though the battle would start later than it really would. He wondered if something like the spur Sykes had constructed towards the fake

240

railhead at Depot No. 2 might be the answer. Barkas replied that he and Ayrton had come up with exactly the same idea, but this time it would not be a dummy railway spur, but a pipeline leading south to a false supply depot as far away from the main battle area as they could manage. The construction of the pipeline could be timed to make it look like it would be completed at the beginning of October, by which time the battle should be nearly over.

Barkas went on to explain that he didn't plan to hide the armour or the lorries; he was going to make their presence very obvious. What's more, the Germans would never know the tanks had moved until they saw them in battle. The meeting ended. De Guingand called for an officer to take the plan to Montgomery and promised a quick response. Barkas and Ayrton walked back to the jeep in silence. Ahead of them a staff car accompanied by a small convoy of armoured cars with a motorcycle escort roared through the gates. In the car they could just glimpse Monty. Barkas had got his wish to catch a sight of the legendary leader.

Back in the caravan Richardson explained to de Guingand that he was negotiating with the RAF to have some of their Wellington bombers fitted with wireless telegraphy-jamming equipment to further confuse the enemy. He also confessed to having deep worries about Bertram: nothing had ever been done like this before, not on such a large scale. It would need the involvement of elements throughout the Eighth Army. One wrong word at Grey Pillars, a loud-mouthed soldier, could sabotage everything. De Guingand suggested that Montgomery should write a letter to all the corps commanders explaining the importance of the deception initiative, which Richardson could deliver in person, and so make Operation Bertram Monty's own private scheme, carrying with it all the weight of his authority as commander.

The blueprint for Bertram was accepted, although Montgomery was not satisfied with the creation of two phantom armoured brigade groups. He doubled it, demanding a complete phantom armoured corps. Barkas wondered how they were going to magic more than six hundred tanks and support vehicles out of thin air.

* * *

Work on Bertram started on 27 September. Barkas had twenty-eight days before the attack. He decided that Ayrton and the cartoonist Brian Robb would supervise the concealment and display side of things in the field, while he and Southron would take responsibility for the provision of all the materials and supervise the execution of the scheme in the rear areas.

The tank forming-up area, situated to the north end of the Alamein line, was codenamed 'Martello'. Barkas wanted to draw the enemy's attention to Martello, and persuade him that it was unimportant. He arranged for more than seven hundred lorries to be driven into the zone and parked. This was done very quickly, and enemy observers became used to seeing the large concentration of soft-skinned vehicles sitting harmlessly on the desert, not a tank in sight.

Next Barkas had to make the Germans turn their attentions south. He knew that the Germans would be especially interested in any build-up of stores. So he chose an area to the south-east of the Alamein line, which he codenamed 'Brian' after Brian Robb. Seven hundred separate stacks of dummy stores were created on Brian, made from simple canvas shapes supported on boxes, sticks, anything that came to hand. When finished, it would look from the air as though thousands of tons of assorted stores were being accumulated— ammunition, petrol, oil, food, water and engineering equipment.

The Germans had now been shown two things: the harmless lorries in the north and the dummy stores twenty miles away to the south. Barkas then had to persuade them that the supply dump in the south was important, which is where the dummy water pipeline came into play. The pipeline was codenamed 'Diamond' and started at the end of a real pipe to look as if it was being extended to join up with the false supply dump at Brian. If the enemy ever got the chance to take a much closer look, he would be in for a shock. He would find artist Phillip Cornish and a young officer from the Tank Regiment, Lieutenant Sidney Robinson, supervising a crew of local labourers hammering the ubiquitous four-gallon petrol cans over circular formers, the same technique that Sykes had used to create his dummy railway lines. They made enough sections to create a five-mile-long pipe, the distance the engineers reckoned they could lay in a day if they were doing the job for real.

On 27 September, heavy earth-moving equipment was used to dig the first five-mile length of trench. The dummy pipe was laid alongside, as if being made ready to be welded and buried. At night

243

the trench was filled in and the pipe moved up ready for the next five-mile section the following day. Ayrton gave a lot of thought to the extra elements the pipeline would have had if it was real; as a result the installation rapidly took on a life of its own as he embellished it with water towers, control boxes and supply dumps. Written-off vehicles and scarecrow men were dotted about and moved around as often as possible. To enhance the illusion of a construction site, real vehicles were diverted to drive parallel to the trench, throwing up dust and leaving visible tracks. The work was constantly scrutinised from the air to check its plausibility.

The pipe's steady progress towards Brian was carefully calculated to make it seem that Diamond was destined for completion around 4 October, twelve days after the battle had started. Thanks to Jasper Maskelyne, the store contained almost enough lightweight Sunshields to convert all 600 tanks into lorries. What the unit didn't have was any way to convert the same number of lorries into 600 tanks, plus all their supporting vehicles and artillery. They had nothing to make them with. Working in the Development Centre at Helwan was John Baker, the young architect Barkas had managed to get seconded from the Eighth Army. Baker was a sapper with a lot of experience of camouflage in the desert. Colonel Barkas was certain that, if anyone could, this unflappable officer would come up with a solution. And he was right. It was Baker who had a brainwave. The Egyptians used locally grown reed to make simple bedframes and flimsy packing cases. There were thousands of Egyptian workers who did nothing but make the frond hurdles and they made them in comparatively few patterns.

Baker thought he could use the panels to prefabricate everything. Geoffrey Barkas was doubtful; he didn't think the existing patterns were big enough. Within thirty-six hours the architect had designed a prototype dummy tank using only the existing varieties of hurdle—'That's brilliant John.' Two days later the works, services, ordnance and local purchase departments, where everything normally moved slowly and cautiously, had placed orders for vast quantities of hurdles. A workshop was set up near Martello and 113 General Transport Company RASC took on the gigantic task of hauling and delivering thousands of hurdles from all over the Nile Delta. Everyone was press-ganged to work on the job; other ranks and officers alike were soon toiling on the makeshift production line.

At the southern end of the Alamein line, a risky double bluff was organised. Three-and-a-half dummy regiments of twenty-five-pounder field guns were put in place. Units of real personnel manned some of the batteries to give the element of reality. Three batteries (nine guns) were deliberately exposed at the end of a rock formation called the Munassib Depression. The units manning the guns slowly and deliberately let their camouflage discipline slip, until it became clear to an observer that the guns were fake. The idea was that when the attack started, real guns would be substituted for the dummy ones. German armour got a very unpleasant surprise when what they thought were decoy guns started firing at them over open sites at point-blank range.

Ayrton solved the problem of hiding the

245

thousands of tons of real fuel, ammunition, food and equipment earmarked to be stockpiled in the north. Near the train station at El Alamein were hundreds of yards of slit trenches, which had been dug and lined with cement, the hard edges of which cast strong black shadows, making them very obvious from the air. They had never been used. Ayrton found that if the petrol cans were stacked one deep against the cement facings, they disappeared into the shadows. More than two thousand gallons of petrol were delivered to the trenches by convoys travelling only at night. The cans were stacked in the shadows, then reconnaissance was asked to overfly the area to see if they could find the hidden petrol; they couldn't.

An equally ingenious way was found to squirrel away other supplies. The boxes of food and ammunition were taken to the lorry park at Martello by truck, each one of which was unloaded in a specific place. The boxes of stores were piled in such a way that if a tarpaulin was tied down over them they would look like thirty-hundredweight trucks. Any overspill cases were stacked beside the 'lorry' and covered with another tarpaulin, shaped to look like a soldier's bivvy. From the air it looked as though the Eighth Army was adding to the 700 lorries already parked there and that the lorries were being guarded by men in tents. Even though the dumps were guarded, quartermasters voiced concerns about the problem of pilfering supplies, particularly items such as boiled sweets and cigarettes. It was decided to put the most tempting items in the middle of the dumps, as far from light fingers as possible.

Other pieces were placed on the battlefield, the

most important of which were the twenty-five-pounder field guns and their ammunition limbers, disguised as small trucks and deployed in form-up areas near the front line, codenamed 'Cannibal' I and II, and ready to move up twenty-four hours before being taken into action. They would remain disguised until the last minute and the Desert Air Force would keep away an enemy reconnaissance flights.

They now had the problem of the tanks. The Royal Engineers had spent the previous month bulldozing access roads from the rear assembly areas to the front line. Barkas got them to do this in such a way that seemed to suggest that they were creating roads to move the armour south to the supposed build-up of supplies at Brian. The real armour would make its way to the battlefield in two stages. First transporters would haul the tanks onto three assembly areas (codenamed 'Murrayfield North', 'Murrayfield South' and 'Melting Pot'), where they would wait before moving under their own power to Martello, to the north-west. On 18 and 19 October, with 'D-Day' four days away, the tanks were transported to the rear holding areas; nothing was done to hide the huge assembly of vehicles. The Germans knew that while the tanks were parked miles from the front line, the battle could not start for at least two, or even three, days.

Every tank and piece of supporting equipment was numbered and allotted its own parking spot at Martello, forty miles away. The parking bays were given the same number as the tank that would use them. Every tank had its own Sunshield, the double-sectioned disguise that fitted over it to make it look like a lorry. Each Sunshield was allotted to a tank and given the same number. Synchronising the numbering was a complex task. The shields were then driven to Martello and each one dropped at their tank bay. The tank crews were taken to Martello, shown their parking bays and how to erect the Sunshields. This was a matter of lifting each half above the tank, lowering it over the turret and then bolting the two halves together. The whole tank, including tracks, was then hidden. Close up the 'lorries' looked like vast toys, but from 1,000 feet in the air they looked like the real thing.

Thanks to John Baker's Herculean efforts, each tank now had its own dummy counterpart. Barkas planned that as each tank went off to Martello its place would be taken by a dummy. From the air it would be impossible to tell that the tanks had moved.

With four days to go, all the pieces of the jigsaw were in place. In the north, real field guns, petrol and stores were hidden or disguised as thin-skinned lorries. In the south, at Brian, were all the signs of a 10,000-ton storage depot waiting in readiness for the battle, which wouldn't be for some days because the water pipeline was not nearly ready. The conclusive evidence was the tanks, forty miles in the rear, without which the battle couldn't start. Now came the job of moving the real armour, hundreds of killing machines, without the Germans knowing.

On 20 October, a coded signal was sent ordering the start of the transformation of the scene. At five o'clock, as the sun sank over the desert and the nearly full moon took its place, the magic trick began. Tank engines roared and the first vehicles rumbled off, heading north-west to Martello. As soon as each tank was gone, Royal Engineers erased the tracks and assembled the dummy counterparts. When the tanks arrived at Martello, military police guided them into their parking bays and the crews fitted the Sunshields. Before the sun rose, all activity stopped; the dust settled. To an aerial observer it looked as though nothing had changed. The same manoeuvre was repeated the next night, and as dawn broke on the second day the operation was complete. A whole army of tanks had been spirited onto their front-line start positions, right in front of the enemy's eyes. As far as the Germans could tell, the tanks hadn't moved.

*   *   *

The next night, 22 October, under cover of darkness, nearly two hundred thousand men—infantry, tank crews, gunners, engineers, drivers, medics and cooks—move into their starting positions, with orders that once the sun rises, no one is to budge. They must remain hidden until dark for the start of the battle. The first rays of light creep above the horizon and there they wait, a whole day, while the scorching sun makes its slow progress through the sky.

Bombers of the Desert Air Force take off, heading west to begin their daily task of blasting the enemy with high explosives. Spitfires and Hurricanes follow in their wake, shooting up anything they see, turning the day into misery for the Germans. In the south, on the ground, General Horrocks, the commander of British XIII Corps, which is to mount the feint, has been ordered to stand fast and behave aggressively. Horrocks will be

249

supported by the Phantom Army, straw men and canvas tanks with cardboard barrels.

The soldiers do what they can to pass the time, their stomachs permanently clenched in anticipation of the battle to come. They play cards, write letters home, make stupid jokes in quiet, tense voices; anything to forget what lies ahead. At noon the blinding light bounces off the pinky-grey sand of the desert, objects lose their shape, shimmer and melt into nothing. Anything more than 400 yards away is invisible in the glare. The temperature reaches thirty-five degrees centigrade. Huge, disgusting flies hover around the sweating men, crawling at their mouths, buzzing in their ears, sucking the sweat from their backs, their armpits and groins. What all the soldiers, armoured and infantry, fear are the mines, Rommel's 'Devil's Garden'.

The mines are the first obstacle the Allied troops have to deal with. The engineers must lead, and clear and mark three paths, codenamed 'Sun' 'Moon' and 'Stars'. Some engineers are equipped with the new mine detectors, long-handled objects with elliptical discs on the end, the invention of a Polish officer named Jósef Kosacki. The discs contain two coils of wire that are connected to headphones worn by the operator, who has a heavy battery strapped to his back. The operator has to walk forward holding the disc parallel to the ground. When it passes over a metal object a signal is emitted; the place will be marked and the engineers will lift the mine. The equipment weighs thirty pounds and is fragile and exhausting to use. Worst of all, it must be operated standing up by men straining to hear the electric signals through the cacophony of battle, terrified that at any minute they will be chopped to the ground by machine-gun fire. Those who don't have the new equipment will find the mines the old-fashioned way, crawling forward on their stomachs, probing the sand with bayonets. The engineers with the mine detectors can clear over two hundred mines an hour; the men with bayonets can only manage a hundred.

They are looking for two sorts of mine: anti-tank and anti-personnel. The German anti-tank Teller mine is a flat metal drum containing twelve pounds of explosive. It needs at least the weight of a lorry to set it off. These large mines can rip the tread of a tank or overturn a three-and-three-quarter-ton Bren-gun carrier. There are also Italian anti-tank mines and some captured British ones. But it is not so much the anti-tank mines that scare the engineers, but the deadly little anti-personnel mines that are sown in with the anti-tanks, the 'S-mines'. There are thousands of them, each triggered by little spikes that stick up above the sand, invisible in the dark. These mines are planted to booby-trap the anti-tanks; some have been laid with trip wires joining them up. Once triggered, a small cylindrical canister containing 350 shrapnel balls is thrown three to five feet in the air, at which height it explodes. The troops have nicknamed them 'de-bollockers'. They are designed to blind, maim and castrate, to disrupt the battle and lower morale. Men who have lost a foot or both hands, men with no eyes, or with great bleeding gashes ripped in their groins, must be carried screaming and bloody from the fight to dressing stations where they will patched up and sent on their long journey back home, to spend the rest of their lives as

251

invalids. There are also some Italian 'B4' anti-personnel mines, and the dreaded *Schu*-mine, a wooden box that is almost impossible to detect with the new electronic equipment.

The men have been told that to sweep the area effectively; they must remain level-headed and calm, whatever is going on around them. They need to clear lanes sixteen feet wide, just enough for tanks to pass through in single file. The edges of the three lanes will be marked with Tilly lamps, placed inside petrol cans with sun, moon and star shapes punched into them. The men have spent the previous week preparing the cans, a mindless job that took their thoughts off the coming battle.

Hours later the sun disappears in the west and the Allied bombers turn for home. Weary German soldiers emerge from their trenches, blockhouses and strongpoints, grateful to have survived another day. The bombing has stopped; they can relax. The men brew coffee and open tins of sausages with the letters 'AM' (for *Adminastrazione Militaire*) stamped on the sides. The German troops call the contents '*Alt Mann*' (Old Man), the Italian soldiers call them 'Dead Arabs' and the water they use for tea 'Arab Piss', because it is so heavily treated with chemicals. The cleverer soldiers dine on chicken or goat, traded with the locals. The really lucky ones receive delicacies from home.

In the dim moonlight, a sentry from 21st Panzer thinks he can see something moving about on the other side of the minefields. He calls the alarm: 'Stand to!' The men groan, half-shaved machine gunners slide back into their emplacements; the eleven-man teams on the 88s run back to their posts, choking on their disgusting sausages and

252

gulping back the last dregs of their coffee. The radio men, their faces lit by the soft glow from the dials of their equipment, tap out signals to General Stumme at *Afrika Korps* HQ, telling him there is a possibility of enemy action. Everyone holds their breath, the silence of the night only broken by the odd clink of metal on metal: a Spandau round being chambered, an 88 shell being eased quietly into its breach.

The soldiers of the Eighth Army, suddenly cold, shiver and huddle into their uniforms. The cooks bring round a last ration of cooked food, bully-beef stew, tinned potatoes and carrots, the vegetables slopping around in the processed meat, washed down with hot tea, the brackish taste of the sterilised water hidden by sweet condensed milk. The cooks ladle the food into mess tins, moving quietly from gun-pit to gun-pit, tank to tank, slit trench to slit trench. They murmur words of encouragement and comfort to their comrades who will soon be in action, and may be dead before another meal is served.

Soldiers start working on the lorries, pulling off the Sunshields to reveal the tanks. In other parts of the line, small, harmless vehicles have turned, as if by magic, into deadly twenty-five-pounder field guns. On each field gun the crews wait for the order to load. Behind the dial sight, the No. 3s, the layers, fidget in their seats, checking and rechecking the settings. Then, crackling over the Tannoy speakers strapped to the limber of each weapon: 'HE 117 WM charge super—LOAD!' The infantry stiffen: this is it. Any minute and they'll be off.

The No. 2, the rammer, heaves on the heavy brass handle to open the breech, which swings

253

down with a satisfying clunk. The loader, No. 4, rams a high-explosive shell into the barrel, followed by a brass cartridge that has been primed with a sack of cordite. 'Charge super' is the strongest charge for extra range.

The engineers form up on the start line, bumping into each other in the dark, carrying 80,000 lanterns, 130 miles of white marker tape, 100,000 metal stakes: all the paraphernalia for marking the lanes through the minefields. The infantry draw their bayonets from canvas scabbards and lock them into place on the tips of their .303 rifles. The Rifle Brigade, who will be right at the front, protecting the mine-clearing lads, call their bayonets 'swords'. Their job is to protect the engineers.

The order is given: 'One up the spout, safety catches on.'

The first rounds are chambered, brass cartridges with deadly nickel tips. The men have practised what they are to do many times during the preceding month. The night is full of the sound of metal clicking against metal. The noise makes the soldiers nervous; it'll give the game away. The gun-layers peer into their sights, for the last time checking the cross-hairs against the black-and-white aiming posts that have been hammered into place in front of the guns. The aimers' right hands curl round the wooden handles of the firing levers, shoulders tense.

Twenty-five miles to the east, Geoffrey Barkas and Tony Southron sit beside their battered Chevrolet staff car. Driver Ashman sits with them. They are drinking the tea he has made them. The three men smoke, never taking their eyes off the

254

western horizon. It is 21:23 hours. The three men fall silent, staring into the deep black night.

21:24 Egyptian Summertime on 23 October 1942. On the Allied side of the minefield, a green Verey light rises silently into the night sky.

'Fire!' The order crackles out of the speakers.

The Allied artillery layers push down their firing levers and the guns roar. Lights flicker along the length of the horizon, the ground shakes and the thundering noise of the largest artillery barrage since the First World War sweeps over the German lines.

11

THE BATTLE OF EL ALAMEIN

Barkas's little camp was too far away for the noise of the opening barrage to reach him. In the eerie silence he wondered what it was like for the troops in the first wave, remembering the night, twenty-six years before, when as a junior officer he had stood in a trench on the Western Front waiting for the whistle that would send him over the top. Operation Bertram was the climax of his work in the desert; he prayed it would be a success, that it might save the lives of his fighting comrades.

Some of the Eighth Army batteries were aimed at targets on the extreme edge of their range. Shells launched just seconds earlier, struck artillery and communication positions more than seven miles away. The roar of the twenty-five-pounders was soon joined by the deeper boom of the sixty-pounders positioned behind them; further back still, the 105mm self-propelled howitzers, newly arrived from America, added to the tumult.

The barrage concentrated on enemy positions to the south of the line, keeping up the Bertram deception until the last moment. For fifteen terrifying minutes, hundreds of shells landed on units of the Italian Folgore Parachute Division and the German 21st Panzer Division. The bombardment tore thousands of yards of coiled barbed wire to pieces, demolished blockhouses and caved in the sides of dugouts and trenches. Tanks weighing tons were blown to pieces and heavy howitzers reduced to shredded metal. Support vehicles bowled across the desert like giant, blazing toys. Men running for cover were vaporised by blast, or sliced to ribbons by red-hot shrapnel. An experienced twenty-five-pounder gun crew could get off eight rounds a minute. In a quarter of an hour over thirty thousand shells had exploded on the German and Italian lines.

At 21:40, the 456 guns of British X Corps and XXX Corps to the north of the Alamein line opened up on the 15th Panzer Division: a gun for every thirty yards of the front line. The combined thunder of the guns produced the loudest manmade noise ever heard in Africa, a sound so intense that it caused some men's eardrums to bleed. Out to sea, the guns from the Royal Navy joined in the chorus; the shells from their batteries soared overhead, wailing like deep, jagged organ notes. Explosions flashed red and yellow on the desert sand as the moon disappeared behind drifting smoke. The second barrage destroyed communication and command centres. At 21:55 hours the range lowered to the enemy front lines.

At 22:00 hours the Allied infantry started to move.

Engineers and infantry, men from all over the British Empire—Australia, New Zealand, India and South Africa—clambered to their feet and set off through the minefields, walking into the lethal glittering thunder. In front were the Royal Engineers, whose task it was to clear lanes for the tanks. The Bren-gun carriers of the Rifle Brigade bounced alongside them, keeping pace. Many of the mines had been booby trapped, causing terrible injuries. Once cleared, pathways were marked with tape and lit with the specially prepared lanterns. Behind, the tanks waited their turn to move forward; behind them the supply vehicles, ambulances, staff cars, canteens, workshops and the other multitude of vehicles needed to keep the army supplied and moving.

On the German side, no one knew what was happening: the initial barrage had cut many of the links between the *Panzerarmee*'s corps and divisional headquarters. Information that could not be sent across the shattered wireless nets was handed to despatch riders, who disappeared for ever into the storm.

The shocked and bewildered survivors soon began to fire back. Rapid-fire Spandaus wracked the lanes at 1,200 rounds a minute and the crash of mortar bombs joined the cacophony. For some it was all too much. One British soldier noticed that a 'bloke was missing, hiding in a slit trench behind the gun. So I dragged him by the scruff of the neck . . . I would have shot him if I had to. He went back to the gun but was never quite the same again.'

At midnight the Allied tanks started to enter the minefields, some of them directly in line with the German 88s. The big dual-purpose guns began to take their toll, but advancing towards them were Sherman tanks equipped with 75mm gyro-stabilised guns that could be aimed and fired on the move. The Shermans were the best armoured vehicles on the battlefield. Their rate of fire was faster than the cumbersome 88s, which they began to knock out.

The tanks stirred up giant dust clouds, making it impossible to see, choking the troops and ruining

258

the neat uniforms of the military police struggling to keep the advance to schedule. Lanes quickly became blocked by crippled and destroyed armour and carriers, as tank drivers, blinded by the billowing fog of sand, steered their vehicles off the safe lanes and fell into the 'Devil's Garden'. Lanterns and marker tape became obscured or obliterated, creating chaos for those behind. Exploding mines ripped into the tanks' steel hulls and the screams of the wounded rose above the noise of battle. Huge traffic jams developed, stretching back for miles. The mines blew the tracks off the Bren-gun carriers and the crews struggled to repair the heavy metal links under fire, heaving on them while bullets zipped round their heads. A platoon of kilted Scotsman marched forward, bayonets fixed, striding in perfect parade-ground formation, led by a skirling piper. The piper fell just before they disappeared into the smoke and flames.

The sun rose on 24 October to reveal chaos behind the Axis lines. Signallers tried to re-establish contact and the messages that did get through were often confused and hysterical. At ten o'clock in the morning, the 15th Panzer Division received a transmission saying that the Littorio Infantry Regiment 328 had been wiped out by 'drunken negroes with tanks'. At the north end of the line, Stumme received a signal from the commander of 15th Panzer, *Generalmajor* Gustav von Vaerst, saying that he was under heavy attack and needed support. Stumme, convinced that the main thrust was against 21st Panzer in the south, refused to move any of his armour north.

Eventually Stumme, starved of information by the destruction of his communications systems, set out to assess the situation for himself. He left at 10:40 hours and took with him his driver, Corporal Wolf, and a signals officer, Colonel Büchting, who was eager to see if he could repair the damage to the field telephone net. Stumme declined to take either an escort or a wireless vehicle, saying that they were only going as far as the 90th Light Panzer Division, just behind the front line on the coast. Stumme did not believe that the bombardment and the events of the night were anything to do with the expected Allied offensive. He left telling his staff that intelligence had told him that the real battle was not expected 'for several weeks'. Operation Bertram and the Phantom Army had helped fool him.

When Stumme arrived at the 90th HQ he found they knew even less about the situation than he did, so he decided to move nearer the front. No one is certain what happened next—whether Stumme's vehicle was attacked and strafed by fighter aircraft, or whether he went too near to the anti-tank and machine-gun fire near the front. Something hit his vehicle, mortally wounding Büchting in the head. Driver Wolf slewed the heavy staff car into a U-turn of such violence that Stumme lost his balance; half in and half out of his staff car, he had a heart attack and fell. The car tore off, leaving him dying in the sand. Wolf was a mile or so away before he realised that he had lost his chief. Stumme had never opened the yellow envelope given to him by Rommel. Had he done so he would have read: 'Should the enemy break through at a single point, concentrate a counterattack reserve and aim straight for the heart of the attacking formation. Destroy it before it succeeds in creating a salient.'

The *Panzerarmee Afrika* was leaderless and remained so for several hours until Stumme was replaced by fifty-one-year-old Lieutenant General Wilhelm Ritter von Thoma, an aristocrat and a veteran of the war in Poland and the Eastern Front, and a man prone to violent and unpredictable rages.

*   *   *

That afternoon, Rommel got a call from Rome informing him of the catastrophic events that had overtaken his army. He wanted to set off at once for North Africa, but Hitler had other plans for his *Generalfeldmarshal*, including the possibility of sending him to Russia. Rommel waited near his aircraft at Wiener Neustadt as his Führer deliberated.

Precious hours were lost. It was not until half past five the next evening, 25 October, that Rommel returned to his forward headquarters at Alamein. Shortly before midnight every German unit received the signal: 'I have taken command of the army again—Rommel.'

Lieutenant Colonel David Gibbs of the Queen's Battalion had been taken prisoner and was lying behind barbed wire, huddled in a blanket trying to sleep, when he heard the news. He and his men had been forced to surrender after fighting for eighteen hours under heavy artillery and mortar fire. Gibbs asked the guards what all the cheering was about. They told him everything was going to be all right, Germany would win: Rommel was back.

The battle had stalled. The Axis forces were still not certain where the main thrust of the Allied attack was coming from. In the south, the 21st Panzer and the Ariete Division were still heavily engaged by General Horrocks's XIII Corps.

On the afternoon of the twenty-sixth, three days after the start of the battle, Rommel finally decided that the attack in the south was a bluff and ordered the 21st Panzer north to take 'Point 29', where his 15th Panzer Division had lost nearly seventy per cent of its armour. This was a risky move because it left only the troops and armour of the Ariete Division troops to hold the line. Rommel would not have enough petrol to go back if Montgomery suddenly wheeled south. Things became so desperate that Rommel considered flying in untrained troops from Crete.

The 21st Panzer tanks were delayed by bombing from the Desert Air Force. Then, near Point 29, at a feature known as Kidney Ridge and codenamed Snipe, they ran into the 2nd Battalion the Rifle Brigade and 239 Anti-Tank Battery, who were fighting a desperate action. The small force of twenty-seven anti-tank guns and about 300 men had been ordered onto Snipe the day before, but their advance was complicated by conflicting map references, which led to uncertainty as to exactly where Snipe was. When the battalion arrived at what they thought was the right spot they fired two green Verey lights, the signal for success and the cue for the anti-tank guns and the support vehicles to move up.

As dawn broke, the Riflemen realised they were in the wrong place. Surrounding them were hundreds of soft-skinned vehicles, ambulances and tanks—it was like being 'in the middle of a huge car park', one soldier reflected. The vehicles belonged to 15th Panzer and the Italian Littorio Divisions, who were massing for a counterattack the following day. The Riflemen fought for their lives from dawn of the twenty-seventh until night. Unloading their equipment under fire, the battalion's six-pounders were rushed into action. Wave upon wave of advancing Axis tanks were disabled, some by direct hits at point-blank range. During the defence, the battalion's CO, Victor Turner, though wounded, acted as loader to a six-pounder operated by Sergeant Charles Calistan, for which Turner received a Victoria Cross.

Calistan was awarded the Distinguished Conduct Medal. His commendation, countersigned by Montgomery and Alexander, reads: 'Sgt Calistan's troop was engaged by enemy tanks both during the night and the following morning. By midday on 27 October, all the other guns in his troop had been knocked out, and all the other numbers of his own gun crew but himself wounded and incapacitated. The troop was almost out of ammunition. At about 13:00 hours, fifteen German tanks attacked his sector. The commanding officer [Turner] arrived at his position and acted as loader while he [Calistan] laid the gun and acted as No. 1. With the greatest courage and coolness he waited until the tanks were 200–300 yards away, and hit and set nine of them on fire. He then had no more ammunition left. Unperturbed he waited while his troop commander fetched more ammunition and when it arrived, hit three more enemy tanks in as many shots, and so broke and repelled the enemy attack.' The three rounds were the only rounds that Calistan had left. Sergeant Calistan was originally recommended for a Victoria Cross, but Montgomery, for reasons that are unclear, downgraded the award to the next best, the DCM.

Towards the end of the afternoon of 27 October, the 21st Panzer arrived and counterattacked. The fighting went on until darkness provided enough cover for the Rifle Brigade to withdraw. Their resistance had destroyed or badly damaged fifty-six German tanks, five self-propelled guns and an assortment of trucks and other vehicles. When the fighting stopped, less than half the 106 tanks 21st Panzer had set out with were usable. Rommel wrote home: 'No one can imagine the fear hanging over me. Once again, everything is at stake. The circumstances we are in could not be worse.'

Montgomery decided to re-form XXX Corps and hold it in reserve. Churchill interpreted this as a retreat, and was only just dissuaded from sending a blistering telegram asking, 'Have we not got a general who could even win one single battle?'

Under great pressure to get the campaign moving again, Monty came up with Operation Supercharge, which he described as 'the master plan' (and claimed later that 'only the master could write it'). When one of his staff commented that the scheme was 'suicide', Montgomery replied: 'It's got to be done. If necessary, I'm prepared to accept a hundred per cent casualties in both personnel and tanks.' Supercharge took the Eighth Army south. The day before the attack Montgomery wrote to his bosses in London saying: 'We have got all the Germans up in the north in the Sidi Rahman area and I am attacking well to the south of that place.'

The attack went in at 01:00 hours on the night of 2 November, preceded by a seven-hour aerial bombardment. Luck ran with Monty. The *Afrika*

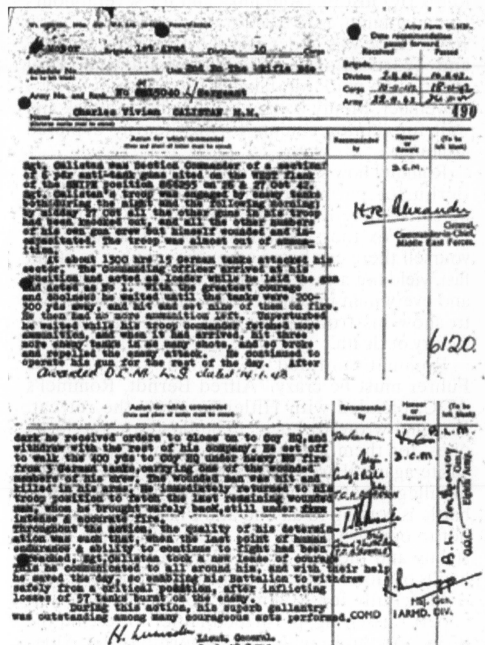

Sergeant Charles Calistan's commendation, originally for a VC. Monty turned it into a DCM.

Korps HQ lost its radio links and for several hours Rommel endured a frustrating radio blackout. By 16:45, Snipe was under attack by the 151st Infantry and 133rd (Lorried) Brigades and this vital observation point was taken a few hours later. By 3 November, Monty was forced to halt the attack and wait for reinforcements for his heavily depleted armour.

Rommel now saw his chance to retreat and asked Berlin for permission to withdraw. At 13:30 a personal directive from Hitler arrived telling the Desert Fox that: 'In the situation that you find yourself there can be no other thought but to stand fast, yield not a yard of ground and throw every gun and every man into the battle.' Hitler ordered him to show his troops 'no other road than that to victory or death'.

Rommel confided to a junior officer: 'The Führer must be crazy.' Alfred Berndt, Rommel's ADC, pleaded with Hitler to allow the retreat. Rommel wrote to Lucie: 'The dead are the lucky ones, for them it is all over.' Later that night he wrote again: 'Farewell to you and our lad . . .'. To his illegitimate daughter Trudie he wrote: 'The battle is coming to an end and I'm sorry to say it is not to our own profit. The enemy's strength is too strong and they are overwhelming us. It is in the hands of God whether my soldiers will survive.'

Mercifully for Rommel's troops, his superior, Albert Kesselring, persuaded Hitler to rescind the order. Around eight in the morning, the Allies heard deep explosions from the south as Rommel began to blow up his ammunition dumps. He was leaving.

On 4 November, General Ritter von Thoma,

who had been given command of the *Afrika Korps* after the loss of Stumme, was captured by Captain Allen Singer of the 10th Royal Hussars. Von Thoma, 'a born enthusiast who lives in a world of tanks', had watched as his men and armour were almost annihilated. That morning, he commandeered a tank and drove it to the heart of the battle, west of El Alamein. His vehicle was hit several times and he was captured sitting calmly on the battlefield, surrounded by his blazing armour and dead comrades. One British officer who saw him said he looked like 'a big strong thoroughbred with the head of a sugar daddy and blond wavy hair slightly tinged with grey. His eyes were blue and his gestures lively'. Rommel speculated that the general had wanted to die in the field, or possibly to negotiate a surrender, as he too believed Hitler's order to be 'madness'.

That night von Thoma was invited to discuss the battle over dinner with Monty in his caravan. (When he heard, Churchill responded caustically: 'I sympathise with General von Thoma, defeated, in captivity and [*dramatic pause*] dinner with Montgomery!') Monty asked the *General der Panzertruppe* what he thought his armies had been up to in the days prior to the battle of Alamein. Von Thoma said he thought the Allies had at least one armoured division more than they actually did, and declared he had believed this until the third or fourth day of the battle. He said the *Panzerarmee* command had expected the battle to start in the south because of the considerable build-up of supplies and equipment they had observed.

General Thoma's confusion and Georg Stumme's conviction, as he set off on his last, fatal, reconnaissance mission across the desert, that the Allied attack was not expected for several weeks, is a tribute to the effectiveness of Bertram and proof that German intelligence had been duped. A captured Italian map records the build-up of Allied armour in the south. Asked whether he knew of any fake Allied tanks or dummies in the area, von Thoma replied with an emphatic 'No'. For him the Phantom Army was real and a deadly threat.

* * *

After the war von Thoma claimed that Montgomery had won his battles because in 'modern mobile warfare' the decisive factors were less tactics and more the 'organisation of one's resources'. Though the German general meant this as a snub to Monty's skills as a commander, in one sense he was right. The British had organised the most unlikely of their resources—an eclectic bunch of bohemians and artists, equipped with little more than straw, cardboard and cloth—and deployed them in the most audacious way imaginable. Monty's men and equipment had been boosted by the Phantom Army, a mirage created by the Camouflage Unit in the best British traditions of 'making do'. Battles are won by an accumulation of small events and every advantage helps. If by deception a commander can confuse his enemy and make him act according to a misconception, then he has stacked the cards in his favour.

On 15 November 1942 church bells rang out through Britain for the first time since the start of the war and in the House of Commons a relieved PM was delighted to report that 'by a marvellous system

268

of camouflage, complete tactical surprise was achieved in the desert'. He was referring, of course, to Operation Bertram. Alamein handed the Allies their first major victory of the Second World War. 'It may almost be said that before Alamein we never had a victory,' Churchill later reflected. 'After Alamein we never had a defeat'—classic Churchillian hyperbole that contained a general truth.

Casualties on both sides had been heavy. Axis forces lost 20,000 men, dead, wounded or taken prisoner, and ninety-five per cent of their guns and tanks—a scale of loss unprecedented for Rommel. The Eighth Army casualties were 13,560 men—six per cent of Montgomery's army—half of whom were dead or missing, plus approximately a hundred guns and 150 tanks. Richard Heseltine, the young hussar who had had wanted to arrest Montgomery, remembers that in the weeks after the battle a verse appeared and became popular among the men of the armoured divisions:

I rode my tank to Alamein
Prepared to do or die.
I led my few to victory
Now all I do is cry.

Geoffrey Barkas, the film director-turned-magician who, in the blink of an eye, had conjured an army of tanks across the desert, had every reason to feel satisfied. He had risen to Buckley's challenge and helped build the Camouflage Unit from a tiny outfit in a cramped office into a respected and integral part of the British Army. Barkas and the men under his command had played a key role in what would prove to be a turning point in the war.

The Eighth Army chased Rommel out of North Africa and the Phantom Army vanished, its job done. The battlefields moved to Italy and northern Europe and Barkas went back to London, where he carried on his work at the War Office. On the vast sands of the Western Desert all that remained to tell of the Phantom Army's existence were the discarded Sunshields that had turned deadly tanks into harmless lorries, the hundreds of dummy tanks, quietly falling apart, and the flapping canvas remains of the 'stores' so carefully planted in the south, all watched over by the scarecrow figures of straw troops leaning drunkenly into the wind, their work done, now left to rot in the scorching desert sun.

12

AFTER THE BATTLE

Barkas and the Camouflage Unit were the last people to practise truly large-scale physical deception. For the invasion of Europe—Overlord— the Phantom Army of Alamein would be replaced by two, far bigger phantom armies, made not of straw or canvas, but conjured from the airwaves with wireless and radar.

Operation Bodyguard, the most ambitious deception plan in the history of warfare, comprised six main and thirty-six minor schemes to protect Overlord, the operation to invade Europe. At its heart was Fortitude, the scheme to mislead Hitler as to the timing and location of the D-Day landings. Two fake invasion forces were spirited into being: Fortitude South, comprising US First Army and led by the flamboyant General George C. Patton, would land at the Pas-de-Calais, a decoy to the actual landing sites in Normandy. Fortitude North, comprising Fourth Army and led by early camouflage pioneer Lieutenant General Andrew 'Bulgy' Thorne, would land in Norway. The movements of both virtual armies were simulated by a handful of radio signallers working to a meticulously devised and controlled script.

In addition, diplomatic channels were used to leak false information via embassies in neutral countries. German double agents sent false information to Berlin. There were about fifty of these, including Garbo, a Spaniard whose approaches had at first been spurned by the British. Garbo created a substantial network of non-existent spies in the six months before D-Day and these dummy agents flooded Berlin with misleading information. Other details of the Fortitude fiction were impressive: field-dressing stations, cash offices and army film and photographic sections were incorporated into the picture. The airwaves of the Fourth Army were crammed with signals about ski training, specialist equipment, the demands on vehicles operating at sub-zero temperatures; while First Army generated thousands of movement orders, urgent queries about tides, beach conditions and air cover. Sudden, random radio silences were imposed, simulating the real silences that would accompany Operation Overlord.

Some physical deception was used. Dummy tanks, false invasion barges, full-scale model aircraft and mock supply dumps were created to help create the illusion of a massing army. Even real troop movements were worked into the scheme. The 3rd Infantry Division, who were training in assault techniques in the Moray Firth for the real invasion, doubled as elements of the phantom Fourth Army. In Dundee harbour, snow-clearing equipment, including bulldozers and snowploughs, was parked in full view on the quay, apparently ready to be shipped to Norway. In the Firth of Forth dummy ships and landing craft were crammed in amongst the real thing.

The Allied Air Force was worked into the scheme. Whatever aircraft were thrown at the real landing sites in Normandy, the Pas de Calais would receive double, twice as many bombs and twice as many reconnaissance patrols. This tactic was so successful that Rommel, in charge of organising the coastal defences of northern Europe, reported to his superior, Gerd von Rundstedt, that 'concentrated air attacks on the coastal defences between Dunkirk and Dieppe strengthen the prospects of a large-scale landing in that area'. Hitler was so certain that the Allies would invade the Pas-de-Calais that he deployed most of his troops in the area. He and his staff read the build-up in Scotland as a decoy to distract them from Patton's First Army Group.

Another element of physical deception was fake shipping. Everything from huge tank-landing craft to the much smaller infantry carriers, was deployed around the south-east coast of England. Camouflage officers swung into action. The young architect Basil Spence, who had spent the early part of the war in intelligence, transferred to the Royal Engineers as a camouflage officer and was put in charge of creating a giant oil storage and docking facility near Dover. Technicians drafted from film studios built an enormous complex, complete with storage tanks, miles of connecting pipe, jetties, control points, and anti-aircraft defences. The structures were lit at night to imply round-the-clock work. Oil was poured into the water to simulate spillage from refuelling and the vast amount of completely imaginary naval maintenance work. King George VI and Montgomery visited the site. The RAF allowed German reconnaissance planes to fly over at very high level, from which the illusion was perfect.

The port was shelled by a German long-range

cannon at Cap Gris Nez. Remembering the lessons learned by Peter Proud at Tobruk, the camoufleurs went to work simulating bomb damage, complete with decoy fires and smoke. *General Der Panzergruppe* Hans Cramer, commander of the *Afrika Korps* and now POW of the Allies, became an unwitting player in the ruse. He had developed serious asthma and so was eligible for repatriation. The general was told he would be taken home via Dover on a Swedish ship, and that he would travel to the port by road. It was 'accidentally' revealed to him en route that he was travelling through the south-east of England; in fact, the road went right through the area of the full-scale build-up in the south-west and Cramer was allowed to see the enormity of it.

That night Cramer was invited to dine with General Patton, who was introduced as the 'Commander-in-Chief, First Army Group'. Patton, who had a reputation as a loudmouth, let slip the word 'Calais'. Cramer arrived in Berlin convinced that he had seen the build-up for the invasion of Europe and that it was heading for the Pas-de-Calais. His reports were so pessimistic that Goering reprimanded him for defeatism.

A false threat to the Balkans was mounted to stop Axis troops being transferred to northern France. This was entrusted to Dudley Clarke. He crafted a double bluff involving real and phantom troops, radio deception and propaganda. Axis intelligence was fooled into thinking that all the activity in north-west Europe was a cover for a real invasion launched from Africa across the Mediterranean. By May, a German intelligence appreciation asserted that 'unquestionable' sources had it that the invasion would be against the Balkans and would be mounted from Libya and Egypt.

On D-Day itself, the RAF pulled off a large-scale feat of electronic deception. By 1944 the Germans had built radar stations along the coast of Europe from Norway to Spain. On the night of 5/6 June many of these were bombed, and others were jammed. The surviving stations were fed false electronic information. The RAF's 617 Squadron, the 'Dambusters', flew very complex and precise sorties over the Channel, dropping bundles of foil chaff known as 'window'. On the German radar screens it looked as though hundreds of ships were moving steadily towards the Pas-de-Calais at a speed of eight knots. The Phantom Navy came under attack from the air and from shore batteries.

Hitler did not believe that the Allies would start the invasion without such a formidable soldier as Patton in a key role. When the troops went ashore in Normandy, Hitler convinced himself that they, too, were a diversion and kept several divisions on standby, waiting for the 'real' invasion which, he believed, would set out from Dover. The Allied deception schemes were so successful that as late as 18 July, more than six weeks after the Normandy landings, von Rundstedt sent a signal from his headquarters stating: 'There are no grounds for changing our appreciation of the intentions of General Patton's First Army Group assembled in the south-east of England.' US commander Omar Bradley later wrote: 'For seven decisive weeks, the German Fifteenth Army waited for an invasion that never came, convinced beyond all reasonable doubt that Patton would lead the main Allied assault

275

across the narrow neck of the Channel . . . The enemy immobilised nineteen divisions and played into our hands in the biggest single hoax of the war.'

* * *

Bradley wasn't quite right. Huge though the scale of Bodyguard was, the Russians had become expert in even larger-scale deception work. *Maskirovka* is a Russian word often translated as 'camouflage', but as the camouflage tutors at Farnham knew, *maskirovka* went far beyond basic concealment, which is why they went to the trouble of translating a two-volume Russian camouflage manual into English and using some of its theories in their own programmes.

The Russians embraced the importance of camouflage and deception while, thousands of miles away in the Western Desert, Geoffrey Barkas and his handful of zealots were trying to persuade the British Army that there was more to concealment than sticking a few twigs in your helmet, or throwing an ungarnished net over your lorry. *Maskirovka* involved a 'complexity of measures, directed to mislead the enemy regarding the presence and disposition of forces'. The tradition can been traced back to 1380 when, at the battle of Kulikovo Field, the Russian commander Dmitry Donsky used a small force to encourage the Mongol enemy to attack while concealing a much larger force, which overwhelmed the attackers.

The Russian army became skilled at making themselves invisible. Those deployed against the Germans near Moscow in November 1942 moved at night and were careful to enforce absolute radio silence. Camouflage techniques were used to disguise supply depots and rail and road communications along the deployment routes. When the Russians attacked, three of its ten armies had not even been plotted on the German commanders' maps. At Stalingrad in February 1942, the Red Army deployed huge numbers of dummy tanks, vehicles and artillery to distract German attention away from their attack across the Lama River west of Moscow. Their scheme included simulated firing and the use of loudspeakers to broadcast the noise of tank engines. German reconnaissance aircraft flew over a thousand sorties over the dummy build-up area.

By 1943, all Russian commanders about to take part in an offensive had to prepare comprehensive deception plans. Barkas's Soviet counterparts had even drawn up tables showing just how many men and materials would be needed to mock-up larger units: to simulate troops in brigade strength required a rifle company, three tanks, three anti-aircraft machine guns and three anti-aircraft guns. At Stalingrad, the German commander General Paulus was reassured by his Chief of Staff that the Russians 'no longer have any reserves worth mentioning and are not capable of launching a large-scale offensive'. In fact the Russians had moved 160,00 men, 10,000 horses, 430 tanks 14,000 soft-skinned vehicles and over 7,000 tons of ammunition onto the battlefield under cover of darkness, without the Germans realising what was happening. In addition, twenty-two concealed bridges were built across the battlefield, five of which were false and several of which were constructed actually in the water, hidden just below the surface they crossed—a brilliant example of taking advantage of the local environment. The surprise attack paralysed the Germans and led to a defeat from which they would never recover.

The lessons the Russians learned in the Second World War were carried into the Cold War and beyond. The Soviets were determined that they would never again be surprised by an attack in the way they had been by Hitler. In 1976, the *Soviet Military Encyclopaedia* declared that 'surprise is one of the most important principles of military art involving secrecy, camouflage and darkness'. It went on to refine its definitions of what was needed, including the disciplines of activity, plausibility, variety and contrast. By activity it meant the use light, heat, sound and reality. This meant the application of nets, camouflage, special clothing, the manipulation of heat sources and dummy equipment. The Soviet army developed reflectors which, properly used, could give wooden tanks a false radar signal, hide roads and create fake bridges. In the 1970s every Soviet motorised battalion was issued with them and trained in their use. The philosophy of *maskirovka* was summed up by a Russian strategist who wrote: 'a more important condition for achieving victory than overall superiority in weapons and manpower is the ability to use concealment in preparations for a major strike and surprise in launching an attack against important enemy targets'.

*   *   *

In the post-war years, camouflage and deception have become increasingly more difficult. Night-vision

278

and thermal-imaging equipment scan the battlefield. Satellites monitor troop movements in far greater detail than was ever achieved by photographic reconnaissance from aircraft. Computers listen in on, remember, and analyse radio traffic. Every new surveillance technique conjures a new and equally ingenious counter-surveillance technique.

The search for a magic cloak of invisibility has never stopped. Today stealth bombers are almost invisible to radar. During the Gulf War in 1991, Colonel Barry Horne of the US Air Force was surprised to find the bodies of dead bats on the floor of a hanger holding USF-117A Nighthawk stealth fighter-bombers. He realised that the bats, which use natural radar to find their way in the dark, had not been able to detect the aircraft and had been crashing blindly into them.

One company in North Carolina has been working on counter-thermal-imaging solutions and has reportedly come up with a paint containing microscopic silver ceramic balls made from a by-product of coal ash. It is claimed the paint can cancel out heat emissions from the human body, vehicles and equipment of all sorts, making them undetectable by heat-sensitive equipment. The paint can be used on transportation, worked into the materials used to make combat clothes, or worn on the face as camouflage cream.

The Holy Grail of the camoufleur is 'active camouflage', which is the ability of some creatures, such as octopuses and chameleons, to change colour and apparent skin texture at will. A Chinese design team working at the Southeast University in Nanjing has found a way to change the way radar waves interact with an object. Using concentric rings of circuit boards etched with metal-lined channels, they can manipulate the incoming radar waves to make an object look like something else. Researchers claim that similar illusion devices could, in time, convert the radar image of an aircraft into a flying bird.

Nanotechnology makes it theoretically possible to produce a lightweight combat suit that serves as body armour, biological warfare protection, muscle enhancer and active camouflage all in one. Scientists at the University of California think that an invisibility cloak might be within reach. They claim to have 'come up with a new solution to the problem of invisibility based on the use of dielectric [non-conduction materials]. Our optical cloak not only suggests that true invisibility materials are within reach, it also represents a major step towards transformation optics, opening the door to manipulating light at will for the creation of powerful new microscopes and faster computers'. At the moment, the cloaking effect can only be observed through a microscope.

The uses of some of these developments may lie far in the future. For now in the West military camouflage is still the poor relation, just as it was for the Camouflage Unit when they arrived in North Africa. For the 'poor bloody infantry' on the battlefield, things are not so very different from the way they were for our ancestors, who would put on the disguise of a reindeer skin to make themselves invisible. Every day in the press we see troops wearing camouflage designed to make them blend into whatever environment they are fighting in. Back home, when their spokesmen speak on the television they wear the same camouflage, not to hide from the camera, or disappear into the gleaming stone and green grass of the White House, but to show that, they too, carry the magic.

Epilogue

BACK IN THE STUDIO

By 1943, as the fighting moved to Italy and then France, the Middle East became a backwater. Almost all of Barkas's camouflage personnel were sent away, mostly to follow the fighting, with one particular exception, Steven Sykes, who, having missed out on Bertram, found himself marooned as Camouflage Instructor G2 Major at the Combined Training Centre, Suez. The posting was for an obligatory six months and the army refused to listen to his pleas to be sent somewhere more lively. While he kicked his heels, he learned the terrible news that Tony Ayrton, the stalwart of camouflage development in the Western Desert, had died of meningitis. Brian Robb took over from Ayrton and, along with many other old desert hands, set to work on schemes for Operation Husky, the invasion of Sicily.

Sykes was desperate to be back in the thick of things. He accepted a demotion from captain to major and, despite still suffering from recurrent bouts of malaria, volunteered to become a glider pilot with the newly formed Glider Pilot Regiment. (Paratroop and mobile airforces were in the fashion of military thinking at the time.) Sykes was turned down. He finally got back to England on 10 February 1943, his wedding anniversary. It had been 1,241 days since he had last seen his wife. He spent fourteen uneasy days with his family and was treated like a stranger by his young son Simon.

Soon Sykes was drafted to Elgin in Scotland to train with No. 5 Beach Group for the Normandy landings. Here he met up with Basil Spence, a fellow graduate of Farnham, whom he had encountered before the war. Spence was the camouflage officer in charge of No. 5 and 6 'Beach Groups'; these were cross-service units tasked with landing the assault groups and maintaining the beaches as so that reinforcements, food and ammunition could be passed safely across them to the troops at the front line. Spence told Sykes that he hated the job, felt like a stooge and was not able to get on with any genuine camouflage work.

On 6 June 1944, D-Day itself, Sykes landed safely on Queen Red Sector, Gold beach at H+195 minutes, with orders to establish a Beach Group HQ. Sykes quickly became embroiled in the work and wrote after the war: 'I lost all sense of time as one task followed another.' The days passed; friends were killed and wounded, and Spence and Sykes even found themselves part of a group storming a pillbox. As ever, Sykes found opportunities in the weeks after the fighting to paint watercolours—of the movement of troops, the landings, and of the dead.

The Allies broke out of Normandy and began the long slog to the Rhine and Germany. Eventually Sykes and Basil Spence found themselves working on camouflage schemes for the air defences around Antwerp. They were joined by the glass engraver John Hutton and he and Spence began what was to be a long and fruitful friendship. Hutton had been shipped back to England from the Middle East in

May 1943 to recover his health. Throughout his time in the desert he had looked forward to being reunited with Nell and their twin boys, who had been born just before the war. He had hoped to pick up on the happy ties they had all shared together before he was posted to Egypt. The reality of the family reunion was very different. Like Sykes, Hutton felt like an unwelcome intruder, a frightening stranger to his children who resented his presence, and someone who came between them and their mother. Nell was growing more extreme in her left-wing views, something that did not sit easily with Hutton's liberalism. Eventually, and with some relief, he went back to the war.

By the spring of 1945 the interminable and bloody march on the German frontier was over. On 23 March the Allies crossed the Rhine in an operation called Plunder. Hutton was put in charge of the 21st Army Group Camouflage Pool, known as 'Swan Lake', which was in part responsible for camouflaging the crossing. The camouflage work was so successful that the Allied build-up was completely hidden. Hutton's war ended where it had begun, at Farnham, where he was made Chief Camouflage Instructor, with Basil Spence as his second-in-command. He was demobbed in October 1945, having been mentioned in despatches three times. Freddie de Guingand wrote of Hutton: 'His unlimited enthusiasm in the face of the greatest difficulties has been an inspiration to all those who served under him, and his outstanding devotion to duty has greatly contributed to the concealment of our forces prior to major operations.'

Steven Sykes celebrated New Year's Eve 1944 at the Palace Hotel in Brussels in the company of

285

Hutton and Spence. By March he was back in London with another illness: he had developed a patch on his lung. Three years later he began teaching at the Chelsea School of Art. His creative output was huge—painting, pottery, sculpture—he had an insatiable appetite for making things. He wanted to be known as a war artist but it would take until 1989 before his D-Day watercolours appeared in *The Sunday Times* magazine and in an exhibition organised by Guillaume Gallozzi at the Redfern Gallery, London. Sykes's most touching memorial is the garden and house he created at Hopkiln in Sussex. The house is a reflection of Sykes's impetuous personality. He was always adding to it and built a maze, a grotto, a waterfall and a small raised canal. He peopled it with family, friends and peacocks and became a sun worshipper, standing naked by his swimming pool to welcome his guests.

Other members of the Camouflage Unit were picking up the pieces of their lives they had been forced to drop in 1939. Peter Proud returned to film design and worked on several popular television series, including *The Buccaneers* and *Robin Hood*, and set up his own successful film production company. Proud used the techniques he had learned in the desert to pioneer a method of designing scenery so that it was almost completely flexible and mobile. He claimed that he could turn Sherwood Forest into a banqueting hall in an hour and that during the run of one of his film or television productions nothing was ever thrown away or wasted—the old Camouflage Unit adage of 'make do with what you've got'.

The Beddington brothers went on their enigmatic way. Jack, who in the thirties had been so helpful to struggling artists, spent the war making films for the Ministry of Information, including, in 1943, the acclaimed documentary *Desert Victory*, which detailed the duels between Montgomery and Rommel at Alamein. After the war he founded the successful advertising agency Colman Prentis and Varley. His brother Freddie became a director of Wildenstein's, the art dealers, and died in 1979.

After the war Hugh Cott went back to his research as a zoologist: he travelled and worked in Africa, and developed a particular interest in the Nile crocodile. He became a Fellow of the Royal Photographic Society and displayed his skills in three books: *Zoological Photography in Practice*, *Uganda in Black and White* and *Looking at Animals, A Zoologist in Africa*.

William Murray Dixon, whom Peter Proud stole from the Rifle Brigade in 1941, ended his war in Baghdad as art advisor to the chief education officer at the Army Education Centre. After the war he returned to the Royal College of Art and then joined De La Rue's plastics division, where he pioneered the use of Formica in furniture and exhibition design.

Bainbridge Copnall, who had sent the whimsical message about the camouflage officers going into action for Operation Crusader, returned to the hammer and chisel, carving in stone and wood and casting in bronze. His statue *The Boy David*, an unusual memorial to the Machine Gun Corps, stands on Chelsea Embankment. Possibly his best-known work is a large bronze *Thomas Becket*, in the garden of St Paul's Cathedral. He died in 1973.

Blair Hughes-Stanton, who had been badly wounded in Greece and spent two years as POW of the Germans, was repatriated to England in 1943, but because of his wounds he never sculpted or engraved again. He was employed as a lecturer at St Martin's School of Art and the Central School of Art and died in 1981.

Julian Trevelyan spent most of the rest of the war teaching camouflage: at Farnham, where he became a confidant of 'Buckles'—the name he gave to Richard Buckley. He lectured on camouflage to army units all over Britain. At a camp in Seaford he presented himself to the colonel in charge, who asked him: 'So you are to be our new camouflage officer?'

'Yes, sir.'

'Do you know another camouflage bloke called Hickory?'

'Yes sir, charming fellow; gifted, too, as a painter.'

'I dare say, but, as a matter of fact, he's run off with my wife.'

Trevelyan continued to be confronted by the surreal. His abiding memory of the army tour is lecturing to a thousand men who had all been ordered to wear their gas masks from eleven to eleven thirty each morning. The masks steamed up and none of the audience could see or hear what was being said. In the mess afterwards the officer of the day offered him a pink gin, saying, 'Terribly sorry, old boy, a bit of a balls-up.'

Trevelyan returned to his beloved Durham Wharf by the Thames at Hammersmith, which he had bought in 1935. He lived and worked there for the rest of his life. He taught etching and art at Chelsea School of Art. In 1986 he was awarded a Senior Fellowship of the Royal College of Art and became a Royal Academician in 1987. He died in 1988.

Roland Penrose became senior lecturer during the war at the Eastern Command Camouflage School in Norwich and in 1947 married his camouflage muse, Lee Miller. He was knighted for services to the visual arts.

Possibly the strangest post-war transformation was that of Jasper Maskelyne. He moved to South Africa, where he found it hard to earn a living as an illusionist and became, instead, a driving instructor. Before he left the camouflage workshops of the Western Desert he told Barkas that he planned one day to write a memoir about what he had done, and call it *Magic Top Secret*. He wasn't sure what he would put in it, but said there would be lots of action and adventure, because that's what the public liked.

Maskelyne's book, ghost-written by Frank S. Stuart, appeared in 1949. Jasper claimed to have been the mastermind behind Operation Bertram and of several other major camouflage ruses. He asserts that as a soldier, his war work started in May 1940 with 'the biggest Magic Show in history, helping disguise the South Coast of England against enemy invasion'. However, Maskelyne did not enlist in the army until October of that year, when he joined the school at Farnham. Julian Trevelyan, who trained with him, wrote in his memoir *Indigo Days*: 'The course included others who'd espoused camouflage for one reason or another. Jasper Maskelyne's connection with it was obvious, since disappearing was his profession and he was called in when anyone wished to make something invisible. He entertained us with his tricks in the evening, and tried, rather unsuccessfully, to apply his techniques to the disguise of the concrete pillboxes that were then appearing everywhere overnight. He was at once innocent and urbane and ended up Entertainments Officer in the Middle East.'

In the desert, Maskelyne says that as the 'Officer in Charge of the Experimental Unit', he set up a group of camoufleurs called The Magic Gang. They hid, he claims, Alexandria harbour and created a dummy port at Mayrut Bay: 'a mile along the coast . . . it is sufficiently like Alexandria in shape to attract a bomber pilot'. At the bay the Magic Gang laid down lights, explosives, and a dummy lighthouse, while Alexandria itself was blacked out. Unfortunately for Maskelyne, Mayrut Bay is not on the coast but an inland saltwater lake and there is nothing in the official record about such schemes. The dummy port is most likely to have existed only in Maskelyne's mind, and was possibly inspired by Sykes's abandoned project.

Maskelyne also made extraordinary claims for the 'Dazzle Light' which, he wrote, 'creates beams nine miles long, twenty-four of them from each searchlight . . . the magic mirrors were a success and the next job was to get the device into mass production. We made twenty-one searchlights for the entire one-hundred mile length of the Suez Canal'. One camoufleur who served with Maskelyne in North Africa describes Suez as having been protected by anti-aircraft guns, searchlights and barrage balloons. The most vulnerable section of the canal was protected by a huge net: anything dropped from an enemy aircraft tore through it, leaving a hole that enabled the engineers to see exactly where the mines had landed. Divers regularly walked the length of the section in teams of six, three from each end. He has no memory of the Dazzle Lights being used.

The journalist and historical researcher Richard Stokes has made a careful study of the contradictions between what is known to have happened and what Maskelyne claimed happened. When Stokes asked Maskelyne's son, Alistair, about the lights, he wrote in reply: 'The Dazzle Lights were an idea which was, I believe, constructed only in one prototype and tested on one occasion.' This is also the view of the artist and model-maker John Morton, who served with Maskelyne in the desert. A top-secret report written by Geoffrey Barkas called 'Visual Deception in the Western Desert', now in the National Archives in London, does not mention any of Maskelyne's grandiose schemes. In his memoir, Barkas talks about Maskelyne and credits him with the development of the prototype Sunshields, dummy tanks and the Fire Cream.

After the war Geoffrey Barkas himself almost vanishes from the official record. We know he went back into the film business, making children's films for the Rank Organisation; his work for them included *Dusty Bates* and *The Little Ballerina*. In 1946 he received an OBE and went back to Shell-Mex and BP as a producer. He stayed in this role until 1956 when he joined his last film production company, Random Film Productions. He also wrote a book about his time in the desert called *The Camouflage Story*. His achievements in Cairo were probably the most important of his career, especially Operation Bertram, which he describes as 'the biggest film production of my life'. It gave him the chance to work on a scale that was grander and more important than anything he had done before or was later to do. William Murray Dixon, whose work helped to establish the reputation of the Camouflage Unit in Tobruk, sums Barkas up and provides his epithet: 'He wasn't just my commanding officer, he was my best friend, he was a gorgeous man.' Barkas died in 1979.

*　　*　　*

In 1951, the Festival of Britain on the South Bank brought together many of the artists who had worked in the Camouflage Unit. Basil Spence was the exhibition's director of architecture, John Hutton was asked to create a mural for the 'Sea and Ships Pavilion' and Steven Sykes contributed items of pottery. John Morton, who had worked with Peter Proud as a draughtsman in Cairo, worked on designs for the Lion and Unicorn Pavilion.

Perhaps the most moving memorial to the creative friendships formed in the Camouflage Unit is Coventry Cathedral. On the night of 14 November 1940, over five hundred German bombers attacked Coventry in the industrial heartland of Britain. They came in waves, carrying high explosives, air mines, and petrol and magnesium incendiaries. The bomb loads were designed to destroy industrial plant, kill civilians and make it impossible for the emergency services to operate. The raid was codenamed Moonlight Sonata.

Coventry's air-raid sirens sounded just before

19:00 hours and at 19:20 hours. At midnight the raid reached its climax. Water mains all over the city had burst, the roads were impassable, the fire brigade HQ received a direct hit and a firestorm started in the city centre. Red-hot winds howled, forming a lethal vortex that sucked the living and the dead into the air. The all-clear sounded at 06:15 the next morning. Dawn revealed over two thousand people dead or injured, the centre city a ruin and over four thousand homes destroyed.

A young intelligence officer, Basil Spence, was told to report that the raid had also destroyed the Daimler Factory, the Humber Hillman factory, the Alfred Herbert machine-tool works, nine aircraft factories, two naval ordnance stores and the city's seven-hundred-year-old Gothic cathedral.

Four years later, Basil Spence was in Normandy as a camouflage officer and appalled at the damage the war had done to the magnificent Romanesque churches of northern France. And so was born the ambition to build a cathedral.

In 1950 his chance came: a competition was announced to find an architect to design the new Coventry Cathedral. Spence won the competition and central to his thinking was the idea that the ruins of the old cathedral should be visible from the new by means of a huge glass screen, the full height of the west end of the building. He wanted the screen to be engraved with angels; the artist he chose to make the screen was John Hutton, who had been his commanding officer at Farnham. Spence wrote of Hutton: 'He had worked with me on many exhibitions and I had found him an artist of great quality, a true draughtsman and one who knew the glass-engraving technique backwards.

Moreover, he was a delight to work with, practical and trustworthy.'

To draw the angels Hutton devised new engraving techniques and recruited the artist's model Marigold Dodson to sit for him. For the next decade Hutton and Marigold worked together. Their relationship deepened and in 1963 they married. Some of Hutton's engravings can be seen at Clifton Hampden, where Marigold still lives.

It took Hutton ten years to complete the seventy-foot screen, which was unveiled on 25 May 1962. Spence wrote to his friend, congratulating him: 'I think your screen is a triumph and everybody I speak to is very moved by the floating saints.' John Hutton's ashes are buried beneath a stone at the foot of *The Screen of Saints and Angels*, which is arguably his finest work.

Basil Spence also recruited Steven Sykes to create a mosaic for the Chapel of Christ in Gethsemane at the end of the cathedral's south aisle. Sykes created a gold, Byzantine-inspired Angel of Agony offering a chalice while, near him, a small group of Apostles sleep. The gold mosaic is beautiful, and troubling. The crown of thorns, through which the mosaic can be seen, was crafted and presented by the Royal Engineers at Chatham. Sykes, Spence and Hutton had all been, and were proud of having been, members of the regiment.

In his book *From the Ashes*, Basil Spence describes Coventry Cathedral as a symbol of faith, courage and sacrifice. The cathedral was born out of violence and death and is a fitting memorial to the artists who went into battle, not with guns, but with their imaginations and whose fragile creations helped win a world war.

NOTES

The main sources I have used in the writing of this book have been the reports on the operations of the Camouflage Unit and the papers of individual members held in the National Archives, Kew (NA), the Imperial War Museum, London (IWM), and the Royal Engineers Museum Library and Archive, Gillingham, Kent. In addition I found the memoirs of Geoffrey Barkas (*The Camouflage Story*) and Steven Sykes (*Deceivers Ever*) to be particularly helpful sources of detail and local colour.

Prologue

'In Martinique-Avanti': G. Hartcup, *Camouflage, the History of Concealment and Deception in War*, David and Charles, New York, 1979.
'The Great War': Wikipedia/wiki/camouflage, 7 Jun 2012.
'In six short weeks': 'Report on Camouflage in Western Desert, Aug–Dec 1942, (Battle of Egypt)', NA WO 201/2024.

Chapter 1: The Art of War

'The old terror': Major General J. F. C. Fuller, *The Conduct of War,* 1962.
'One officer was only prevented': T. Newark,

Camouflage, Pen and Sword, 2002, and Sir P. Cadell, 'Beginning of Khaki', *Journal of the Society for Army Historical Research*, Vol. XXXI, 1953.

'At the outbreak of war': Olga S. Phillips, *Solomon J. Solomon: A Memoir of Peace and War*, Leon and Underwood, 1974, Chapter 6, *passim.*

'Another team led': N. Wilkinson, *A Brush with Life,* Seeley, 1969.

'Good for morale': Hartcup, op. cit..

'All civilian movement': B. H. Liddell Hart, *Thoughts on War*, Faber and Faber, 1944.

'The campaign "had, in fact': General Sir A. Wavell, *Allenby: A Study in Greatness*, Harrap, 1940, Chapters 8–10, *passim.*

Chapter 2: Hitler, Smoke and Mirrors

'At the risk': Hitler to a British journalist, Berlin, June 1933, cited by 'Northampton University Holocaust Education and Research Team, Guest Publication Dr Martin Friedhaus', www.holocaustresearchproject.org.

'Are you Aryan?': S. Haffner, translated by Oliver Pretzel, *Defying Hitler,* Phoenix, 2002.

'We even had': ibid.

'Hitler instinctively understood': B. H. Liddell Hart, *The Strategy of Indirect Approach,* Faber and Faber, 1946.

'This was an understanding shared': Peter Caddick-Adams, *Monty and Rommel: Parallel Lives,* Preface/Random House, 2011, Chapter 3, *passim.*

'The brothers created': author interview with Henry Korda, March 2012.

'But Churchill was': G. Valiunas, *Churchill's Military Histories*, Rowman and Littlefield Publishing Inc., 2002.

'A small or': G. Best, *Churchill's War*, Hambledon and Continuum, 2005, and T. Bridgeland, *Sea Killers in Disguise: The Story of Q Ships and Decoy Ships in the First World War*, Naval Institute Press, 1999.

'Liddell Hart was': Liddell Hart, op. cit., Preface.

'In an attempt': Hartcup, op. cit., Chapter 3, *passim*.

'Ernö Goldfinger's offices': N. Warburton, *Ernö Goldfinger: The Life of an Architect*, Routledge, 2004.

'Nature, he thought': author interview with Christopher Long, January 2012.

'Freddie's older brother': author interview with Candida Lycett Green, November 2011.

'One of the artists': M. Brentnall, *John Hutton Artist and Glass Engraver*, Art Alliance Press, 1986, Chapter 3, *passim*.

'Trying to find': Geoffrey Barkas, *The Camouflage Story*, Cassell and Company Ltd, 1952.

'Barkas explained his': see www.imdb.com.

'His grandfather John': see en.wikipedia.org: wiki/john_neville_maskelyne.

'When they reached': S. Sykes, *Deceivers Ever: The Memoirs of a Camouflage Officer*, Spellmont Ltd, 1990.

'The notion of': K. H. Frieser and J. T. Greenwood, *The Blitzkrieg Legend: The 1940*

Campaign in the West, Naval Institute Press, 2005.
'Sykes stumbled down': Sykes, op. cit.

Chapter 3: A Matter of Life and Death

'Barkas soon realised': Barkas, op. cit.
'The intake for': ibid.
'On the first night': ibid.
'The silence was': ibid.
'Julian Trevelyan grew': J. Trevelyan, *Indigo Days*, Scolar Press, 1957.
'Afterwards Buckley wrote': Papers of Major D. A. J. Pavitt, Documents Archive, IWM 86/50/3.
'On that day': Barkas, op. cit.
'Penrose stressed the': R. Penrose, *Home Guard Manual of Camouflage,* IWM 25/60.

Chapter 4: GHQ Cairo and Operation Compass

'Diffident or not': C. Barnett, *The Desert Generals*, Phoenix, 1960, Chapter 1, *passim*.
'Buckley told Barkas': Barkas, op. cit.
'The pair made': Sykes, op. cit.
'Joining Sykes on': 'Middle East Camouflage Report', NA WO 201/2843.
'The first phase': Barnett, op. cit.
'The smell of fresh': A. Cooper, *Cairo in the War* 1939–45, Hamish Hamilton Ltd., 1989.
'Outside, other ranks': author interview with Rifleman Victor Gregg, May 2010.
'At the foot': Barkas, op. cit.

298

'Large armies, with': Winston Churchill to the House of Commons, 8 September 1942.
'Into the two vehicles': Barkas, op. cit.
'The Londoner was': ibid.
'For Barkas it': ibid.
'The Italians continued': R.H.W.S. Hastings, *The Rifle Brigade in the Second World War*, Gale and Polden Ltd, 1950.
'Surrendered to Captain Pearson': letter to author from General Sir Thomas Pearson, KCB, CBE, DSO.

Chapter 5: Tobruk: The Camouflage Unit's Lucky Break

'My Dear Maskelyne': Jasper Maskelyne's undated copy of letter from H. M. Davis, the Officer Commanding Troops, to Maskelyne, written shortly before disembarkation from the *Samaria*. Documents Archive, IWM 267, item 3635.
'Later Maskelyne wrote': Letter to R. V. Hood, held in a small collection of papers and memorabilia catalogued as: 'misc. documents, one from Maskelyne': Documents Archive, IWM 13714.
'The canopy was': author interview with Alistair Maskelyne, January 2012.
'A Camouflage Unit': 'Middle East Camouflage Report'.
'It was John Hutton': ibid.
'The ingredients they': ibid.
To their horror': author interview with Marigold Hutton, spring 2012.

'Back at GHQ': Barkas, op. cit.

'Barkas devised two': 'Middle East Camouflage Report'.

'Ayrton was a man': Barkas, op. cit.

'The design called': ibid.

'The first edition': 'Middle East Camouflage Report'.

'He was spotted': author interview with William Murray Dixon, February 2012.

'Tobruk was under': Captain Ashley Havinden, 'Summary of Report on Camouflage Work in Tobruk Fortress, 18 Apr–11 Jul 1941', Documents Archive, IWM 74/165/3.

'An early success': ibid.

'The recipe for': ibid.

'Report on large': ibid.

'To disguise': ibid.

'In June, with the siege': ibid.

'The port itself': ibid.

'The camouflage teams': author interview with Murray Dixon.

'The ferocity of': 'Middle East Camouflage Report'.

'Proud and Murray Dixon': Havinden, IWM 74/165/3.

'The team's artificial': 'Middle East Camouflage Report'.

'By the end': author interview with Murray Dixon and drawings from Murray Dixon's private collection.

'The latest ROME': 'Middle East Camouflage Report'.

'Especially satisfying were': ibid.

'Barkas summed up': ibid.

'A general appreciation': ibid.

Chapter 6: Operation Crusader

'Hughes Stanton made it onto the beach and collapsed': G. Roddon, unpublished manuscript, in the author's possession.

'It included studying': 'Middle East Camouflage Report'.

'Another Barkas initiative': ibid.

'The new Camouflage Branch': ibid.

'He remembers his': author interview with John Morton, September 2011.

'Jasper Maskelyne provided': my account of the Fire Cream demonstration is based on interviews with Alistair Maskelyne and Richard Stokes, June 2011; photographs provided by Alistair Maskelyne; photographs on Richard Stokes's website (www.maskelynemagic.com).

'In a letter': letter from Maskelyne, IWM 267, item 3635.

'Back in his headquarters': Barkas, op. cit.

'Barkas calculated the amount': 'Middle East Camouflage Report'.

'The *Egyptian Mail*': Barkas, op. cit.

'Regulations required that': ibid.

'The committee was': ibid.

'In the early': ibid.

'Then he remembered': ibid.

'Later driving along': Sykes, op. cit.

'Between escapades': ibid.

'He scuttled through': ibid.

'Sykes now focused': Sykes interview, Sound Archive, IWM 12265.

'Soon they were': Sykes, op. cit.

'Thousands of feet': ibid.

'To add authenticity': 'Middle East Camouflage Report'.
'All was ready': Sykes, op. cit.
'The battle proper started': Barnett, op. cit.
'At the dummy railhead': Sykes, op. cit.
'The fighting raged on': author interview with Jon Pusey, January 2012.
'Most Secret': 'Middle East Camouflage Report'.

Chapter 7: The No. 1 Deception Unit

'By the end': 'Middle East Camouflage Report'.
'But Helwan came': author interview with Alistair Maskelyne, January 2012.
'Then there was': ibid.
'He would merge': 'Middle East Camouflage Report'.
'After the interview': letter from Maskelyne, IWM 267, item 3635.
'There is film footage': 'Tea Party, Governor's House', Film Archive, IWM AYY210/4 (undated).
'Word of Steven Sykes': Sykes, op. cit.
'The plan was approved': ibid.
'Pusey was the talented': author interview with Pusey.
'Apart from the': Sykes, op. cit.
'First year from': ibid.
'Pusey undertook the': author interview with Pusey.
'Encouraged by the way': Sykes, op. cit.
'As the site grew': ibid.
'One of the camoufleurs': E. Copnall

Bainbridge, unpublished memoir, in the possession of his daughter, Jill Neff.
'On the evening': ibid.

Chapter 8: Retreat: The Gazala Stakes

'Fellers had the complete': J. Latimer, *Alamein*, John Murray, 2002.
'Run Away, Someone's Coming': author interview with Major Tom Bird, DSO, MC, January 2010.
'He had another': Lieutenant Colonel P. Richards, 'Rommel—*Fingerspitzengefühl*', *British Army Review*, No. 131, and Caddick-Adams, op. cit., Part 3, Chapter 15.
'The camoufleurs were': author interview with Nick Sykes, December 2011.
'Cornish, Rolfe and Bainbridge Copnall': Bainbridge Copnall, unpublished memoir.
'One British officer': author interview with Major Tom Bird.
'Dorman-Smith recommended': Latimer, op. cit.
'The column roared by': description based on interview with Gregg.
'Barkas remembered that': Barkas, op. cit.
'The importance of': *Rifle Brigade Journal*, Vol. XXI (2012).
'In his diary': S. Sykes, op. cit.
'He had one very strange': ibid.
'He was the brains': T. Holt, *The Deceivers*, Weidenfeld and Nicolson, 2004.
'In an attempt': 'Middle East Camouflage Report'.

'He returned minutes': author interview with Murray Dixon.

'The argument went on': reported to the author by General Sir John Hackett, December 1990.

'The news of Rommel's': author interview with General Sir Thomas Pearson, May 2010.

'At Helwan, the': author interview with Morton.

'On 24 June': Barkas, op. cit.

'The day was christened "Ash Wednesday"': author interview with Pearson.

'Although I was': Sykes, op. cit.

'Sykes was not': Brentnall, op. cit.

'Sentinel was the brainchild': Holt, op. cit.

'To make a dummy': 'Middle East Camouflage Report'.

Chapter 9: Monty

'Heseltine, was a small': 'Pippin's Progress', memoir of Richard Heseltine, 3rd Hussars. Document Archive, IWM 03/1348; and Richard Heseltine, *Pippin's Progress*, Silver Horse Press, 2001.

'The next day': author telephone interview with Richard Heseltine, December 2011.

'Bernard Montgomery was': Caddick-Adams, op. cit., *passim*.

'Life is very black': ibid.

Chapter 10: Bertram Steals the Show

'Rommel had been promised': E. Bergot,

translated by R. Barry, *The Afrika Korps*, Allen Wingate, 1976.

'Rommel's replacement was': ibid.

'Rommel's last act': ibid.

'They drove towards': Barkas, op. cit.

'Geoffrey Barkas was': ibid.

'On the beach': ibid.

'Back in the caravan': M. Young and G. Stamp, *The Trojan Horses*, The Bodley Head, 1989.

'The tank forming': 'Report on Camouflage in Western Desert', NA WO 201/2024.

'On 27 September': ibid.

'The mines are the': author interview with Pearson.

'There are also some': Latimer, op. cit.

'The men have': ibid.

'Then, crackling over the Tannoy': author interview with Brigadier John Keeling, May 2012.

'Twenty-five miles': Barkas, op. cit.

Chapter 11: The Battle of Alamein

'Engineers and infantry': author interviews with Major Tom Bird (February 2010), Gregg and Pearson.

'drunken negroes with tanks': enemy documents files and papers, Cabinet Office Historical Section, NA CAB 146/17. Also see 'Captured Enemy Documents, Apr 1942–Mar 1943', NA WO 210/2150 GSI(S) GHQ MEF.

'He left telling his staff': ibid.

'The small force': author interviews with Bird and Gregg.

'He described as': Bergot, op. cit.
'I rode my tank to Alamein': author telephone interview with Heseltine.

Chapter 12: After the Battle

'Diplomatic channels were': Thaddeus Holt, *The Deceivers: Allied Military Deception in World War Two*, Weidenfeld and Nicolson, 2004.
'Huge though the': V. V. Kuibishev, *Russian Camouflage Manual*, V.V.4/c/106 623.77 KUI, Royal Engineers Museum.
'*Maskirovka* is a Russian word': author interview with Clementine Cecil, March 2012.
'The Russians embraced': J. Latimer, *Deception in War*, John Murray, 2001. Also see G. K. Zhukov, *The Memoirs of Marshall Zhukov*, Jonathan Cape, 1971. The Soviet armed forces learned to preserve in deep secrecy the intentions to execute disinformation on a large scale. Also author interview with Clementine Cecil, February 2012.
'The philosophy of *maskirovka*': A. Postovalov, 'Modelling the Combat Operations of the Ground Forces', *Voennaya Mysl*, No. 3. (1969). Also see Latimer, *Deception in War*, op. cit.

Epilogue: Back in the Studio

'Freddie de Guingand wrote': photocopy of citation in private collection of Marigold Hutton.

'He was always': author interview with Nick Sykes.

'William Murray Dixon': letter dated 19 September 1983, private collection of William Murray Dixon.

'Bainbridge Copnall who': author interview with Bainbridge Copnall's daughter, Jill Neff, September 2011.

'Possibly the strangest': author interviews with Alistair Maskelyne and Stokes.

'To draw the angels': author interview with Marigold Hutton.

BIBLIOGRAPHY

Addison, G., *The Work of the Royal Engineers in the European War* 1914–1918. Institution of Royal Engineers, 1926

Barkas, G., *The Camouflage Story*. Cassell, 1952

Barnett, C., *The Desert Generals*. Kimber, 1960

Beaton, C., *Near East*. Batsford, 1943

Beaumont, R., Maskirovka, *Soviet Camouflage, Concealment and Deception*. Centre for Strategic Technology, Texas Engineering Experiment Station, Texas A&M University System, 1982

Behrendt, H-O., *Rommel's Intelligence in the Desert Campaign*. Kimber, 1985

Behrens, R. R., *False Colours: Art Design and Modern Camouflage*. Bobolink Books, 2002

—, *Art and Camouflage: An Annotated Bibliography*. Leonardo Online. www.boblinkbooks.com 9 December 2008

Behrens, R. R., *Camopedia: A Compendium of Research on Art, Architecture and Camouflage*. Blackwell Publishing, 2010

Bergot, E., trans. R. Barry. *The Afrika Korps*. Wingate, 1976

Bierman, J., & C. Smith. *Alamein: War Without Hate*. Viking, 2002

Breckenridge, R. P., *Modern Camouflage: The New Art of Protective Concealment*. Farrar and Rinehart, 1942

Brentnall, M., *John Hutton: Artist and Glass Engraver*. Associated University Press, 1986

Brooks, A. J., *Photo Reconnaissance*. Littlehampton Book Services Ltd, 1975

Bungay, S., *Alamein*. Aurum, 2002

Carver, M., *El Alamein*. Batsford, 1979

Cave Brown, A., *Bodyguard of Lies*. Harper and Row, 1975

Clarke, D., *Seven Assignments*. Jonathan Cape, 1949

Cott, H., *Adaptive Colouration in Animals*. Methuen, 1975

Coward, Noël *Middle East Diary*. Heinemann, 1944

Cruickshank, C., *Deception in World War II*. Oxford University Press, 1981

De Arcangelis, M., *Electronic Warfare*. Blandford, 1985

Dobinson, C., *Fields of Deception: Britain's Bombing Decoys of World War II*. Methuen, 2000

Douglas, K., *Alamein to Zem Zem*. Faber and Faber, 1992

Dunninger, J., *The Complete Encyclopaedia of Magic*. Spring Books, 1970

Fisher, D., *War Magician*. Putnam, 1983

Ford, K., *El Alamein 1942: The Turning of the Tide*. Osprey, 2005

Goodden, H., *Camouflage and Art: Design for Deception in World War II*. Unicorn Press, 2007

Gregg, V., and R. Stroud, *Rifleman: A Front Line Life*. Bloomsbury, 2011

Haffner, S., *Defying Hitler*. Weidenfeld and Nicolson, 2002

Hartcup, G., *Camouflage: The History of Concealment and Deception in War*. Pen and Sword Military, 2008

Hastings, R.H.W.S., *The Rifle Brigade in the Second World War 1939–1945*. Gale and Polden, 1950

Haswell, J., *The Intelligence and Deception of the D-Day Landings.* Batsford, 1979

Hoffman, Prof. L. A., *Modern Magic.* George Routledge, 1891

Holland, J., *Together We Stand: North Africa 1942–1943: Turning the Tide in the West.* HarperCollins, 2006.

Holt, T., *The Deceivers: Allied Military Deception in the Second World War.* Weidenfeld and Nicolson, 2004

Keegan, J., *Churchill's Generals.* Cassell Military, 2005

—, *The Battle for History: Re-Fighting World War II.* Longman Group Ltd, 1998

Latimer, J., *Alamein.* John Murray, 2002

—, *Deception in War.* John Murray, 2001

Liddell Hart, B., *The Strategy of Indirect Approach.* Faber and Faber, 1951

Lucas, J., *Panzer Army Africa.* Arms and Armour Press, 1982

Lucas, J., *War in the Desert.* Macdonald and James, 1977

Lucas Phillips, C. E., *Alamein.* Heinemann, 1962

Luck, H. von, *Panzer Commander.* Cassell, 2002

Macintyre, B., *Operation Mincemeat.* Bloomsbury, 2010

Maskelyne, J., *Magic—Top Secret.* Stanley Paul and Co., 1949 (An amusing insight into the mind of a fantasist. This book should be read with a very large pinch of salt.)

Mellenthin, F. W. von, *Panzer Battles: A Study of the Employment of Armour in the Second World War.* Cassell, 1956

Moorehead, A., *The Desert War.* Hamish Hamilton, 1965

Newark, T., *The Future of Camouflage*. No Nonsense Books, 2002

Newark, T., *Camouflage*. Thames and Hudson, 2009

Owen, D., *Battle of Wits: A History of Psychology and Deception in Modern Warfare*. Cooper, 1978

Penrose, R., *The Friendly Surrealist*. Prestel, 2001

Penrose, R., *The Home Guard Manual of Camouflage*. George Routledge, 1941

Rankin, N., *Churchill's Wizards*. Faber and Faber, 2008

Reit, S., *Masquerade: The Amazing Camouflage Deceptions of World War II*. Hawthorn Books, 1978

Robb, B., *My Middle East Campaigns*. Collins, 1944

Solomon, S. J., *Strategic Camouflage*. John Murray, 1920

Stanley, R. M., *To Fool a Glass Eye*. Airlife, 1998

Sykes, S., *Deceivers Ever: The Memoirs of a Camouflage Officer*. Spelmount, 1990

Tarbell, H., *Tarbell Course in Magic*. A. S. Barnes, 1956

Thayer Abbot, H., *Concealing Coloration in the Animal Kingdom*. Macmillan and Co., 1909

Travers, S., *Tomorrow to Be Brave: A Memoir of the Only Woman ever to Serve in the French Foreign Legion*. The Free Press, 2001

Trevelyan, J., *Indigo Days*. MacGibbon and Kee, 1957

Whaley, B., *Stratagem: Deception and Surprise in War*. Artech House, 2007

Wilkinson, N., *A Brush with Life*. Steeley, 1965

Wilmot, C., *Tobruk 1941: Concealment—Siege—Capture—Relief*. Robertson, 1945

Young, D., *Rommel*. Collins, 1947

Young, M., and R. Stamp, *Trojan Horses: Deception*

Operations in the Second World War. The Bodley
  Head, 1989
Zhukov, G. K., *The Memoirs of Marshal Zhukov.*
  Jonathan Cape, 1971

ACKNOWLEDGEMENTS

Camouflage and deception are essentially ephemeral arts and those who practise them leave little trace of what they have done. This is especially true of the men who worked to deceive Rommel in the scorching heat of the Western Desert seventy years ago. They used whatever came to hand: canvas, string, paint and old four-gallon petrol cans, materials which, once the job was done and the battle had moved on, simply rotted away. The camouflage men themselves have proved equally elusive and I am grateful to many people who helped me piece together just what the raggle-taggle group of artists, sculptors, designers and technicians actually did in those tense days when the war was going badly and North Africa looked as though it might become just another Axis dominion.

Sadly, most of those who fought with the Camouflage Unit in the Western Desert are no longer with us. Of those who are, I would like to thank John Morton for his descriptions of life at GHQ in Cairo and at the Helwan workshops. John was also very generous with his memories of the cartoonist Brian Robb and lent me his own copy of Robb's book, *My Middle East Campaigns*. I would like to thank Richard 'Pippin' Heseltine, who as a young officer berated Monty for being ill-prepared for desert warfare. I owe special thanks to William Murray Dixon, who spent an afternoon telling me about his experiences in Fortress Tobruk. As he spoke, his wife Ann laid on one of the finest teas I have ever eaten. Murray Dixon has allowed me to use his beautiful working drawings of camouflage and deception schemes, some of which were made while under attack from dive-bombers. Their son Peter ferried me around Northumberland and took on the laborious task of scanning his father's pictures, for which many thanks.

The families and friends of the camouflage men who are no longer around responded to my endless questions with patience and enthusiasm. I would particularly like to mention Carola Zagolavich, who talked to me about her father, Hugh Casson, and showed me her collection of his drawings and sketches relating to airfield camouflage in the United Kingdom; John Hutton's wife, Marigold, who was the model for the angel engravings in Coventry Cathedral, spent many hours talking to me and lent me rare and useful materials from her personal archive; Jill Neff for her memories of her father, Edward Bainbridge Copnall, and for allowing me to photograph his unpublished autobiography and other materials; my good friend Jon Pusey, himself a distinguished film designer, who told me about his father Fred and allowed me to use his father's photographs of life in Tobruk. I must thank Nick Sykes, who took time at an especially busy moment in his life to dig up a wealth of material about his father, Steven, and who allowed me to interview him for the better part of a day. Tanya Harrod talked to me about Steven and lent me her research materials, for which many thanks.

Louise Rodden lent me her father Guy Rodden's unpublished diary, which gave me some excellent background; her sister the Revd Diana Glover was also very helpful. Guy himself is not in the book because his camouflage duties kept him in England, but his memories were a valuable insight into life at Farnham. I wish that space had allowed the inclusion of two of Murray McCheyne's drawings, 'Guy Rodden Farnham' and the sketch 'Rodden Shaving', both in the Imperial War Museum.

When I began this book Vicki Hallam got me off to a very good start, as did Virginia Ironside. Both had camouflage officer fathers and both pointed me towards people who took me along the elusive trail that led deep into the Western Desert. Henrietta Goodden was an invaluable resource, generously sharing her contacts and the research from her own book, *Art and Camouflage.*

Christopher Long and Candida Lycett Green both helped me understand the elusive Freddie Beddington and his brother Jack, known to some as 'Bedders'. Freddie Beddington served in the First World War as a sniper, during which he learned how to hide, a skill he seems to have applied to the rest of his life. Another man who was skilled at making things vanish was the illusionist Jasper Maskelyne, whose son, Alistair, talked to me at length. Alistair was very candid about what his father did and didn't do, and lent me photographs, letters and other materials from his own collection. The researcher and historian Richard Stokes was more than generous with his own research into Jasper and his website www.maskelynemagic.com is well worth a visit.

The Chelsea Arts Club was very helpful in my bid to track down material, especially Don Grant, Hugh Gilbert, Derek Bloom and Warwick Woodhouse, who introduced me to Getty Images. Henry Korda gave me some fascinating insights into the relationship between his uncle Sir Alexander Korda and Winston Churchill. Finally, thanks to the incomparable club secretary, Dudley Winterbottom, who racked his brains to come up with past club members who served with the Camouflage Unit.

Many soldiers have come to my aid. I must thank my friend and collaborator on another book, Vic Gregg, who fought at Alamein with the Rifle Brigade and was at the Snipe action. Vic spent many hours describing life as a soldier in the desert, as did Major Tom Bird, who also fought and was wounded at Snipe. I am very grateful to General Sir Thomas Pearson, who fought in the desert and as a young captain took the surrender of General Bergonzoli after Beda Fomm. General Pearson explained the dangerous and essential business of 'gapping the mines'—clearing lanes for the tanks. Other military men who have been very kind and helpful are: Major Ron Cassidy of the Rifle Brigade; Brigadiers John Keeling and Dennis Blease, both gunners, who provided valuable information into the workings of the twenty-five-pounder field gun and especially the ballistic characteristics of that gun's shells when loaded with 'charge super'; John Keeling also agreed to read the manuscript, for which many thanks; Captain Max Wakefield, who shared his experiences of armoured combat in the desert; Lieutenant Colonel Andrew Mills RE, who helped me understand the business of being a Royal Engineer; and Brigadier Jock Hamilton Baillie, who died long before this book was even an idea, but whose reminiscences of life in the Royal Engineers have stayed in my mind and informed the writing of this story. Also Lieutenant Colonel Charles Holman

318

and Lt Col John McLennan, both Royal Engineers, and Andrew Davis and Amy Adams of the Royal Engineers Museum. The staffs of the London Library, the Imperial War Museum, the British Library and the National Archive at Kew have all been very helpful.

Others I must thank are Philip Athill of Abbott and Holder; Neil Parkinson at the Royal College of Art; Luigi Di Dio of Getty Images; and Robbie Stamp, who spent time trying to track down information from his own researches into deception. Thanks to Clementine Cecil for aiding me with Russian translation. I would also like to thank Alan Afriat for screening the Western Desert episode of the series *The World at War*, on which he was supervising editor. Thanks too to Viet Tran and the Notes Plus team, who have devised one of the most useful iPad research apps I have ever come across

I also want thank my grandson Jimmy Joe Hughes for his encouragement and genuine interest in a period which must, to him, seem immeasurably long ago. I am lucky to have as my agent Victoria Hobbs of A. M. Heath.

This is the second time I have worked with the people at Bloomsbury and I would like to thank them all for their Rolls-Royce service, in particular Nick Humphrey, who was always there on the telephone and for whom my continual demands were never a problem; Greg Heinimann who designed the cover and exactly captured the feel of the Phantom Army; Phil Beresford for his miracle-working on the clarity of some of the pictures; John Gilkes for his maps and especially for his rendering of 'Bomb Alley' in Tobruk; Kate Johnson for her beautiful copy edit and ideas that went beyond the call of duty; Emily Sweet for her care in crafting the book; and of course my editor, the incomparable Bill Swainson, whose friendly but stern and scholarly eye kept me on the right track, and who above all was always enthusiastic about the project.

Needless to say any errors in this book are entirely my responsibility.

Finally I must thank my wife, to whom this book is dedicated.